The Ark
on Ararat

The Ark on Ararat

by Tim F. LaHaye
and John D. Morris

Jointly published by

**THOMAS NELSON INC.,
PUBLISHERS**

Nashville / New York

Dedicated to the Creation Research Society . . .
that group of dedicated scientists
who in the space of a few short years
have succeeded in restructuring
all of scientific thought concerning origins,
sometimes in spite of
professional censure and personal sacrifice.

Second printing

Copyright © 1976 by Creation-Life Publishers

All rights reserved under International and Pan-American Conventions.
Published by Thomas Nelson, Inc., Publishers, Nashville, Tennessee
Manufactured in the United States of America

Library of Congress Cataloging in Publication Data

LaHaye, Tim F
    The ark on Ararat.

    Includes bibliographies and index.
    1. Noah's ark. 2. Mt. Ararat. I. Morris, John David, 1946– joint author.
II. Title.
DS51.A66L34   001.9'4   76–25027
ISBN 0–89051–019–9
ISBN 0–8407–5110–9
ISBN 0–8407–5607–0 pbk
ISBN 0–8407–5608–9 prepack

This Amazing Book

"This amazing book shows the very real possibility that in this day when the authority and inspiration of the Bible is being rejected, God may give us proof-positive that one of the greatest historical events in this planet's history is absolutely true. This would leave the doubting world with no excuse for their unbelief. This is a thrilling book that all should read."

Hal Lindsey

Contents

The Mystery of Noah's Ark

The official Turkish guide electrified my memory as he gave a travelog of his native country. The forty-two people on our Holy Land tour were in the conference room of the grand, marble-faced Izmir Hotel. That evening the guide, a former Turkish Army captain, flashed a picture of beautiful 17,000-foot Mount Ararat on the screen. He had been stationed at its base for two years, during which time he took the pictures.

Immediately my mind went back to the exciting stories I had heard of those who claimed they had actually seen the Ark. As an Air Force G.I., I had been astounded by the story printed in *Stars and Stripes* about the 8th Air Force crewmen flying out of Tunisia who had looked out of their B-17 to see the Ark nestled among the crags and glaciers of Ararat. I had just assumed that the Ark, by this time 4,500 years old, had rotted away. The possibility that it had been deep-frozen and preserved for future exposure to a skeptical world had never really gripped me.

Shortly after World War II, I had heard about the Russian flyers who had seen the Ark in 1916, resulting in the Czar sending an expedition to Ararat to investigate. Since then, there have been other stories, including that of the Frenchman, Navarra, who claimed to have touched the Ark and brought back a piece of hand-tooled timber 9 inches x 9 inches x 5 feet long. Even *Life* magazine had carried the abortive story of the Turkish Air Force photographs that showed a man-made object that appeared to be the same size as the Ark of Noah.

I asked our guide some questions: "Did you climb Mt. Ararat?" "Did you see Noah's Ark?" "Did you meet anyone who did?" He was more than happy to discuss it, but unfortunately his college training had convinced him that the story of Noah was fictional. Consequently, he had never climbed the mountain "because it was too dangerous." He did admit that he had talked to "many people who claimed to have seen the Ark" and that "they all believed it was still up there." But his humanistic education had convinced him that the Ark story was "unbelievable." Consequently he had never attempted to investigate.

When the guide realized that I was seriously interested and really expected the Ark to be discovered someday, he said, "If it is ever found, I will have to change a lot of my beliefs." And that is the very point! Such humanistic ideas would have to change if Noah's Ark were ever discovered. No doubt that fact is the reason so many Christians have earnestly tried to find the Ark, and so many skeptics have tried to hinder the search.

It has been interesting to observe the almost unanimous response of humanistic-oriented newsmen, magazine editors, authors, and professors when confronted with a report of an Ark sighting. Often they place it in the same category as Alice in Wonderland. Perhaps they have a subconscious fear that if the Ark were found they would be forced to do some real heart searching and re-evaluation.

Evolutionists Fear the Ark

The theory of evolution undergirds the entire secular educational system today and, consequently, its thinking process. Until a large number of Christians became well-qualified scientists, educators seemed to have the "facts of science" in their favor. Now there are many competent voices being raised to challenge the scientific "evidence" of evolution, using the same scientific discoveries to support the concept of creation instead.

Dr. Henry Morris, director of the Institute for Creation Research, and vice-president of Academic Affairs at Christian Heritage College in San Diego, has said,

. . . the only evidence for organic evolution which is more than trivial and circumstantial is the supposed testimony of the fossil record in the sedimentary rocks. This gigantic graveyard of plants and animals, now found buried in water-deposited sediments all over the world, has been interpreted by most geologists in terms of a long chronologic series of evolutionary stages, purportedly tracing out the gradual evolution of the earth and all its inhabitants.

A worldwide Flood, of course, is impossible in the context of this standard system of evolutionary geology—*and vice versa*! Even without the testimony of the Ark, however, an abundance of evidence for the worldwide Flood has already come to light in recent years and a real revival of interest in scientific catastrophism is already under way. As a matter of fact, all the real factual data of observable geology are potentially capable of systematic reinterpretation in terms of the complex dynamics of a worldwide Flood and its associated residual catastrophism.

It is still true, however, that the majority of geologists (and, because of the geologists' presumed authority in such matters, other scientists as well) remain committed to the basic evolutionary system of interpretation of earth history. In turn, because most natural scientists are evolutionists, most laymen also believe that evolution must be true. The evolutionary system of thought has therefore long been taken as the basic philosophy in sociology and psychology, in politics and economics, in law and religion, and indeed in every other field as well.

I think one can easily see that, in the light of these conditions, the confirmed discovery of the Ark would have worldwide repercussions. It would provide conclusive evidence confirming the global nature of the Flood, and thus the mortal blow to any further belief that evolution is a *scientific* theory (as distinct from its true character as a religious philosophy).

Furthermore, such a discovery should also have profound sociological effects. Men would suddenly have to realize that they are all of *one* human race, descended in very recent times from the sons of Noah. They would have to realize that there really is a Creator, a God who judges and punishes sin.[1]

In recent years the stories of those who maintain they have seen the Ark have been repeated, written, and distributed so widely that no amount of repression or ridicule has been able to stifle the curiosity of millions. Books on the subject have appeared in English, Danish, German, and French. In 1975 *Reader's Digest* carried an article considering the possibility. In fact, so many people have shown an interest in the Ark's discovery that skeptics often ridicule researchers in this field by calling them "arkeologists."

It has been my privilege to meet personally many of these "arkeologists" and study their research materials. In addition, John Morris, co-author of this book, has made two expeditions to Mt. Ararat as well as several other trips to Turkey and is eager to return as soon as the political climate in Turkey clears up. All these people have sufficient reason to believe the Ark really has been preserved by God in the upper ice-covered regions of the mountain, where the Bible states it came to rest.

Most people cannot spend the time to do all the research necessary to reach a conclusion on this mystery. We have gathered, and are still gathering, more material. This book ties all the past research together with recent explorations of Mt. Ararat and brings the reader up to the present findings in the hope that he can reach his own decision. Frankly, I have rarely studied anything I thought was more factual.

It has been almost one hundred years since Mt. Ararat, a mountain with a long history of earthquakes, has experienced a major earthquake. The previous ones exposed the Ark for several years by altering the glacial cap. Another could shake that old mountain at any time, and this could be the one that God will use to stop the mouths of skeptics, atheists, and doubters the world over by revealing, so that all can see, the remains of Noah's Ark. Certainly that is possible, but we hope such an extreme measure is not necessary. We would rather see several years of low precipitation in the Ararat region, when the hot winds from the desert below melt back the snow and part of the glacier to an all-time low. At such a time God, who still works in the affairs of men to perfect His will and pleasure, could create a political climate of peace in Turkey, conducive to another I.C.R. expedition to find and photograph what is left of Noah's Ark. Even better, God could make it possible during such a season for a helicopter or airplane to fly up and do the photography necessary to convince the unbelieving people of this age.

We sincerely hope it will occur in our lifetime!

Tim F. LaHaye
President Christian Heritage College

---

1. Violet Cummings, "Foreword," *Noah's Ark: Fact or Fable?* (San Diego: Creation Science Research Center, 1972), pp. 13, 14.

The Ark on Ararat

Adventure On Ararat

You are about to embark on one of the most exciting adventures of all time. It has everything. Danger, hardship, world travel, international intrigue, sabotage. Evidence leading to blind alleys, contrasting reports, even fraudulent testimony stand in the way.

The adventurers who embark on this quest must be prepared to give everything to it. It quickly becomes a life's work. They must in many cases sacrifice what most could call a normal life. Months spent in foreign countries facing strange diseases, hostile natives, political opposition, violent weather, savage beasts, and the rigors of exploring a rugged mountain substitute for the comforts of a home and family.

Be careful now, the story presented in this book is gripping and a word of caution must be extended to the reader. Every one of the explorers now involved in the search for Noah's Ark became "hooked" on much less evidence.

Skeptics have ridiculed the search from the start. Some have compared it to looking for the Holy Grail, the Loch Ness Monster, or the abominable snowman. Those who have not considered the significance of the potential find or who fear its implications point to a waste of time and money to find remains of a boat that they hope never existed at all.

And perhaps they have a point. If finding the Ark has no significance, the search is relegated to the status of a "mere" adventure, but if it never existed, then it is indeed folly.

But the point is that every true interpretation of the facts of history points to the Ark as real. And in spite of all logic to the contrary, the evidence indicates that the remains of the Ark survived the turmoil since the Flood and still exist today.

The factor that sets this adventure on a level by itself is its significance. If the Ark were found and conclusively documented, an overwhelming impact would register on every front. Potential finding of the Ark has been billed as the "greatest archaeological find of all time, more newsworthy than the walk on the moon," because a successful search would ring the death knell to the already fragile theory of evolution. In the spiritual realm, one of the most ridiculed stories in all the Bible would be vindicated. The world would realize (perhaps the first time for many) that the Bible is true and that millions of intelligent men and women accept it as God's Eternal Word.

The significance of finding the Ark would extend into the personal lives of each one of us, for we would be reminded of God's past method of purging the world of sinful people, and our attention would be focused on God's promise of another judgment in the very near future. By seeing evidence of His love and mercy in His providing the Ark as a method of salvation, we would be reminded of the present-day Way of Salvation, Jesus Christ, and the urgent message of accepting that Way would be evident to all who stop to realize that in Noah's day, those who refused faced an overwhelming judgment, worldwide in scope. Yes, the search for Noah's Ark is an adventure that has no equal in today's world. It is no wonder that many are willing to risk physisical abuse, even death, to bring the project to a successful conclusion.

This book could be considered a step in that direction. It might even be called a biography of the search, for its chronological nature takes you, the reader, from the birth of Mt. Ararat itself to its use as a resting place for Noah's Ark. Then it closely watches the Ark through the following millennia until the present time. All known verified sightings have been included, discussed, and evaluated here. In the proper chronological order, all major expectations are reported truthfully, even though that truth is not always flattering.

You, the reader, will be quick to recognize that any individual piece of evidence is not sufficient to prove the Ark's existence, and the authors also recognize this. However, we know you will be impressed by the amount of evidence gathered supporting the theory, and you will no doubt agree with us that the search should continue.

Much of the evidence is rather frustrating. Ephemeral in nature, it seems to tease the researcher, promising to provide substantive information but never fulfilling its promise. Each report looks good on the surface, but look further, the documentation is always elusive, just around the corner.

This book tells the story of the old Armenian whose deathbed account was destroyed in an explosion; the newspaper whose files were destroyed by fire; the bishop who reported seeing the Ark was scoffed at and left no written proof; the beautifully written story that was admittedly 95 percent

John Morris taking a long look into the awesome Ahora Gorge. The vertical ice wall in the background is several hundred feet thick. The Ark could be in this general area.

fiction, but what of the other 5 percent; the letter delivered twenty years after it was written, after the eyewitnesses had died; the old Armenian and the aging Kurd whose health would not permit them to return to the discovery site before they died. The list could go on and on: the March of Times newsreel, the *Stars and Stripes* article, the Defense Department spy photographs that no one seems to be able to find, but everyone knows about. This book also tells the story of the "unidentified object," the Ark-like structure in a photograph on an unidentified section of Mt. Ararat, and many, many other stories.

It is the authors' hope that this book will bring to light additional evidence. Perhaps as the news spreads, some will come forward with a new account and perhaps even with firm documentation. If you have something of interest, do not hesitate to pass it on. You can be assured that you will find in us a willing ear, for even what seems to be a rather insignificant piece of information might be just the clue necessary to understand the puzzle that has intrigued us for so long.

How there could be so much evidence and so little proof defies reason.

It almost seems that by design, the proof is kept from the hands of those who would make it public.

Make up your own mind. The evidence is presented in as factual a manner as possible. Original documents are quoted wherever available. With the information in this book you have almost as much as the veteran researcher; you're lacking only the firsthand knowledge gained by personal discussion with eyewitnesses and the experience acquired through years of work on the vast mountain itself.

2

Ararat:
Creation to the Flood

The Mountain Has Its Face Lifted

Today the mere sight of Mt. Ararat is inspiring. A huge mountain, one of the largest in the world, it dominates the barren, semiarid plains of Eastern Turkey. But with all its symmetry and gracefulness, it also displays the stark reality of the destructive tendencies of the forces of nature.

Mt. Ararat was not always as it is today. In the very beginning, the Bible tells us, the entire world was covered with water and darkness. But on the third day of Creation Week, God called the waters together. He formed the ocean basins, and the dry land appeared. Neither the total amount of water nor the total amount of rock and soil needed to change, just their relative positions. As the water rushed to fill these newly formed basins, the land appeared. The deepening and widening of the oceans caused the land to shift, in places tilting and buckling. Mt. Ararat, along with most of the world's mountains and mountain ranges, burst forth.

In the beginning God created the heaven and the earth.

And the earth was without form, and void; and darkness was upon the face of the deep. And the Spirit of God moved upon the face of the waters.

And God said, Let the waters under the heaven be gathered together unto one place, and let the dry land appear: and it was so.

And God called the dry land Earth; and the gathering together of the waters called he Seas: and God saw that it was good.

(Gen. 1:1-2, 9-10)

Original Ararat Lower

Dr. Clifford Burdick, structural geologist from Tucson, Arizona, in

The Deluge, from *An Illustrated History of the Holy Bible* by John Kitto, published in 1866.

the summers of 1966, 1967, and 1973 carried out an extensive geologic survey on Mt. Ararat and in Eastern Turkey. The heart of the mountain lies exposed on the northeastern face, and, after examining the area, he explained as follows:

Evidence gathered at Mount Ararat indicates that the original mountain was much lower than the present one and was of a different composition or at least of a different texture and different color. . . . the original Mount Ararat apparently was not more than 10,000 to 12,000 feet in height. The present peak is about 17,000 feet, and at its greatest height perhaps measured nearer 20,000 feet.

The Ahora gulch exposes the inner core of the original mountain which is distinct in color and texture from the volcanic rock. It is course-grained porphyry with a light buff color and much pyrite. This indicates a deep-seated intrusive that cooled slowly, permitting the coarse phenocrysts to form first. Then the whole mass was uplifted through the cover rock, allowing the remainder of the magma to cool more quickly and form fine-grained crystals and glass. This inner core may represent the original mountain dating from Creation.[1]

At the end of Creation Week, God pronounced His completed work "very good." He had created a perfect world, designed to last forever, with the natural forces precisely balanced. But Adam sinned, and God

Upturned strata surround Mt. Ararat. A remnant of a larger, taller mountain.

A field of pillow lava—very dense, thick, and heavy with conchoidal fractures. It was formed by extrusion under great depths of water.

cursed not only the human race, but the entire creation. "Cursed is the ground for thy sake" (Gen. 3:17), and "the whole creation groaneth and travaileth in pain together until now" (Rom. 8:22). The earth systems no longer functioned quite as smoothly, but continued with a marvelous degree of efficiency until the time when man's wickedness increased to the point that God once again had to intervene.

And God said unto Noah, The end of all flesh is come before me; for the earth is filled with violence through them; and, behold, I will destroy them with the earth (Gen. 6:13).

Note that God not only vowed to destroy sinful man but all flesh as well. Moreover, He promised to destroy the earth, and destroy it He did!

It is not our purpose here to discuss the geological implications of the Flood. Space does not permit us to detail the effects of such a catastrophe. The many extensive fossil graveyards—the great coal and oil deposits, overwhelming thickness of sedimentary rock, volcanic and tectonic activity on an unprecedented scale, continents splitting apart, ocean basins forming, tidal waves, hurricanes—can only be mentioned. Suffice it to say that in the original Hebrew text the word which is translated *flood* implies more than a deluge, even more than a catastrophe; indeed, it is the root from which we derive our concept of cataclysm. This can mean nothing less than an earth-changing, world-restructuring event.[2]

Geologic Evidence

As one might imagine, Mt. Ararat did not survive unscathed. In fact, the geology of Eastern Turkey, and Mt. Ararat in particular, virtually cries out in support of Flood geology. Again quoting from Dr. Burdick:

Apparently the Paleozoic-Mesozoic limestone complex which covered parts of the region was severely deformed, compressed, folded, and in places like the Ararat area domed up when the rising magma burst through. This doming effect is most evident when one views the same limestone formations on all sides of Mt. Ararat. The beds dip away from the mountain on the Turkish, the Russian, and the Persian (Iranian) sides.

During the Flood period—in the broad sense—at least three blankets of basaltic or andesitic lava were extruded over the first Ararat. Volcanic eruptions have taken place periodically ever since, but with subsiding activity. More recent flows have been extruded from cracks lower down on the mountain as each succeeding extrusion had less force than the preceding one.[3]

A great deal of evidence exists indicating that not only was Mt. Ararat once covered by water, but it even erupted while submerged under great depths of water. In common with many mountains around the world, Mt. Ararat exhibits fossil-bearing strata. Sedimentary rock (by definition laid down by flood waters) containing the fossilized remains of ocean creatures has been found as high as the snow line, approximately a 14,000-foot elevation. Furthermore, on the exposed northeastern face, layers of lava are intermingled with layers of sediments.

More evidence was revealed when a certain type of lava was discovered on Mt. Ararat as high up as rocks are exposed, at least to the 15,000-foot level. This lava is known as "pillow" lava, because of its pillow-like appearance, and is formed only when the lava is spewed out under great depths of water. The heat sink of the water "freezes" the lava almost immediately, so quickly that only very small crystals are formed. Because of the intense water pressure, gasses in the lava are trapped inside, having no time to bubble out. Consequently, the resulting rock is very dense and hard and has a high glass content. The quick cooling also causes the rock to take on a smooth rounded shape, resembling a pillow.[4]

Around Mt. Ararat, one sees more evidence of catastrophe. A few miles northwest of Mt. Ararat, salt is being mined. Evidently, as the flood waters covered the area and volcanism was rampant, vast amounts of salt which were underground were forced to the surface. Such an extensive deposit could not be the result of slow evaporation.

Southwest of Mt. Ararat, where hundreds of gypsies make their summer camp, lava, in all likelihood from the Flood period, is still hot. A blanket of limestone covers the basalt, but groundwater trickles below, is heated, and returns to the surface in the form of geysers and hot springs. The very existence of this hot layer does not fit long ages geology but conforms quite well to the concept of a global Flood a few thousand years ago, causing unequaled volcanic activity and laying down thicknesses of sediments.

During the Flood period, Mt. Ararat grew to its greatest height, estimated at 20,000 feet. A shield-type volcano, it repeatedly erupted, not only adding to its height with the addition of the lava above but also the pressures below simply shoving the mountain up. Since that time erosion has worn the mountain down. As the subterranean pressures were relieved, the massive mountain sank, forming a moat around its base. This is a poorly drained area, especially on the south side where today remains an uninhabitable, snake-infested swamp, and the rivers run toward the mountain.

Far below the surface of the ground lies the reason for all of this

Entrance to mines in an extensive salt deposit within sight of Mt. Ararat.

After the flood waters subsided, Mt. Ararat sunk, forming a swamp that now encircles its base.

activity. Mt. Ararat lies along a twisting and complex earthquake fault system trending east-west. It is referred to as the Ararat-Alagoz Fault and is part of a larger system running generally in a north-south direction from Europe to Africa known as the East African Rift. This Rift dwarfs the potentially dangerous San Andreas Fault in California and Mexico and is responsible for the formation of the Dead Sea and the Sea of Galilee in Israel and the Red Sea in Egypt. No wonder Mt. Ararat bears so many scars.

Very likely some time after the flood waters had subsided, almost the whole northeast side of the mountain blew up. A long deep gash was opened in the mountain, now known as the Ahora Gulch. This is many miles long and thousands of feet deep and wide, and a conservative estimate would be that from one to two cubic miles of rock debris and volcanic ash were blown from the mountain.

Large surface fragments were hurled miles away down toward the lower slopes of the northeast side, where they are yet visible. Lighter volcanic ash was blown into the upper atmosphere and settled down as light colored whitish tuff on the east and northeast sides of the mountain.

The ash covered some 100 square miles of surface to a thickness of from hundreds of feet near the mountain to a few feet ten miles away. . . . As a result, varied rock specimens of the whole Ararat area are found in the Ahora Gulch.

This is the type of volcanic eruption that buried Pompei and Herculaneum. Presumably, Noah and his family had left the area by that time. The original Ararat had been deeply blanketed before that, and the only part of the original Ararat now exposed is that at the head of the Ahora Gulch where the giant explosion opened it up.[5]

[1]Clifford L. Burdick, "Ararat, The Mother of Mountains," in *Creation Research Society Journal* (Ann Arbor, Mich.: Creation Research Society, 1967), pp. 9, 10.
[2]Henry M. Morris, *Scientific Creationism* (San Diego: Creation-Life Publishers, 1974). See Also Henry M. Morris, *The Genesis Record* (San Diego: Creation-Life Publishers, 1976).
[3]Ibid., pp. 8, 9.
[4]One of the foremost authorities on volcanic processes, Dr. J. G. Moore, states, "Pillow lava is probably the most abundant form of volcanic rock on earth, though most of it is hidden beneath the world's oceans and mantled by younger sediments." "Mechanism of Formation of Pillow Lava, *American Scientist*, vol. 63, May-June, 1975, p. 269.
[5]Burdick, "Ararat," p. 9.

Sightings
Throughout History

Could the remains of Noah's Ark have survived the turmoil that followed its landing on Mt. Ararat? Could it possibly have withstood the anger of an erupting volcano or the onslaught of an unstable glacier? All logic dictates that it should not have.

The Bible, outside of a few possible intimations in still-to-be-fulfilled prophecy, sheds absolutely no light on the subject. No mention of the status of the Ark appears after its occupants abandoned it. But a few other voices from the ancient past beg to be heard. More often than not these dim voices are barely audible, but their testimony remains consistent. They claim that the Ark has in fact survived. Can they be trusted? Are they reliable or simply folklore? Perhaps they are simply echoes of traditions passed down for thousands of years. Perhaps not.

Time and again, even in this "enlightened" century, one persistent tradition surfaces. The Armenians (who once lived in the Ararat region and even now, though dispersed throughout the world, preserve their national integrity as well as traditions) maintain that the remains of the Ark still exist. Frequently, the story is told of how angels watch over the Ark of Noah, protecting it from almost certain destruction. But, so the tradition goes, the ancient Armenians—who seemingly have always lived in this area—as well as the other believers in the true God made regular pilgrimages to the Ark to worship there and remove portions of the wood for talismans and good luck charms. This continued for many generations until man once again became so wicked that God refused to allow even the righteous to visit the relic, and eventually the Ark became entirely buried by ice and snow.

Evidently, as each generation succeeded the previous one, the location of the Ark was passed on from father to son, and even though few people visited it or even saw it from a distance, everyone knew its hiding place. And each generation knew that near the end of time once again the Ark of Noah would be revealed to an unbelieving world, calling attention to the

Mt. Ararat, drawn by James Morier, Esq., 1822.

truth of the Scriptures and reminding people to turn from their evil ways.

Just when the remains became inaccessible or whether it occasionally was exposed, of course, is not known. However, many non-Armenian accounts have filtered down through the ages that support the tradition. Keeping in mind that the Armenians trace their ancestry to Noah's grandson and claim to have lived in the Ararat region since that time, let us examine some of the more significant ones.

Reports from Antiquity

The brilliant and seemingly prolific historian of Babylon, Berosus, compiled his *History of Babylonia* in Greek in approximately 275 B.C. Even though his works have never been recovered by modern archaeologists, excerpts of his work have been quoted by many later historians who had access to his work in their day. Alexander Polyhistor, in the last century B.C., attributes the following statements to Berosus:

A. But of this ship that grounded in Armenia some part still remains in the mountains of the Gordyaeans in Armenia, and some get pitch from the ship by scraping it off and use it for amulets.[1]

And later in the same work:

But the vessel in Armenia furnished the inhabitants with wooden amulets to ward off evil.[2]

Flavius Josephus was a Jewish historian. He lived during the time when the New Testament was being written and has provided graphic insight into the lives of the early Christians and the spread of Christianity as well as the persecution of the Jewish race. He mentions the remains of Noah's Ark three times. In his best-known work, *The Antiquities of the Jews*, speaking of Mt. Ararat, he states the following:

B. The Armenians call that spot the Landing-Place, for it was there that the Ark came safe to land, and they show the relics of it to this day. This flood and the Ark are mentioned by all who have written histories of the barbarians. Among these is Berosus the Chaldean, who in his description of the events of the flood writes somewhere as follows: "It is said, moreover, that a portion of the vessel still

Flavius Josephus made reference to the Ark in his historical writings (artist unknown).

survives in Armenia on the mountains of the Gordyaeans, and that persons carry off pieces of bitumen, which they use as talismans." These matters are also mentioned by Hieronymus the Egyptian, author of the ancient history of Phoenicia, by Mnaseas and by many others. Nicholas of Damascus in his ninety-sixth book relates the story as follows: "There is above the country of the Minyas in Armenia a great mountain called Baris, where, as the story goes, many refugees found safety at the time of the flood, and one man, transported upon an ark, grounded upon the summit; and relics of the timber were for long preserved."[3]

Later Josephus continues:

. . . the country called Carrae; it was a soil that bare amomum in great plenty: there are also in it the remains of that ark, wherein it is related that Noah escaped the deluge, and where they are still shown to such as are desirous to see them.[4]

It is hard to say, at this point, just how many of the early writers who mentioned the survival of the Ark were merely relying on previous accounts and how many actually had knowledge of its whereabouts. The early church fathers did write about the Ark's existence with conviction. It seemed unnecessary to attempt to prove or document their claims; indeed, they wrote as if it were an accepted truth. For example, Theophilus of Antioch wrote in A.D. 180:

C. And of the Ark, the remains are to this day to be seen in the Arabian mountains.[5]

The Armenian Bishop

The source of one of the more common stories concerning the existence of the Ark comes from the fertile pen of Faustus of Byzantium. The work of this fourth-century historian has been copied and adopted by several later writers. It tells the story of one St. Jacob of Medzpin, a devout man who prayed for years that God would allow him to view the remains of Noah's Ark. His story follows:

D. About this time the great Bishop of Medzpin, that admirable old man, tireless in the works of Christian truth, that chosen of God, Jacob by name, of Persian origin, set off from his city to the mountains of Armenia, that is to say, to Mt. Ararat in the principality of Ararat and the canton of Gortouk. He was full of the graces of Christ and had the power to do miracles and marvels. Arriving at his destination, he prayed God most fervently to allow him to see the Ark of deliverance built by Noah—the Ark which has come to rest on that mountain at the time of the Deluge. Now Jacob generally obtained from God all that he asked.

While he was climbing the stony side of the inaccessible and arid Mt. Ararat, he and those who accompanied him felt thirsty from fatigue. Then the great Jacob bent his knees and remained in prayer before the Lord. At the place where he laid his head, a spring of water broke forth by which he and his companions quenched their thirst. It is for this reason that to this day that spring is called "Jacob's well." Meanwhile, he applied himself zealously to catch sight of the object of his desire, and not cease to pray for it to the Lord God.

Already he had arrived near the summit of the mountain, and thoroughly exhaused as he was, he fell asleep. Then the angel of God came and said to him: "Jacob! Jacob!" He answered, "Here am I, Lord." And the angel said: "The Lord gives ear to your prayer and grants what you desire. That which you find beside your bed is wood from the Ark. There it is: I bring it to you: it comes from it. Henceforth, you will cease desiring to see the Ark, for such is the will of the Lord." Jacob woke with the greatest joy, praising and thanking the Lord. He saw the plank, which seemed to have been peeled off a large piece of wood with the blow of an axe. Taking up what had been entrusted to him, he went back, followed by his companions in the trip.

The joy felt by the great prophet Moses, that man who had seen God, could not have been greater than Jacob's—and perhaps was even less—when after receiving the commandments written by the finger of God and with them in his very hands, he descended Mt. Sinai with the tablets for a rebel people—that people who, having turned their faces from the holy places to the earth, having departed from the Lord's pathway, worshipped a metal calf, and deeply grieved the bearer of the Law, for the broken tablets already proved the annoyance of the one who brought them. But in the case of the blessed Jacob, the object of our narration, it was not the same, for, full of spiritual consolation, he returned bringing to all the nations of the earth the good news bestowed clearly and secretly by the Almighty God.

While this man of God was approaching with the wood of the deliverance—that relic of the Ark built by our father Noah, that eternal symbol of the great punishment inflicted by God on man and beast—the inhabitants of the city and the surrounding neighborhood came forth to meet him with boundless joy and happiness. From the moment they laid their eyes upon the holy man, they surrounded him as an envoy from Christ and kissed his footprints. The people eagerly accepted the gracious gift of the wood, and it is preserved to this day among them as the visible sign of the Ark of the patriarch Noah.[6]

Dark Ages Shed More Light on St. Jacob

In 1255, Guillaume of Ruysbroeck detailed an account of the same story after talking with a bishop from the area.

E. Many have tried to climb it, but none has been able. This bishop told me that there had been a monk who was most (desirous of climbing it), but that an angel appeared to him bearing a piece of the wood of the Ark, and told him to try no more. They had this piece of wood in his church, he told me.[7]

Vincent of Beauvais doubtless relied on the account of Faustus when he produced his extensive work *Speculum Quadruples* in 1259. However he furnishes some additional information not in the previous work. Picking up the story where Jacob is physically unable to continue:

F. When he had climbed part of the way, he would fall asleep on account of his tired limbs, and on waking he would always find himself at the foot of the mountain. Finally, however, the Lord gave in to his persistence: He harkened to the monks, vows, and prayers and so instructed him by His angel that he might ascend the mountain on one occasion—but for the future he would not seek to do so again. Thus he safely made the ascent, and when he returned he brought one of the beams from the Ark back with him. At the foot of the mountain he built a monastery in which he faithfully placed this same beam as a holy relic.[8]

In approximately the year 1360, Sir John Mandeville penned his *Travels*, after visiting the Ararat region in 1356. Note that his rehashing of the Jacob account reintroduces the idea that each morning he found that he had been returned to the base of the mountain.

G. . . . and there besides another mountain that men call Ararat, but the Jews call it Taneez, where Noah's Ark rested, and yet is upon that mountain, and men may see it afar in clear weather. That mountain is at least seven miles high. And some men say that they have seen and touched the Ark, and put their fingers in the parts where the fiend went out when Noah said "Benedicte." But they that say such words say without knowledge, for a man may not go up the mountain for the great amount of snow that is always on that mountain, both summer and winter; so that no man may go up there: no, never a man did, since the time of Noah: save a monk that by God's grace brought one of the planks down, that yet is in the monastery at the foot of the mountain. And beside is the city of Dayne, that Noah founded. And fast by is the city of Any, in which were one thousand churches. But upon that mountain to go up, this monk had great desire; and so upon a day, he went up. And when he was upward the third part of the mountain, he was so weary, that he might go no farther. And he rested and fell asleep; and when he awoke, he found himself lying at the foot of the mountain. And then he prayed devoutly to God that He would vouchsafe to suffer him to go up. And an angel came to him and said he should go up; and so he did. And since that time no one ever went up; wherefore men should not believe such words.[9]

The last ancient scholar and traveler that we shall mention who reviewed the story of St. Jacob is Sir John Chardin. In his work *Voyages*

Sir John Chardin, by David Loggan. Chardin visited Mt. Ararat in the seventeenth century.

he detailed his travels throughout the Ararat area, and, keeping in mind that the Armenian name for Mt. Ararat is Mt. Massis, we quote:

H. The Armenian traditions relate that the ark is still upon the point of Mount Massis. Ararat is thus called by the Armenians from Mash or Mesech, the son of Aram, from whom they would derive their name and origin. No one, however, as they report, has been able to climb to the place where it rested. This they firmly believe, on the faith of a miracle said to have occurred to one James, a monk of Eitch-mai-adzen, who subsequently was Bishop of Nisbis. This monk, prepossessed with the vulgar opinion of the hill being assuredly that on which the ark rested after the deluge, formed the design of going to its top, or of dying in the attempt. He got half way up, but never could mount higher; for, after climbing all the day, he was miraculously carried back, in his sleep at night, to the spot whence he had set out in the morning. This continued for a considerable time; when at length God listened to the monk's prayers, and agreed to satisfy his desire in part. For this object, He sent to James by an angel a piece of the ark; exhorting him through the same messenger not to fatigue himself to no purpose in climbing the mountain, as God had forbidden its access by mankind. Upon which I shall make two remarks—first, it is at variance with the ancient writers, such as Josephus, Berosus, and Nicholas of Damascus; who assure us, that in their days, the remains of the ark were still shown, and that the powder of the bitumen, with which it was pitched, was taken as a preservative of health; secondly, instead of its being a miracle that no one could ever reach the top of the mountain, I should deem as a grand miracle that any one ever got to the top of it; for there is not an habitation upon the hill, and from its middle to the summit it is covered with snow perpetually; so that at all seasons it has the appearance of a vast heap of snow.[10]

Chardin was quite familiar with Ararat, having spent some time there. The inhabitants of the area not only told him the story of Jacob but also indicated on which shoulder of the mountain the Ark reportedly lay hidden. When he etched out an engraving of the mountain, he added a rendition of the Ark in that spot. Interestingly enough, it is just that location that is still under consideration.

It seems that the story of Jacob changed with time, but it also seems that if a correct version exists or at least a version most likely to be correct, it must be the original story as laid down by Faustus of Byzantium, since it was written during Jacob's own century.

Early Historians

There are many other ancient witnesses. Two early church fathers, Bishop Epiphanius of Salamis and John Chrysostom, mentioned the existence of the Ark in their day. Both of them wrote in the latter part of the fourth century. Their respective quotes follow:

I. Do you seriously suppose that we are unable to prove our point, when even to this day the remains of Noah's Ark are shown in the country of the Kurds? Why, were one to search diligently, doubtless one would also find at the foot of the mountain the remnants of the altar where Noah, on leaving the Ark, tarried to offer clean and fatly animals as a sacrifice to the Lord God.[11]

And speaking of the destruction of Noah's Flood, Chrysostom writes:

J. Do not the mountains of Armenia testify to it, where the Ark rested? And are not the remains of the Ark preserved there to this very day for our admonition?[12]

Etymologies, compiled circa 610 by Isidore of Seville, also makes mention of Noah's Ark. Isidore compiled the facts or knowledge of his day and his tone in the following quote is definitely positive.

K. Ararat is a mountain in Armenia, where the historians testify that the Ark came to rest after the Flood. So even to this day wood remains of it are to be seen there.[13]

L. An interesting account of a visit to the Ark by the East Roman emperor Heraclius early in the seventh century comes to us from Hussein El Macin of Baghdad, who claims that the emperor visited the remains of the Ark after conquering the Persian city of Thamanin, near the base of Mt. Ararat.[14]

Reports from the Middle Ages

Nearly every school child in this country studies the life and travels of Marco Polo, who passed through Armenia on his way to the Far East.

M. In the central part of Armenia stands an exceedingly large and high mountain, upon which, it is said, the Ark of Noah rested, and for this reason it is termed the mountain of the Ark.[15]

A very interesting comment comes to us from Jehan Haithon, a monk who wrote in 1254:

N. Upon the snows of Ararat a black speck is visible at all times: this is Noah's Ark.[16]

Some have interpreted this to mean that he himself observed the object.

A Franciscan monk by the name of Odoric ventured near the mountain in 1316 and was bitten by the desire to visit the remains. He did not, but his comment is intriguing.

O. . . . and in that country is the mountain whereon is Noah's Ark. And I would fain have ascended it, if my companions would have waited for me. But the folk of the country told us that no one ever could ascend the mountain, for this, as it is said, hath seemed not to be the pleasure of the Most High.[17]

Seemingly a long silence as to the whereabouts of the Ark is broken in 1647 by Adam Olearius, in his book *Voyages and Travels of the Ambassadors*. Olearius lived near Ararat in 1633 and related:

P. The Armenians, and the Persians themselves, are of opinion that there are still upon the said mountain some remainders of the Ark, but that Time hath so hardened them, that they seem absolutely petrify'd. At Schamachy in Media Persia, we were shown a Crosse of a black and hard Wood, which the Inhabitants affirmed to have been made of the Wood of the Ark[18]

The Two Ararats, by Boulé Legouze. This French traveler sketched this crude rendering in 1647. His numbered locations represent: (1) the resting place of the Ark, (2) snow, (3) fog, (4) the mountains of Ararat, (5) St. Jacob himself, (6) the voice that speaks, and (7) foothills. From *Penashkharik Pararan.*

Probably the most intriguing of all ancient accounts is that experienced by Jans Janszoon Struys in 1670. Much of the following narrative is not only hard to believe but is highly unlikely. It is included here because it does possess many details that would not be accessible to one who has not climbed on Ararat and indeed would not even be recognizable to most readers, and also because it is a beautiful and highly exciting tale.

Q. This mountain is between Media and Armenia. It is like a range of Mountains of Dagestan. The Armenians call it Messine and the Persians, Agri. It is higher than Mount Caucase or Tarus and even than any mountains of Persia, Media, and Armenia. The rocks are of a clear brown, shaded a little toward blue, and I saw some quarried rocks, some yellow, some heavy and some light. I took a few of each kind to examine when I had leisure, but the "Anglois" relieved me of that trouble, taking all that I had when they made me a prisoner, as we shall tell of in its place.

My Patron desired to sell me at Erivan, but the people didn't want to buy me. Since he didn't care any longer, two Carmese men came to ask if I was a surgeon, and they assured me that if I had some intelligence in that art, they would give me some work for which I would be well paid if they saw that I would succeed.

I answered that surgeon was not my trade, and that I had never tried it. These good men did not believe me. After conferring together for some time, I saw from their faces that they took me for a skilled man, but that I didn't dare to acknowledge it in the presence of my Patron. They then took him aside and asked what my talent was. Without waiting for him to answer, one of the two said, "you can't deny us, my brother is sick with a rupture and if your slave can cure him, I'll give you 50 'ecurs.'' Let me go, said my Patron, I answer that your brother will be healed. He claimed he had known one of my comrades, who said I excelled in this . . . "Do you know," he said to me, "that here is a chance to recover your freedom. Take it if you are wise, for you will perhaps never have another so fine or sure." Then he held out his hand and told me I must undertake this cure which would perhaps bring me success. I thought the proposition over and resolved to try it even though I might be beaten if I failed. They settled on the price and on the next day we left to find the patient who lived as a hermit on Mount Ararat. His hermitage was so far from the base of the mountain that we traveled seven days, making five luus per day. Every evening we found a hut where we rested. The hermit there would give us the next day a country-man and donkey; the first as a guide and the other to carry our food and wood.

Engraving of Mt. Ararat showing reported resting place of the Ark. From *Travels in Persia* by Sir John Chardin.

This last provision is so useful, because without it the mountain is uninhabitable; and the cold there, is such that a horseman can run without risk with full rein on the ice for three hours. There is nothing to warm by unless one carries it, for one sees neither trees nor shrubs and in all the mountain there is not a bit of earth. The first clouds we passed were dark and thick. The others were extremely cold and full of snow, although a little lower down the heat was intense, and the grapes and other fruits were in perfect máturity. In the third cloud we thought we would die of the cold, we had to run! Nothing could warm us and so cold was this that we would have died; but when we could go no further we came to another hermit's hut. They made us a great fire, though it took more than an hour for me to feel it. The following days, the more we advanced the more temperate was the air we breathed; and this gentleness continued to the cell of our patient, where we arrived July 7.

This cell is large and hewn out of the rock, and this good hermit told me that it had never been any warmer or cooler than it was then, and it was then neither one nor the other. He added that in the five years he had been there he had not felt the least breath of wind, nor seen a drop of rain fall. With all that, he continued, the air is

Noah's Ark visible on Mt. Ararat in background of this engraving of Erzerom (artist unknown, seventeenth century).

still more quiet on the summit of the mountain, since no one has seen the least change and that it is for this reason the Ark is not decayed, and that it is after so many centuries as complete as the first day it came there.

The hermit continued to get better and I took care of him. I finally ordered him to keep the bandage on until the end of the year. He told me that his profession would not let him have riches and that he could only give me a cross attached to a silver chain which he took from his neck, with a small piece of red and brown wood, and a little piece of the rock on which the Ark rested. He raised the value of these two pieces of wood and stone in the cross, that I would be rich if I would keep them; or if I wished to carry them to the Church of St. Peter's in Rome, he assured me I would be rewarded with a fortune. Then he told me he was a Roman, named Domingo Alexander, son of one of the wealthiest and most prominent men in Rome, that after having given all his wealth to St. Peter he had become a hermit and would finish his days where he was on the mountain, that he was more happy and content than the wealthiest in the world. At our parting I asked him for written proof that I had been on Mount Ararat, which he gave me in the following words:

> I could not pass by John Jansmire's petition to present proof in writing that he was with me forty-five moons on sacred Mount Ararat during which time he saved me from a large rupture. Because of his great kindness and diligence I gave him a cross which was made from the true wood of Noah's Ark with my own hands, carved with a knife. I also gave him a stone which I cut with my own hands from the rock upon which the Ark rests. I declare all these facts to be as true as the fact that I live here in my sacred hermitage.

Mount Ararat, July 22, 1670

In charge of the holy reliques with which they promised I would lack nothing and proud of the success of my first operation, I descended the mountain escorted by a guide and a donkey. This was by the same trail by which I had ascended but it was much harder than the first time, especially through the cold clouds, which felt so hard, so freezing, so sharp that we ran the risk of falling at each step. Toward the foot of the mountain because of the wind, rain, and more difficult path, I almost gave up hope of reaching the bottom. I arrived, however, but not without swearing that I should never in my life return and that neither the Ark nor the stone which recalled the hermit to me would have power to draw me back there again. Thus, I saw the celebrated Mount Ararat and my trip is proof that although the route is bad, it is not inaccessible, as several had imagined.[19]

R. Not until the early 1800s did the emerging Americans claim a part in the mounting evidence supporting the survival of the remains of Noah's Ark, when Claudius James Rich reported contact with a Persian, Aga Hussein, who claimed to have climbed Mt. Ararat and seen the Ark.[20]

These accounts are only some of the many which have been passed down through the centuries. There are many others that make mention of the Ark indirectly, stating that the Ark still remained on the mountain. Doubtless there are many other accounts hidden in archives throughout the world, which have never been translated into English and which have never been studied. The reader is encouraged to search his own city library, for, who knows, perhaps an account of the discovery of the Ark, with pictures and maps, is itself waiting to be rediscovered.

[1] Robert Rogers, *Cuneiform Parallels to the Old Testament* (New York: Eaton & Mains, 1912), P. 112.

[2] Isaac Preston Cory, *Ancient Fragments*, 2nd ed. (London: W. Pickering, 1832), p. 54.

[3] Flavius Josephus, *The Antiquities of the Jews*, trans. William Whiston (Philadelphia: Henry T. Coates & Co.) book 1, chap. 3, sec. 5.

[4] *The Antiquities of the Jews*, book 20, chap. 2, sec. 2.

[5] *Ante-Nicene Fathers*, trans. Marcus Dods (1885) vol. 2, p. 117.

[6] Translated from Jean-Baptist Emine, *Victor Langlois Collection des Historiens Anciens et Modernes de L'Armenie* (1881), p. 218.

[7] Guillaume of Ruysbroeck, *Itinerarium*, trans. W. Rockhill, series 2, vol. 4 (London: Hakluyt Soc., 1900), pp. 269-70.

[8] Vincent of Beauvais, *Speculum Quadruplex* (1259) as cited in John Montgomery, *The Quest for Noah's Ark* (Minneapolis: Bethany Fellowship, 1972), p. 77.

[9] Sir John Mandeville, *Travels* (1360) cited in James Bryce, *Transcaucasia and Ararat* (London: Macmillas, 1877), pp. 205-6.

[10] Sir John Chardin, *Voyages* (1711), cited in Frederika von Fraygang, *Letters from the Caucaus and Georgia* (London: John Murray, 1823), pp. 279-80.

[11] F. Oehler (trans.), *Panarion*, I.i. 18, by Epiphanius of Salamis (Berlin, 1859), pp. 94-95, cited by John Montgomery in *The Quest for Noah's Ark* (Minneapolis: Bethany Fellowship, 1972), pp. 72-73.

[12] John Chrysostom, in a sermon (4th century), ed. Sir Henry Sevile (17th century), cited by John Montgomery in *The Quest for Noah's Ark* (Minneapolis: Bethany Fellowship, 1972), pp. 72-73.

[13] Isidore of Seville, *Etymologiarium sive Originum*, book 20, trans. ed. W. M. Lindsay, *Scriptorum Classicorum Bibliotheca Oxoniensis*, vol. 2 (Oxford: Clarendon Press, 1911), cited by John Montgomery, *The Quest for Noah's Ark* (Minneapolis: Bethany Fellowship, 1972), pp. 75-76.

[14] As cited by Rev. S. Baring-Gould, *Legends of the Patriarchs and Prophets* (New York: Hurst and Co., n.d.), p. 142.

[15] Marco Polo, *Travels of Marco Polo*, trans. Marsden (New York: The Modern Library, 1926), p. 25.

[16] Jehan Haithon (13th century) as cited by Rev. S. Baring-Gould, *Legends of the Patriarchs and Prophets* (New York: Hurst and Co., n.d.), p. 142.

[17] Sir Henry Yule (trans., ed.), *Cathay and the Way Thither* (London: for Hakluyt Society, 1914), vol. 3, Missionary Friars—Rashiduddin, Pegolotti, Marignolli, p. 102.

[18] Adam Olearius, *Voyages and Travels of the Ambassadors*, trans. John Davis (London: 1662), vol 4, p. 187.

[19] A. J. Smith, *The Reported Discovery of Noah's Ark* (Orlando: Christ for the World Publishers, 1949), pp. 25-29.

[20] Claudius James Rich, *Narrative of a Residence in Koordistan* (London: James Duncan, 1836), vol. 2, p. 124.

4

Earthquake: 1840

On June 20, 1840, a dramatic event took place that was destined to herald in the modern era in the search for Noah's Ark. An earthquake of gigantic proportions opened up a massive section of the upper regions of Mt. Ararat. From that date there has been an ever increasing number of sightings of the Ark.

As discussed before, Mt. Ararat lies squarely along a major earthquake fault zone. In fact, the volcanic Ararat is a direct result of the violent tectonic activity associated with that huge crack in the earth's surface. The fissure is still quite active and evidently has always been, for evidence is found all around the area of at least three major periods of volcanism. Surrounding the mountain, and particularly on the south and east sides, layers of lava rest in huge deposits that are thousands of feet thick in places.

As might be expected, the Ararat region frequently undergoes violent earth tremors. The most recent major earthquake in Eastern Turkey occurred on September 6, 1975, wiping out the town of Lice and many nearby villages in the province of Diyarbikir, causing some 2,000 deaths.

As destructive as earthquakes are, we can point to the 1840 quake as the catalyst which produced a reaction and a chain of events of which even this book is only a part.

The Destruction of Ahora

On the evening of the 20th of June, 1840, a terrific earthquake shook the mountain, and not only the shrine and the cloister, but the entire village of Akhury (Arghuri or Ahora) were destroyed and swept away. An eye-witness, who was pasturing cattle on the grassy slopes above the chasm on the side opposite to the shrine and the well, tells us that he was thrown onto his knees by a sudden reeling of the ground, and that, even in this position, he was unable to maintain himself, but was overturned by the continuing shocks. Close by his side the earth cracked; a terrific rolling sound filled his ears; when he dared look up, he could see nothing but a mighty cloud of dust, which glimmered with a reddish hue above the ravine. But the quaking and the cracking were renewed. He lay outstretched upon the ground, and thus awaited death. At length the sounds became fainter, and he was able to look towards the ravine. Through the dusk he perceived a dark mass in the hollow, but of what it was composed he could not see. The sun went down; the great cloud passed away from the valley; as he descended with his cattle in the falling light, he could see nothing within the abyss except the dark mass.

Another spectator has left us an account of the various phases of the phenomenon, as they were experienced from a standpoint below the village. He happened to be working in a garden a few versts from Arkury, on the side of the plain. His wife and daughter were with him; two of his sons appeared towards evening and brought him a report about his cattle. Two riders, returning to the village, exchanged a few words with the party and rode on. The sun was beginning to sink behind the mountains, and he and his people were preparing to go home. In an instant the ground beneath their feet oscillated violently, and all were thrown down. At the same time loud reports and a rolling sound, as of thunder, increased the panic into which they fell. A hurricane of wind swept towards them from the direction of the chasm and overturned every object that was not firm. In the same direction there arose an immense cloud of dust, overtopped towards the upper part of the ravine, by a darker cloud, as of black smoke. After a momentary pause the same phenomena were repeated; only this time a dark mass swept towards them from the direction of the village with a rolling and a rushing sound. It reached the two riders; they were engulfed and disappeared. Immediately afterward, the two sons were overtaken by the same fate. The mass rolled on towards the gardens, and broke down the walled enclosures. Large stones came tumbling about the unfortunate peasants; and a large crag swept down upon the prostrate witness, and settling by his side, caught his mantle fast. Extricating himself with difficulty, he succeeded in lifting his unconscious wife and daughter from the earth, and in flying with them over the quaking ground. After each shock they could hear the sound of cracking in the chasm, accompanied by sharp reports. They were joined by fugitives, escaping from the neighboring gardens, and they endeavored to make their way to Aralykh. It was morning before they reached their goal; during the night the sounds and shocks continued, always fainter but at periodic intervals. This catastrophe was followed on the 24th of June by a second and scarcely less momentous collapse. On this occasion a mass of mud and water burst from the chasm, as though some colossal dam had given way. Blocks of rock and huge pieces of ice were precipitated over the base, and the flood extended for a space of about thirteen miles. Not a trace was left of the gardens and fields which it devastated, and the Kara Su was temporarily dammed by the viscous stream.[1]

The town of Arkury, now known as Ahora, was situated right at the mouth of the Ahora Gorge, at about a 5,000-foot elevation. Since the earthquake it has been rebuilt, and it is from this little village that most expeditions to search for the Ark begin their climb. It is interesting that according to Armenian tradition the first rainbow was seen in Ahora as Noah, soon after leaving the Ark, built his altar and sacrificed to God, thanking Him for His protection. The tradition goes on to say that it was at Ahora that Noah planted his first vineyard. The earthquake destroyed all traces of the town, includings its church which was reported to have been built on the site of Noah's altar at least 1,000 years earlier, a summer palace or fortress for a Russian ruler, vineyards and gardens, and all other structures and landmarks.

Ahora was not the only settlement affected by the explosion. About two miles farther up into the gorge, on a natural terrace, stood the monastery of St. Jacob. Evidently monks had lived in the area since the fourth century when St. Jacob returned with his piece of wood; although the existing monastery buildings dated from the eleventh century.

Dr. Frederick Parrott, who in 1829 became the first to conquer the summit, established his headquarters at this monastery. He tells us that the small facility included a chapel, a walled enclosure, a garden, an orchard, and a small residence area.

James Bryce, the British statesman, author, world traveler, and ex-

Engraving of Mt. Ararat in 1829 from Kanakir from *Journey to Ararat* by Parrot.

plorer, wrote a similar account of the earthquake, based on his research, when he explored Ararat in 1877.

Near the mouth of the chasm there formerly stood a pleasant little Armenian village of some two hundred houses, named Arghuri, or Aghurri. They boasted not only of the Patriarch's vine, bearing grapes delicious to eat, but which Heaven, in memory of the fault they betrayed him into, had forbidden to be made into wine; but also of an ancient willow trunk, which had sprung from one of the planks of the Ark. Not far above the village, on the spot where stood the little monastery of St. Jacob, eight centuries old, and still higher was a tiny shrine beside a spring of bright clear water, the spring of the "tetagush" legend; while on the opposite side of the glen the Persian Sardar or viceroy had erected a sumptuous summer villa to which he was accustomed to retire from the scorching heats of Erivan. . . . Towards sunset in the evening of the 20th of June 1840 (old style), the sudden shock of an earthquake, accompanied by a subterranean roar, and followed by a terrific blast of wind, threw down the houses of Arghuri, and at the same moment detached enormous masses of rock with their superjacent ice from the cliffs that surround the chasm. A shower of falling rocks overwhelmed in an instant the village, the monastery, and a Kurdish encampment on the pastures above. Not a soul survived to tell the tale. Four days afterwards, the masses of snow and ice that had been precipitated into the glen suddenly melted, and, forming an irresistible torrent of water and mud, swept along the channel of the stream and down the outer slopes of the mountain, far away into the Aras plain, bearing with them huge blocks, and covering the ground for miles with a deep bed of mud and gravel. Even now, after thirty-seven years, the traces of this convulsion are distinctly visible; in some places the precipices from which the masses fell show a fracture mark fresh as of yesterday. . . . the dust which accompanies the great rock fall was probably mistaken for smoke by those who saw it from a distance. Doubtless the blast was produced by the fall of the rock masses.[2]

Our modern-day quest certainly would be simplified had the monastery not been destroyed by the explosion, for it is believed the monks there harbored priceless treasures related to the existence of the Ark.

Colonel Alexander A. Koor, an officer in the White Russian Army stationed at the base of Ararat for several years prior to the Bolshevik revolution, visited and explored many sites of archaeological interest in Eastern Turkey which will be discussed later. But his reference to the monastery of St. Jacob can only intrigue the adventurer.

Not far from Arghuri there are the ruins of St. James monastery buried by an earthquake in 1840. Many ancient relics of the epoch of Noah, many ancient manuscripts and books were lost here. . . . This area should be searched.[3]

A tradition passed on by the Armenian people reflects the striking

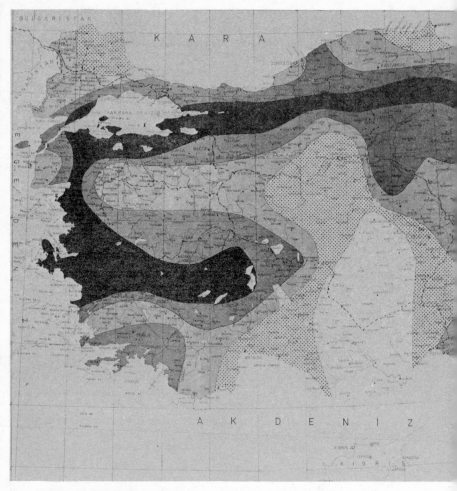

Tectonic map of Turkey. Mt. Ararat is seen to be in an active earthquake zone. (Courtesy Republic of Turkey)

nature of the Ahora Gorge. According to the Armenian historian Father Eprikian:

> . . . the haughty Ardavazd of the Artashesian dynasty, while hunting in the vicinity of the river Kin, suddenly plunged to the bottom of the Ahora Gorge. His father had previously cursed him that he might never again see the light. With his plunge the father's curse materialized. Due to this, there is a well-known legend among the Armenian peasantry that Ardavazd is imprisoned and chained in a cave in the Ahora Gorge, and that some day he might emerge to create disorder in

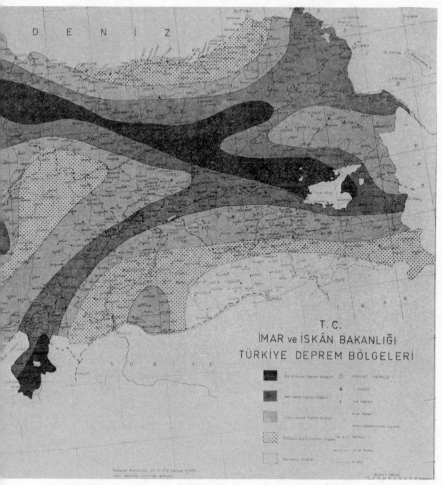

T.C.
İMAR ve İSKÂN BAKANLIĞI
TÜRKİYE DEPREM BÖLGELERİ

the world if the Armenian blacksmiths stop hammering their anvils. This tradition still persists in some sections of Armenia. The superstitious blacksmiths consider it necessary to hammer their anvils a few times each day, even on Sundays and holidays.[4]

Changes in the Ahora Gorge

Dr. Parrott was one of the few scholars who visited Ararat prior to the 1840 disaster. Those who did left us a rich legacy in written form.[5] Note in the following quotes that references to the Ahora Gorge are conspicuous by their near absence. Of course, the major part of today's gorge was

Drawing from Armenian mythology showing the wicked Ardavazd falling into the Ahora Gorge. From *Penashkarhik Pararan.*

blown out at the time of the Flood; but it is entirely possible, indeed very probable, that some of the more striking features were at that time somewhat obscured by sediments, hidden from the view of early travelers. All of the paintings and engravings of the period show only an irregularity in the mountain slopes where the gorge should be; but today anyone who observes the mountain on a clear day from the north side can hardly see anything but that ugly scar. It is much too obvious to have been deleted from descriptions and sketches.

The following is from an old Bible dictionary copyrighted in 1833.

Ararat. a mountain in the country of the same name, on which rested Noah's ark. Part of the province which was formerly so called lies in Turcomania, and the rest is in Persia. It has Georgia on the north, Media on the east, Assyria on the south, and Lesser Asia on the west. Here the rivers Euphrates, Tigris, Araxes, and Phasis have their source. Here stand the famed mountains Taurus and Antitaurus, Niphates, Gordian etc. Mount Ararat, upon which Noah's ark rested, was probably the Ar-dagh or finger-mountain, in Armenia, standing in a large plain, 36 miles east from Erivan, rising in a conical shape to the height of about 12,000 feet above the level of the sea, and visible nearly 200 miles distant. Its top is inaccessible on account of the snow which perpetually covers it. The middle part is haunted by tigers; some poor flocks and small monasteries are at the foot.[6]

Similarly, in another old Bible dictionary, no mention of the rugged features is made. This quote is from two American missionaries, Smith and Dwight, who visited the mountain in 1831.

We passed very near the base of that noble mountain, which is called by the Armenians Massis, and by Europeans generally Ararat, and for more than 20 days had it constantly in sight, except when obscured by clouds. It consists of two peaks, one considerably higher than the other, and is connected with a chain of mountains running off to the north-west and west, which, though high, are not of sufficient elevation to detract at all from the lonely dignity of this stupendous mass. From Nakhchewan, at the distance of at least 100 miles to the south-east, it appeared like an immense isolated cone of extreme regularity, rising out of the valley of the Araxes. Its height is said to be 16,000 feet. The eternal snows upon its summit occasionally form vast avalanches, which precipitate themselves down its sides with a sound not unlike that of an earthquake. When we saw it, it was white to its very base with snow. And certainly not among the mountains of Ararat or Armenia generally, nor those of any part of the world where I have been, have I ever seen one whose majesty could plead half so powerfully its claims to the honor of having once been the stepping-stone between the old world and the new. I gave myself up to the feeling, that on its summit were once congregated all the inhabitants of the earth, and that, while in the valley of the Araxes, I was paying a visit to the second cradle of the human race.[7]

Dr. John Kitto visited Ararat shortly before the earthquake. Later in his two books, he tells of his findings and refers to one James J. Morier, likewise a visitor to Ararat around the turn of the century.

When our own eyes first beheld the "dread magnificence" of Ararat, we had already seen the loftiest and most remarkable mountains of the old world; but yet the effect of the view of this mountain was new and surprising. The reason appeared to be this—most of the loftiest mountains of the world are but peaks of the uppermost ridge of mountain chains. . . .

Now Ararat is not by any means in actual altitude so high as the Caucasian summit; yet the view of it is far more grand and impressive. The reason is, that it is not merely a summit of a ridge; it is a whole and perfect mountain. . . . "Nothing," as Mr. Morier well remarks, "can be more beautiful than its shape; more awful than its height; all the surrounding mountains sink into insignificance when compared with it; it is perfect in all its parts; no hard rugged features, no unnatural prominences, everything is in harmony, and all combine to render it one of the sublimest objects of nature."

Many attempts were made in former times to attain the summit, access to which the native Armenians believe to be supernaturally interdicted; yet with strange incongruity, they sell to pilgrims relics from the wood of the ark, which is still believed to lie upon the summit. It was not till 1829 that a successful attempt was made by Professor Parrot, a German, acting under Russian auspices. (The

The Ahora Gorge as seen today. (Courtesy Hardwicke Knight)

success of this attempt has, however, been much questioned, and is stoutly denied by all persons in the neighborhood of the mountain.)

It remains to be added, that Ararat has since been the scene of a fearful visitation, which in a few moments changed the entire face of the country. This was a dreadful earthquake which commenced in June 1840, and continued at intervals till September in the same year. As the most destructive shock occurred in the daytime, the loss of life did not exceed fifty; but the destruction of property was great, and traces of the calamity will be borne down to future ages in the fissures and landslips of the district. Even the aged mountain did not escape. Vast masses of rock, ice and snow were detached from the summit and lateral points of the mountain, and thrown, "with horrid ruin and combustion down," at a single bound, into the valley of Akhor where the fragments lie to this day, scattered over an extent of several miles.[8]

And in his *Illustrated History of the Holy Bible* he writes:

The Armenians who have many religious establishments in its vicinity, regard the mountain with extreme veneration, and are firmly persuaded that the ark is still preserved at its summit.[9]

The Ahora Gorge as seen before the 1840 earthquake. From *Journey to Ararat* by Parrot.

There are many other accounts which parallel these, but the point to be made is that the appearance of the Ahora Gorge area was significantly altered by the 1840 disaster. It seems only those investigators who examined the mountain closely make mention of the gorge. One such explorer was the French botanist Tournefort, who in 1701 spoke of the "terrible appearance of the ravine." He "trembled" as he "overlooked the precipices" and saw that "one of the loftiest mountains of the world had opened its bosom to a vertical cleft. From the heights above, masses of rocks were continually falling into the abyss with a noise that inspired fear."[10]

Sir Robert Ker Porter, in 1831, recorded the following:

On viewing Mt. Ararat from the northern side of the plain, its two levels are separated by a wide cleft, or glen, in the body of the mountain. The rocky side of the greater head runs almost perpendicularly down to the northeast, and shows to the northeast a broken and abrupt front, opening about half-way down, into a stupendous chasm, deep, rocky, and peculiarly black.[11]

As mentioned before, Parrot spent several days at the entrance to the gorge, living in the monastery. Being a curious individual, he explored it to its end.

On the northern face of Ararat, the first thing that strikes the eye is a deep and wide chasm, which seems to disclose the interior of the mountain. It begins near the summit with a soft depression, which, growing deeper as it descends, and

Inside the awesome Ahora Gorge. Note avalanche debris, black glacier, waterfall, and vertical rock wall.

continuing in the same direction forms, at length, a profound glen with precipitous sides, which are themselves rent and split in a thousand forms. Such is the character of the great chasm about a mile above the monastery of St. James. Near the monastery it widens considerably, and escapes, in some measure, from its rocky barriers. Half a mile lower down it branches into a number of shallow depressions, which lose themselves in the plain of the Araxes.[12]

No mention is made here of the extensive boulder-strewn fields that many times form impassable barriers. No mention is made of the steep slopes composed of alternate layering of sediment beds and lava beds, with so little cohesiveness that even a shout will bring tons of rock down to the valley floor; or the fearsome black glacier at the end of the gorge, impregnated with lava dust and debris to such an extent that it looks perfectly black. The fact that most of the floor of the gorge is really a hidden snowfield—hidden under avalanche debris until it is neither visible nor noticeable unless differential melting causes crevasses to open up, sometimes induced by the weight of one who dares to trespass into the area—is also not mentioned. Neither is it mentioned that ringing the rim of the gorge is the thick glacial ice cap moving toward the edge and eventually breaking off, falling thousands of feet, with such a noise that had he heard it, he would have reported it. Anyone who has ventured into the upper reaches of the gorge is quite familiar with the "perpendicular wall of rock which towered up to the snow cornice of the dome,"[13] but he also knows that huge sections of that wall are dislodged and missing, and at least two distinct fractures are now found in the wall, running from the floor up to the very top of the wall. These cleavages appear even now to be separating, fanning out. And, strangest of all, no mention is made of the beautiful and majestic waterfall at the very end of the gorge, an estimated 450 feet in height, fed by the melting snow above and falling onto the head of the foreboding black glacier.

Ararat Altered

There can be no doubt, the earthquakes and flooding in the summer of 1840 altered the appearance of Mt. Ararat. Not only were five thousand years of sediments washed away, but portions of the inner fabric of the mountain disintegrated, spewing boulders and rock debris for miles in all directions.

Lynch gives his interpretation of the effect of the catastrophe when discussing the findings of the official earthquake investigation team headed up by the Russian Major of Engineers, which investigated the gorge soon after the event:

From his writings we may extract the following explanation of the phenomena to which the destruction of Akhury was due. The upper structure of Ararat had been seriously weakened on the north-eastern side by the slow but persistent action of snow and ice, and by the corrosive tendencies of veins of sulphurate of iron. The earthquake precipitated portions of the higher seams into the chasm, together with masses of snow. A dense cloud of dust was induced by the falling rocks, and the setting sun lent to this cloud a lurid hue. Immense quantities of boulders were hurried down the trough of the chasm, accompanied by a stream of mud and melting ice. The course of this composite current was directed upon the village by the configuration of the left wall of the chasm. As the sides of the valley fell in, its upper portion became obstructed at the neck or narrow which still exists about at the point where the little shrine used to overlook the abyss. A mighty dam was formed by the fallen masses, and the head of the valley became a huge morass.

Further lapses of rock and snow took place from the summit region, and the heats of June dissolved the frozen elements in the morass. On the 24th the dam yielded to the overpowering pressure, and the second act of the catastrophe was fulfilled.

As a result of this earthquake, the ridge enclosing the uppermost end of the chasm was found to have acquired about double its former extent. The height of the precipice had also increased considerably, especially on the eastern side. The summit remained intact, but the fabric of Ararat lay henceforth exposed to its innermost core.[14]

Apparently the earthquake originated right at the heart of the mountain, splitting the awesome cliff. High above, the lip of the canyon broke off and millions of tons of rock fell vertically for over a mile before striking the bottom, accompanied by immense quantities of ice and snow.

There had always been a small stream flowing out of the mouth of the gorge. But the 1840 quake caused the rocks from above to form a natural dam, retaining the melting snow. And, with the addition of the mass of ice from above now at a lower, warmer elevation, the melt was awesome. Several days later when the water pressure built up to the point where the dam could no longer hold it, water and debris burst out in such quantities that more damage was caused then than at the time of the earthquake.

A mature glacier, such as the one found on top of Mt. Ararat at the upper rim of the Ahora Gorge, is characterized by its compact nature and thickness. Such a glacier can only be formed over a period of many, many years by accumulating snow. The two glaciers, now designated as the Abich I and the Abich II glaciers, give every indication of having changed their flow patterns after reaching maturity. Now thicknesses of ice in excess of 600 feet fall off the shoulder of the mountain into the gorge. But a glacier that thick could not form under current conditions. Unless there was previously a restraining factor, probably a rock ridge formation while the glacier was forming, the glacier would not have reached its present thickness. Now the restraining factor is gone, and the previously mature glacier slowly moves toward the edge.

Could the Ark Survive?

"How," the reader might ask, "could a holocaust of this magnitude have heralded the so-called modern era of the search for the remains of Noah's Ark? If it seemed unlikely that the Ark could have survived thousands of years of 'normal' volcanism and glaciation, then it seems almost too much to ask that it also survive such an earthquake."

Once again, we would have to concur. Humanly speaking, it is indeed unlikely that vestiges of the Ark remain. In fact, the possibility seems so remote that we can say without fear of contradiction that if it remains, God has reached down for five thousand years or so and placed His protective hand on the Ark, insuring its preservation.

Suppose for a moment that the 1840 quake dislodged a ridge of rocks that formed the lateral boundary of a mature glacier, and with no boundaries on one side the glacial patterns changed. Within a few years the patterns were established well enough for drainage and melt patterns also to be re-established. Suppose also that somehow the ice pack that holds the remains of Noah's Ark was altered to the point that even now, in periods of exteme glacial melt, the Ark protrudes from the glacier.

This may seem to be a lot to suppose, but it has been a century and a quarter since the earthquake. Before 1840 many people either saw the Ark or saw wood reportedly from the Ark or encountered local legends referring to its existence. The total number of such accounts does not overly impress the researcher; and by no means do these accounts provide conclusive proof that the Ark has survived. Interestingly, however, in this, the modern era, the converse is true. Since 1840, scores of people have claimed to have seen Noah's Ark, personally, up close; many have even walked inside. Many thousands claim to have seen pictures of the remains, and many more have seen a mysterious shiplike shadow through glacial ice. Countless millions have read of these reported discoveries and realized the potential impact on the world a documented study of the artifact would initiate.

Much of the remainder of this book endeavors to present evidence gathered in recent years which indicates that God has indeed preserved the Ark. It also presents speculations on possible answers to the dilemma that "If God has preserved the Ark, why has He done so, and what are His future plans for it?"

Additional References

Abich, H. "Das Erdbeben von Arguri 1840." In *Geologische Forschungen*, part 2. Vienna: 1878-1887.

Freshfield, Douglas W. *Travels in the Central Caucasus and Bashan*. London: Longmans, Green and Co., 1869.

Hodgetts, E. A. Brayley. *Round About Armenia*. London: Sampson Low, Marston and Co., 1896.

Morier, James. *A Journey Through Persia, Armenia and Asia Minor*. London: Longman, Hurst, Rees, Orme, and Brown, 1812.

Morier, James. *The Adventures of Haji Baba*. London: Dulau and Co., 1925.

[1]H.F.B. Lynch, *Armenia: Travels and Studies* (London: 1901), vol. 1, pp. 185-87. Reprinted (Beirut: Khayats, 1965), pp. 189-190.

[2]James Bryce, *Transcaucasia and Ararat* (London: MacMillan, 1877), pp. 239-41.

[3]Alexander A. Koor, unpublished personal memoirs.

[4]Father Eprikian, *Penashkharhik Pararan* (Venice, 1903).

[5]See Bela Bates Edwards, "Ascent of Mount Ararat" in *Biblical Repository and Quarterly Observer* (April, 1836), pp. 390-416.

[6]Howard Malcom, A. M. Copyrighted in 1833, this edition was published in 1844 by Gould, Kendall & Lincoln, Boston, pp. 21 and 22.

[7]*A Dictionary of the Holy Bible* (New York: American Tract Society, 1859), pp. 34-5.

[8]John Kitto, *Daily Bible Illustrations* (London: Robert Carter & Bros., 1874), pp. 160-63.

[9]John Kitto, *An Illustrated History of the Holy Bible* (Norwich, Conn.: Henry Bill, 1866), p. 56.

[10]J. Pitton de Tournefort, *Relation d'un voyage du Levant*, trans. J. Ozell (London, 1741), vol. 3.

[11]Sir R. K. Porter, *Travels in Georgia, Persia, Armenia, etc*. (London: Longman, Hurst, Rees, Orme, and Brown, 1821) p. 170.

[12]Dr. Friedrich Parrot, *Journey to Ararat*, trans. W. D. Cooley (New York: Harper and Brothers, 1846), p. 373.

[13]Ibid, p. 373.

[14]H.F.B. Lynch, *Armenia Travels and Studies* (London: Longman, Hurst, Rees, Orme, and Brown, 1901), vol. 1, pp. 189-190.

5

Haji Yearam: 1856

Haji is a form of the Armenian word *Hadji* or the Turkish word *Haci* meaning holy man or one who has made a pilgrimage to the Holy Land.

With four other men, Haji Yearam visited the Ark during the mid 1850s. At the time he was a teenager, but by the time he told his story he was an old man. Haji was of Armenian descent, that ancient race who throughout history had lived in the Ararat area and who, as we have seen in chapter 3, had kept alive the tradition that the Ark of Noah still remained on the rugged heights of Mt. Ararat.

In 1915, at the age of seventy-four and nearly blind, this formerly rugged individual with such an exciting history lay semi-conscious and totally unable to care for himself or even call for help. He lay in the attic of a deserted mansion that he had rented to store some antiques that he hoped to sell.

With his strength nearly gone, he prayed for help—not necessarily that God would spare his life, but that before he died he would be able to tell his strange story, a story that he knew must be told. Under threat of death, he had kept his story sealed up within his memory for sixty years.

Harold H. Williams was the vehicle God used to answer Haji's prayer. We let him tell the story in his own words in a letter addressed "To Whom It May Concern"[1] and dated 1952, almost 100 years after the actual sighting took place, possibly the first sighting following the 1840 earthquake.

In the year of 1915, Mrs. Williams and I were living at Pacific Union College where I was taking special classes at the College. We were operating a private nursing home. My parents were living on Telegraph Avenue, in Oakland, California.

One day while visiting my parents, a young man was sent by Elder B. E. Beddoe, pastor of the Oakland Seventh-Day Adventist Church, with a request that I go at once to see an old man who had not been to church for some time. They were afraid that he might be ill.

This man's name was Yearam in Armenian, which is Jeremiah in English. When he was a young man he had made a pilgrimage to Jerusalem from Armenia, thus gaining the title of Haji, so was ever afterward known as Haji Yearam, or Jeremiah the Pilgrim.

I found Haji nearly dead with bloody dysentery in the attic of his house. He was so nearly dead that I could not move him for several days, so had to doctor and nurse him where he was. As soon as he was sufficiently recovered, I removed him to the home of my parents, and thence to my own home, where Mrs. Williams and I cared for him for many months, free of charge, because we supposed him to be a pauper.

Haji was one of the most earnest and consecrated Seventh-Day Adventist Christians I have ever known. He was the first foreign convert of our first foreign missionary, J. N. Andrews. I have forgotten the place and circumstances of their meeting, but after his conversion Haji Yearam came to the States and worked in the old Battle Creek (Michigan) Sanitarium. He had formerly been a merchant in the city of Constantinople. Three different times Haji built up fortunes in business in the United States and planned to return to the Old Country, but each time was robbed of everything he had before reaching his destination. For the fourth time, there in Oakland, California, he was working through a real estate and antique business to build up a fortune for his old age. He was then about 74 years old and was growing blind, having cataracts.

In May, 1916, Mrs. Williams and I moved to South Lancaster, Massachusetts, where I had been hired by Prof. Machlan as a member of the faculty. Haji Yearam was by this time almost totally blind, so we took him to the home of my parents in Oakland where he lived until he died. It was finally discovered that he owned considerable property. He willed one home to my mother in return for his care until he died.

One day while living with us at Pacific Union College, Haji asked me to get a "composition book" and write down carefully a story he was very anxious to tell, because he was sure that it would be of use some day after he was dead and gone.

Here is the story as accurately as I can now give it from memory, checked by the memory of Mrs. Williams who also heard it.

Noah's Ark

Haji Yearam's parents and family lived at the foot of Greater Mount Ararat in Armenia. According to their traditions, they were descended directly from those who had come out of the Ark, but who had never migrated from that country. The descendants of Ham and his sympathizers had migrated over into the land of Shinar and built the Tower of Babel; and others had migrated to various countries, but Haji's forebears had always remained near the mount where the Ark came to

Tent village high on the slopes of Mt. Ararat.

rest in a little valley surrounded by some small peaks about three-quarters or more up on the mountain.

For several hundreds of years after the Flood his forebears had made yearly pilgrimages up to the Ark to make sacrifices and to worship there. They had a good trail and steps in the steep places. Finally the enemies of God undertook to go to Ararat and destroy the Ark, but as they neared the location there came a terrible storm that washed away the trail, and lightning blasted the rocks. From that time on, even the pilgrimages ceased, because they feared to betray the way to the ungodly, and they feared God's wrath. They took that terrible storm to be a token that God did not want the Ark disturbed until near the end of the world, when they believed that its presence would be revealed to the whole world. However, the tribesmen there handed down the legends from generation to generation, and from time to time lonely shepherds or hunters in very hot summers came back with stories that they had reached the little valley and had actually seen one end of the Ark where it had been made visible by the melting snow and ice.

When Haji was a large boy, but not yet a man fully grown, there came to his home some strangers. If I remember correctly there were three vile men who did not believe the Bible and did not believe in the existence of a personal God. They were scientists and evolutionists. They were on this expedition specifically to prove the legend of Noah's Ark to be a fraud and a fake. They hired the father of young Haji Yearam as their official guide. (Haji at that time had not yet become a Haji, and was just a large boy). They hired the boy to assist his father as guide.

It was an unusually hot summer, so the snow and glaciers had melted more than usual. The Armenians were very reticent to undertake any expedition to the Ark because they feared God's displeasure, but the father of Haji thought that possibly the time had come when God wanted the world to know the Ark was still there and he wanted to prove to those atheists that the Bible story of the Flood and the Ark is true.

After extreme hardship and peril the party came to the little valley way up on Greater Ararat, not on the very top, but a little down from the top. This little valley is surrounded by a number of small peaks. There the Ark came to rest in a little lake, and the peaks protected it from the tidal waves that rushed back and forth as the Flood subsided. On one side of the valley the water from the melting snows and glacier spills over in a little river that runs down the mountain. As they reached this spot, there they found the prow of a mighty ship protruding out of the ice. They went inside the Ark and did considerable exploring. It was divided up into many floors and stages and compartments and had bars like animal cages of today. The whole structure was covered with a varnish or lacquer that was very thick and strong, both outside and inside the ship. The ship was built more like a great and mighty house on the hull of a ship, but without any windows. There was a great doorway of immense size, but the door was missing. The scientists were appalled and dumbfounded and went into a Satanic rage at finding what they hoped to prove nonexistent. They were so angry and mad that they said they would destroy the ship, but the wood was more like stone than any wood we have

The precise location of Haji Yearam's burial place has perhaps been lost amid the weeds of an abandoned section of an otherwise fashionable Bay Area cemetery. The visible tombstone (perhaps Haji's) serves as a reminder to us that worldly possessions and status are, in the end, meaningless.

now. They did not have tools or means to wreck so mighty a ship and had to give up. They did tear out some timbers and tried to burn the wood, but it was so hard it was almost impossible to burn it.

They held a council, and then took a solemn and fearful death oath. Any man present who would ever breathe a word about what they had found would be tortured and murdered.

They told their guide and his son that they would keep tabs on them and that if they ever told anyone and they found it out they would surely be tortured and murdered. For fear of their lives, Haji and his father had never told what they found except to their best trusted and closest relatives.

Here Haji was in America, an old man about seventy-five years old by this time. These scientists were much older and he doubted if any of them were then living. To be sure the record was left, he wanted his story recorded before he died. So I recorded it very carefully, and he went over it again and again to make sure no mistake had been made. He felt quite sure that the men who had threatened his life if he told were dead and gone by then.

In the year 1918 we moved to Brockton, Massachusetts, where I took the position of Supervisor of Manual Arts in the High School of that city. I was soon put on permanent tenure by the State Board of Education and held that position for nearly eight years until I entered the Gospel ministry.

Now, if some atheistic scientist had found an elephants knee cap that looked something like a skull bone, they would have proclaimed it a missing link and it would have been printed in large letters across the top of the daily newspapers, but any news that would support the Bible is largely ignored.

One evening (I am pretty sure it was in 1918) I sat reading the daily paper in our apartment in Brockton. Suddenly I saw in very small print a short story of a dying man's confession. It was a news item one column wide and, as I remembered it, not more than two inches deep. It stated that an elderly scientist on his death bed in London was afraid to die before making a terrible confession. It gave briefly the very date and facts that Haji Yearam had related to us in his story. I got out the composition book containing the story he had me write. It was identical in every detail. Haji Yearam had died in my parents' home in Oakland, California, about the same time that the old scientist had died in London. We had never for one moment doubted Haji's story, but when this scientist on his death bed on the other side of the world confessed the same story in every detail, we knew positively that the story was true in every detail.

I kept the sheet of that newspaper in the composition book with Haji's story for many years. In 1940 the school and sanitarium that Mrs. Williams and I had worked hard for nine years to build up in Louisiana was destroyed by fire in twenty minutes by a butane explosion. Everything we owned in the world was burned up, and my son Nathan and I were nearly burned to death. The composition book containing Haji's story and the newspaper sheet containing the atheistic scientist's confession on his death bed were burned up in that fire along with all that we owned on earth.

It is with deep regret that I am unable to submit these two testimonials as they were originally written. All I can offer is the vivid memory of the story as it was told to Mrs. Williams and myself as I wrote it down, and the identical story as printed in the paper. At that time there were two daily papers in Brockton. I do not remember whether it was one of these or a Boston paper in which we found the story, as I used to buy first one and then another. But this I feel sure of — Noah's Ark is still on Mount Ararat, and when it pleases God, some expedition will give the news and facts to the world so that skeptics will have no excuse.

Sincerely and in haste,
Harold N. Williams

Several years later in a letter to Eryl Cummings he further stated:

Evidently Haji's father had previously seen the Ark or knew from others exactly where to find it because he took the scientists directly to it—But it was a very exhausting and perilous expedition, high up on the mountain.

The scientists were so enraged . . . they tried to burn it . . . and "chop it," but it was so mammoth in size that they could not have destroyed it anyhow. . . . The great door was removed from the Ark and was lying up on rocks forming a sort of roof under which was an ancient altar and smoke from the altar was on the rocks and underside of the great door. . . . It is my strong impression from memory that Haji believed that Ararat is about 16,000 feet high, but I know that he said it (the Ark) rests in a glacier and that only in a very hot summer could its prow be seen protruding from the melting end of the glacier where it feeds a stream that flows down the mountain.

Ever since this story first came to light, researchers have been trying to locate the clippings or other corroboration of the London deathbed confession. However, the search has not yet borne fruit. It seems incredible, even more incredible than Haji's strange story, that such a newspaper clipping and such information has disappeared from the face of the earth. Undoubtedly, scores of God's people, recognizing the overwhelming implications involved in the relocation of Noah's Ark, clipped out the article and saved it, along with their personal belongings. The authors strongly urge each reader to personally instigate a search for this material and other missing information. Leaf through the family Bible. Hunt through the albums and storage chests in the attic. Carefully investigate the old trunk containing your grandmother's most prized possessions, conveniently stashed away ever since she went to be with the Lord. It's there. It must be.

Perhaps it strikes some people as rather strange that the first recorded sighting of the Ark in modern times was by three unbelieving atheists rather than by a group of Christians. But as we study the true nature of God we find that this is in harmony with the way He generally deals with us. God loves to reveal Himself to man. The original story of Noah's Ark illustrates the way God revealed Himself in the past. He punished the wicked and supernaturally preserved those who trusted and obeyed him.

The reason He may be planning to reveal the Ark may be to help convince the people of this skeptical age in which we live that His Word is true. What better way could be found than to start by revealing it to three atheists? We cannot but wonder if viewing the Ark eventually produced the same effect on the remaining two atheists that it produced on the one.

[1]From the personal files of Eryl and Violet Cummings.

6

James Bryce: 1876

The three egotistical atheists who visited the Ark guided by Haji Yearam and his father have never been identified. In all likelihood they never will be unless the elusive newspaper article turns up. According to Harold Williams, they were highly trained Englishmen. They must have covered their trail well, because no reference can be found in any of the scientific or travel journals of their day.

Keep in mind that these men were ardent evolutionists. Darwin's evolutionary model had recently been introduced to the world's scientific community, and coupled with Charles Lyell's long geological ages hypothesis, produced an "intellectual" alternative to the biblical Creation/Catastrophe model. It was immediately seized upon by the intelligentsia of the day, for the men of a hundred years ago were the same as they are today. Generally speaking, the more education one receives, particularly from secular institutions, the more self-sufficient he becomes and the more egocentric. He fashions himself as the master of his fate, the captain of his soul. He does not relish the thought of an almighty God, more powerful than himself, to whom he is responsible for his every breath and to whom one day he will have to give an account for every deed done here on earth.

If one acknowledges God as Creator, he realizes he must either reckon with Him as Redeemer, or face Him one day as Judge. This is not an easy pill to swallow for any man, but especially one who has become proficient and recognized in his field.

And so when Darwin's *Origin of the Species* was published, scientists flocked to it, recognizing that finally here was a system in which there was no room for a personal God. There was no need to humble yourself before your Maker. There was to be no final day of judgment. In this model, man was the end product of an infinitely long chain of random processes. Man was here by chance, no Designer had anything to do with it.

Darwin had published his speculations. He did not even present them as a theory. He was enough of a scientist to know that his model of variation and natural selection could not be tested. It could never be proved or disproved.

Strange as it may seem, the great majority of scientists of Darwin's day and the overwhelming majority today believe that we are products of evolution. But that is the key. They must believe! They cannot prove evolution; they cannot observe evolution; they cannot test or run experiments on the model; nor can they see from the fossil record that evolution has ever taken place in the past. They choose to believe it, because the natural man does not like to include God in his thinking processes.

This discussion has been included to provide a framework in which to understand the thinking of the three scientists who came to Mt. Ararat to prove that the Ark had never existed and even that the Flood of Noah's day was not an historical event. Evolution was their chosen religion. They were gambling their eternal destiny on their belief. Obviously, they knew that the existence of Noah's Ark and the historicity of Noah's Flood were absolutely incompatible with their theories. So now you understand why three egotistical men flew into a "Satanic rage" as they stood before the huge vessel.

It is hard to believe that three such braggarts could have kept the expedition a secret. Certainly many of their colleagues knew where they were going and wished them well. But when they returned to England, they were under the self-imposed death oath. Of course, none of them wanted to talk much about their discoveries anyway.

But what of all the pre-expedition publicity? What was their answer to those who asked? We don't know. We do know that about that time, several British expeditions attempted the summit. Maybe our scientists used that as a cover up, claiming that they had climbed the mountain, but had not seen anything. More likely, however, they simply cited various circumstances that kept them off the mountain.

The Viscount James Bryce, British statesman and author, must have been deeply grieved by the attitude of his countrymen. He was a devout man and a renowned theologian. Perhaps it was rumors of the atheists' attempt to disprove the Bible that triggered his interest in the relocation of the Ark, for in 1876, his research culminated in an unprecedented solitary summit climb.

Before his ascent, Bryce conducted extensive research, both field and library, and was convinced of the historical accuracy of the Bible and that the remains of the Ark were still preserved on Mt. Ararat. Realizing that

Engraving from *Transcauasia and Ararat* by James Bryce.

his skeptical colleagues would take a lot of convincing, he did his homework well. Two full chapters of his well documented and extensively read book *Transcaucasia and Ararat* are devoted to his research.

Bryce was also concerned that his contemporaries scoffed at the idea that the present-day Ararat and the biblical Ararat were identical. Again, he collected an impressive amount of data supporting his stand. In doing so, he not only conducted a historical and linguistic study, but he also investigated the traditions of the various tribes of people who had lived in the region. His research, when combined with more recent findings, shows that the names of many, if not most, of the villages, towns, and geographical and historical monuments of the entire area stem from words or phrases having to so with some aspect of the Flood, the landing site, the lives of the family after the Flood, or the deaths of the family.

Bryce Finds Wood

Undoubtedly the highlight of Bryce's trip to Ararat occurred not when he stepped to the summit of the mountain but as he was climbing. For at the 13,000-foot level he discovered hand-tooled lumber.

Engraving of Mt. Ararat from Lesser Ararat in 1844 by Herman Abich.

Mounting steadily along the same ridge, I saw at a height of over 13,000 feet, lying on the loose blocks, a piece of wood about four feet long and five inches thick, evidently cut by some tool, and so far above the limit of trees that it could by no possibility be a natural fragment of one. Darting on it with a glee that astonished the Cossack and the Kurd, I held it up to them, made them look at it, and repeated several times the word "Noah." The Cossack grinned, but he was such a cheery, genial fellow that I think he would have grinned whatever I had said, and I cannot be sure that he took my meaning, and recognised the wood as a fragment of the true Ark. Whether it was really gopher wood, of which material the Ark was built, I will not undertake to say, but am willing to submit to the inspection of the curious the bit which I cut off with my ice-axe and brought away. Anyhow, it will be hard to prove that it is not gopher wood. And if there be any remains of the Ark on Ararat at all—a point as to which the natives are perfectly clear—here rather than the top is the place where one might expect to find them, since in the course of ages they would get carried down by the onward movement of the snow-beds along the declivities. This wood, therefore, suits all the requirements of the case. In fact, the argument is, for the case of a relic, exceptionally strong.[1]

It cannot be said that James Bryce found the Ark. But the wood that he found could only have come from one of three possible sources. Before we discuss its origin, let's rule out some possibilities. It could not have come from a tree. There are no trees on Ararat except those few that the villagers have recently planted. And even if there were trees on Ararat, Bryce found the wood far above the timberline. Besides, it had been hand tooled. It could not have been from the antediluvian world, having floated around during the Flood eventually to land on Mt. Ararat, for without the proper preservatives, the wood would have decomposed and deteriorated due to bacteria and water action. Furthermore, it would not have had sufficient internal strength to survive continued freezing and thawing and the stress of a moving glacier.

One real possibility is that some previous climber had carried the wood up the mountain, not as a climbing aid, but as a monument. Dr. Parrot's expedition indeed planted a cross at the summit. This cross was made up of two bars, the longest being five feet long and two inches in diameter. Parrot had also planted a larger cross, ten feet long and six inches square on the broad western shoulder of the mountain,[2] but since Bryce had approached from the southeast, the wood could not be the same. Col. Khodzko's party had planted a seven foot cross on the summit in 1850,[3] similar to one Hermann Abich planted in 1845 on the western slope.[4] Of these relics, only Khodzko's cross could have been transported by the glacier to the spot where Bryce found his tooled wood, and the likelihood of that is remote.

One other remote possibility remains. Bryce's discovery could be part of Noah's Ark.

Additional References

Bryce, James. "Armenia and Mount Ararat." In *Proceedings of the Royal Geographic Society*, vol. 22. London: May, 1878, pp. 169-186.

Bryce, James. "The Ascent of Ararat." In *The Alpine Journal*, vol. 3. Edited by D. W. Freshfield. London: Longmans, Green and Co., 1878, pp. 208-221.

Morris, Henry M. *The Troubled Waters of Evolution*. San Diego: Creation-Life Publishers, 1975.

[1] James Bryce, *Transcaucasia and Ararat* (London: MacMillan, 1877), pp. 264, 265.

[2] Friedrich Parrot, *Journey to Ararat*, trans. W. D. Cooley (New York: Harper & Brothers, 1846), pp. 167, 195.

[3] Longuinoff, D., "Ascension de l'Ararat" Bulletin de la Société de Géographie (Paris), 4 ser., I (1851), pp. 52-65.

[4] Abich, H., "Notice explicative d'une vue du cône de Ararat" Bulletin de la Société Géographie (Paris), 4 ser., I (1851), pp. 515-525.

Earthquake Exposes the Ark: 1883

The late 1800s boast of an attitude of unprecedented ridicule of eternal matters. Atheistic humanistic principles, born out of unbelief and discontent in France and Germany, spread to the English universities and, coupled with unscientific evolutionary philosophies, crossed the Atlantic. Arrogant American scholars championed their cause before the people with all the zeal of evangelists.

Just when the Christian world needed a dose of realism to counteract the atheistic prattling of free thinkers that were poisoning the minds of impressionable youth, God drew back the veil of obscurity allowing a tantalizing glimpse of the great ship He has so precariously preserved.

On May 2, 1883, another major earthquake and avalanche shook Mt. Ararat to its very core. Far less severe than the 1840 quake, but still sufficient to cause huge quantities of rock and ice to bury villages on the slopes of the mountain, it was recorded throughout the world.

Reports of this serious condition prompted the Turkish government to commission an investigation of the area. The expedition was made up of Turkish scientists and soldiers and included as well a member of the British diplomatic core named Captain Gascoyne.

While studying possible avalanche conditions on the upper slopes of the mountain, the team of experts accidentally stumbled onto the remains of Noah's Ark, protruding from the ice cap.

News from Constantinople

The original news release from Constantinople has never been located, but possibly the most complete and accurate account of the discovery appeared in the British *Prophetic Messenger* in the summer of 1883. Quoting as its source the Levant *Herald*, it read as follows:

We have received from our correspondent in Trebizond news of the return of the Commissioners appointed by the Turkish Government to inquire into the reported destruction of Mosul, Ashak, and Bayazid by avalanches, and to render relief to the distressed villages in the glens of the Ararat ranges, who had suffered so severely from the unusual inclemency of the season.

The expedition was fortunate in making a discovery that cannot fail to be of interest to the whole civilized world, for among the vastnesses of one of the glens of Mount Ararat, they came upon a gigantic structure of very dark wood, embedded at the foot of one of the glaciers, with one end protruding, and which they believe to be none other than the old Ark in which Noah and his family navigated the waters of the Deluge. The place where the discovery is made is about five days' journey from Trebizond, in the Department of Van, in Armenia, about four leagues from the Persian frontier.

The villagers of Bayazid, which was situated about a league away, had seen this strange object for nearly six years, but were deterred by a strong superstitious fear of approaching, as there was a rumor, generally believed, that strange voices were heard within it, and it is said that some, more daring than others, who had approached had seen a spirit of fierce aspect gazing out of a hole or door in the upper portion of the structure.

The Commissioners, accompanied by their personal attendants, proceeded to examine it, the villagers positively refusing even to approach the neighborhood of the glacier in which it was embedded. The way led through a dense forest, and the travelers were obliged to follow the course of a stream, wading sometimes waist high in water which was intensely cold being from the melting glacier.

At last they were rewarded by the sight of a huge dark mass, protruding twenty or thirty feet from the glacier, on the left side of the ravine. They found it was formed of wood not grown in these elevated districts, not nearer than the hot valleys of the Euphrates, where it is known by the natives as "izim," said to be the gopher wood of the Scriptures. It was in a good state of preservation, being painted on the outside with a dark brown pigment, and constructed of great strength.

It was a good deal broken at the angles from being subjected to somewhat rough usage by the moraine during the slow descent of the glacier from the lofty peaks towering away beyond the head of the valley to a height of over 17,000 feet, a process which, considering the nature of the country and the slow pace at which these snow rivers travel, especially in the higher altitudes, must have required thousands of years. The projected portion seemed about forty or fifty feet in height, but to what length it penetrated into the glacier they could not estimate.

Effecting an entrance through one of the broken corners, the explorers found it filled for the greater part with ice, the interior being partitioned off into compartments about twelve or fifteen feet high, into three of which only they were able to make their way, owing to the mass of frozen substance with which these were filled, and also because of their fear of the structure collapsing with the overhanging mass of the huge glacier.

Avalanche debris in Ahora Gorge covering about 100 feet of snow. Note crevass.

The Commissioners, one of whom was an Englishman, Captain Gascoyne, formerly attached to the British Embassy in this city, and well known as a scientific investigator, are fully confident that it is the Ark of Noah, and they support the position by maintaining that, having been enveloped in snow and frozen, it has been kept in a state of perfect preservation.

Having rested on one of the peaks of the Ararat range, as described in the Scriptures, the Ark must have lain on soil, for "the waters covered the whole earth, and the high hills and the mountains were covered." In these circumstances the snow that ordinarily covers this lofty mountain—for it is 17,230 feet high— would have been all melted by the waters of the flood when Noah grounded on the peak. But as the waters were slowly receding for some five months, and Noah and his family, following the receding waters, gradually made their way to the lowlands, the mountain would of course resume its great height above the sea level, and in consequence, be again covered with snow, which must have once enveloped the Ark as it lay—it must be supposed—on this slope near the summit of the peak. As perpetual snow covers Mount Ararat more than half way down, it is manifest that the Ark must have been kept in a perfect state of preservation, while slowly, during the lapse of four or five thousand years, creeping down, after the manner of the glaciers, into the valley below, though in later ages to discomfort the scoffer and confirm the sure word of revelation.

Frequently, when we are confronted with unbelieving scholars, educators, and personnel from the news media, whose attitude of scoffing prohibits them from objectively analyzing data conflicting with their assumptions, the statement from Romans comes to mind:

For what if some did not believe? Shall their unbelief make the faith of God without effect? God forbid: yea, let God be true, but every man a liar. (Rom. 3:3,4)

The principle in this: that God is what He is and God's Word is what it is. Truth and fact can also stand alone. It does not matter that some refuse to accept the truth. Their unbelief, even their ridicule cannot change the truth. In fact, the Bible says, "Let God be true and *every* man a liar" if it comes to that.

Consider now the following article which appeared in the secular press following the discovery of 1883. The attitude of the day leaps off the page and grabs the reader. These commentaries did not alter the truth, but unfortunately they were able to mold the thinking of an entire nation, as evidenced by the fact that this, the first publicly reported discovery of Noah's Ark, did not produce a significant impact in either the Christian or the secular communities.

Ararat's Antique

New York Herald, August 10, 1883

Now let the heathen rage and the free-thinkers call on their respective beer cellars to hide them, for has not Noah's Ark been discovered, and right on the mountain where she discharged her cargo and passengers more than four thousand years ago? Of course, it is the Ark, and not an antiquated craft that some tricky showman has bought for a souvenir, taken to pieces, dragged up the mountain and reconstructed, for the printed description indicates a model that cannot be found at the present day except in the mudscow fleet of the New York Street Cleaning Department and the navy of the United States, neither of which has yet disposed of any of its antediluvian hulks.

Well, what are the ungodly going to do about it? There she is, according to the Turkish press, which has no possible reason to go so far back into antiquity if searching merely for something to lie about. It will not do for them to make light of the story, for an Englishman has discovered that the ancient cattle boat is of gopher wood, according to specification, and the stalls are in accordance with the plans of the British Admiralty, which body is the modern substitute for inspiration in marine affairs. All that Colonel Ingersoll and Professor Adler can hope for is to persuade the public that the newly discovered antique, although an ark, is not necessarily the handiwork of an amateur ship carpenter named Noah. If arks were the fashion forty-four hundred years ago, why may not dozens of them have drifted from their moorings during the great November freshet of 2616 B.C. and gone ashore on Mount Ararat?

But whatever they may have to say must be said in a hurry, for an American is reported to have arranged to bring the old tub over here, and argument will stand a poor chance against eyesight. If she is three hundred cubits long, according to contract, it may be quite a job to get her from the top of Mount Ararat to the Mediterranean; but a nation that has seriously thought of a ship railway across Central America cannot doubt that the ark can be brought to deep water. If no American engineers of sufficient ability are on the ground the purchaser need only to send to France for Jules Verne. All but three of her compartments are said to be full of ice, which, at present prices, ought to pay the expense of bringing it over. When she reaches American waters, however, the Navy department ought to purchase her at once, for the world's greatest republic ought to have at least one ship that will not rot as soon as it leaves a navy yard. Her absorption by the government would not prevent the public getting bits of her as relics, even timber enough to make walking canes, pulpit chairs, and poor boxes for all who care to buy; for when our Naval Department does "improve" a vessel it gets rid of so much of the original matter that, in case of the Ark, Noah would not know his staunch old family scow if he saw it.

On the same day the Chicago *Tribune* reprinted an article from a London daily. There is less open ridicule here, but the author, in choosing his words carefully, effectively discredits the discovery.

Has Noah's Ark Been Found?

Chicago *Tribune*: August 10, 1883: A paper at Constantinople announces the discovery of Noah's Ark. It appears that some Turkish commissioners appointed to investigate the question of avalanches on Mount Ararat suddenly came upon a gigantic structure of very dark wood protruding from a glacier. They made inquiries of the inhabitants. They had seen it for six years, but had been afraid to approach it because a spirit of fierce aspect had been seen looking out the upper window. The Turkish commissioners, however, are bold men, not deterred by such trifles, and they determined to reach it. Situated as it was among the fastnesses of one of the glens of Mount Ararat, it was a work of enormous difficulty, and it was only after incredible hardship that they succeeded. The ark was in a good state of preservation, although the angles—observe, not the bow or stern—had been a good deal broken in its descent. They recognized it at once. There was an Englishman among them who had presumably read his Bible, and he saw that it was made of the ancient gopher wood of Scripture, which, as everyone knows, grows only on the plains of the Euphrates. Effecting an entrance into the structure, which was painted brown, they found that the admiralty requirements for the conveyance of horses had been carried out, and the interior was divided into partitions fifteen feet high. Into three of these only could they get, the others being full of ice, and how far the ark extended into the glacier they could not tell. If, however, on being uncovered, it turns out to be 300 cubits long, it will go hard with disbelievers.

Commenting on the Chicago *Tribune* article, the September, 1883, issue of *The Watchtower* said:

The gopher wood of which the ark was built is generally supposed to be the cypress, famous among the ancients, and frequently mentioned in Scripture. It is remarkable for durability. Instances are related of doors and posts made of this wood which lasted 1,100 years. Remembering, also, that Mt. Ararat is covered with perpetual snow and ice for more than 3,000 feet below its summit, and that an earthquake which shook it in the beginning of the present year (1883) broke loose tremendous quantities of this ice, burying under the avalanches whole villages, we cannot but think that the foregoing article is not so unreasonable as might at first appear.

On August 13, the New York *World* produced the following details. Note the reference to a Russian team rather than Turkish. This is understandable, although not excusable for a professional, for even today many people think Mt. Ararat lies on Russian soil, and ownership has changed hands many times.

Great Scientific Find

Considerable competition has recently been shown by the discoverers of ancient manuscripts and the finders of ancient relics. The latter has suddenly come to the front by the discovery of Noah's Ark in that part of the Armenian plateau still known as Mount Ararat.

The find was made by a party of Russian engineers who were surveying a glacier. An extraordinary spell of hot weather had melted away a great portion of the Araxes glacier, and they were surprised to see sticking out of the ice what at first appeared to be the rude facade of an ancient dwelling. On closer examination it was found to be composed of longitudinal layers of gopher wood, supported by immense frames, still in a remarkable state of preservation.

Assistance having been summoned from Nakhchevan, the work of uncovering the find commenced under the most extraordinary difficulties, and in a week's time the indefatigable explorers had uncovered what they claimed to be Noah's Ark, as it bore indisputable evidence of having been used as a boat.

At this point archaeology could afford to rest at any ordinary period of the world and we should expect the luckiest finders to form a syndicate and open a bazaar for the sale of relics.

But in our day antiquarian history takes another turn. It isn't looking for merchandise as much as for testimony. We must not forget that the planting of the Cardiff Giant was not so much to make money as to establish the missing link.

Ataturk, the "Father of Turkey," formerly Mustafa Kemal, took over leadership of the country soon after World War I.

The Noah's Ark syndicate are only following the tactics of the antiquary who recently offered to sell an original manuscript of the Mosaic law signed by Moses to the British Museum.

They are trying to correct the record with facts.

With these principles in view, the reader must not be surprised to learn by the latest dispatches from our representative, Mr. Benjamin—who is not going to Persia for nothing—that the engineers have broken through the third compartment of the ark, and in the true spirit of the age have discovered the original log kept by Noah and his sons.

Startling as this announcement is, it is backed up by the documents, which must stand for what they are worth without any comment of ours. Philology, ethnology, and archaeology must fight it out for themselves. A newspaper can only narrate the occurrence.

Further articles in the secular press around the world proclaimed similar denunciations of the discovery.

Turkey has a history unequaled by any other country in the world for color and flavor and wealth of archaeological findings. Indeed Turkey has been rightly termed an archaeologist's paradise, and in many areas of the country, a farmer can hardly plow his field without uncovering an artifact.

The Turkish people, despite their Arab and Moslem ties, stem from a nation who migrated westward from the Indian peninsula in approximately A.D. 1,000. Ever since 1923, when the great general Ataturk (now rightly labeled "the Father of the country") took control, Turkey has been seeking to modernize and westernize its culture. But one of the holdovers from the mysterious past is the desire in every Turkish mind to maintain an aura of secrecy.

Unfortunately this manifests itself when an outsider attempts to trace such stories as the 1883 expedition. No doubt an official report was made to the Turkish government by the team of scientists. And no doubt the material was not destroyed. In all likelihood, it now lies buried somewhere in the extensive Turkish archives, along with overwhelming amounts of material of value only to historians and researchers.

8

Prince Nouri: 1887

Excluding those who lived on the mountain, the first explorer on record to have visited Noah's Ark by design was John Joseph, Prince of Nouri.

"His Chaldean Excellency, the Venerable Monseignior, the ZAMORRIAN, Earl of the Great House of Nouri, was born at Baghdad, on the 7th, and baptized on the 14th of February, A.D. 1865. Graduated, at Mesopotamia April 5, 1884. Consecrated, Grand-Archdeacon of Babylon, on Pentecost Sunday, May 24, 1885," read his biography.

"Sacred Crown's Supreme Representative—General of the Holy Orthodox Patriarchal Imperiality, the most Venerable Prelate, Monseignior, the ZAMORRIN NOURI, John Joseph, Prince of Nouri, D.D., LLD. (by Divine Providence), Chaldean Patriarchal Archdeacon of Babylon and Jerusalem, Grand Apostolic Ambassador of Malabar, India, and Persia. The First Universal Exploring Traveler of a Million Miles. The Discoverer of Noah's Ark, and the Golden Mountains of the Moon," read his title.

One might rightly assume that an additional title, such as "Most Humble Servant of Mankind" or "First Oriental Potentate to Give All His Riches to the Poor" or "Consistent Example of Christian Humility," would not have fit his character.

No one uses such a list of titles today, for our culture would not allow it. But in the day of John Joseph, Prince of Nouri, etc., his titles were most impressive and useful.

Keep in mind, however, that these titles were earned or bestowed. They were not self-proclaimed. Nouri was indeed a remarkable individual—Archdeacon of Babylon at the age of 20, head of the Nestorian Church of South India at 31, and, in case you were wondering, he discovered gold in a Mid-Eastern mountain range called the Mountains of the Moon.

But his discovery of the Ark in 1887 remains his most sensational

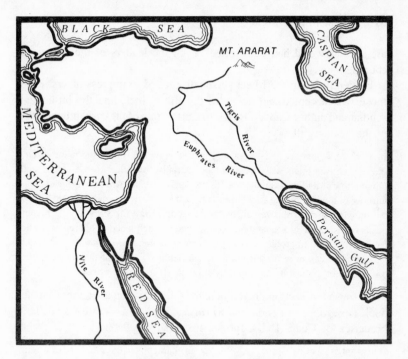

Mt. Ararat and the Tigris-Euphrates River system.

claim. Originally desiring to explore the headwaters of the Euphrates, which were not far from his homeland, Dr. Nouri made three attempts to climb Mt. Ararat and discover the Ark. Finally on the third attempt, he succeeded, finding the Ark almost completely exposed with only its center portions covered with snow. The beams were very thick, a dark reddish-brown in color, and nailed together with long nails.

Under the personal invitations of Dr. John Henry Barrows,[1] President of the World Parliament of Religions, Nouri presented his claim at the Chicago World's Fair in 1893, where the World Parliament of Religions was assembled.

His stories were so convincing that a group of Belgian financiers agreed to sponsor an expedition to relocate the Ark, remove it, and reassemble it at the World's Fair. The deal fell through when Turkish permission proved unattainable.

Nouri's claim failed to impress the liberal clergymen grouped in Chicago to "promote love, harmony, and cooperation between the world's religions." As a matter of fact, all mention of Nouri and the discovery was omitted in the official account of the proceedings of the convention. It seems that the philosophy of higher criticism so rampant in the secular world had "converted" even the leaders of the organized church.

Evidently Nouri's off-beat personality failed to impress others, even those who accepted and defended the Bible, including the influential scholar and author Captain R. Kelso Carter, one of the early propagators of the "canopy theory."

In 1892 an Armenian priest appeared in San Francisco under the name of Dr. Nouri, who narrated with great circumstantiality of detail to the author and others, how he had made eight separate attempts to ascend Ararat with the express purpose of looking for the ark. The last attempt he claimed succeeded, and he saw the remains of the great vessel, partly projecting from the snow on the higher peaks of Ararat. Unfortunately no confidence can be placed in his report, as he has utterly failed to produce any satisfactory credentials or indorsements. There is, however, certainly no objection (scientifically) worthy of the name, to the possibility of the ark being found by someone if it were ever there.[2]

To finish this section, let us quote for substantiation a section from the book *Yesterdays in Persia and Kurdistan* by Nouri's close friend, Dr. Frederick B. Coan, D.D., former missionary to Persia.

One is apt to meet with some very interesting characters in the East, one of whom comes to mind, and is worth describing. About 35 years ago . . . one of our Assyrian friends told us of a very interesting guest who had dropped in on him, by the name of Archbishop Nouri. He had come from Malabar, in southern India, where there are today (1939) some 500,000 Nestorian Christians, a remnant of the work of the Nestorian missionaries, who in the very earliest centuries carried the gospel to India and far beyond. Archbishop Nouri said he had been sent by them to be consecrated as Bishop over them by the Nestorian Patriarch MarShimun who, as Patriarch of all the Nestorians in Kurdistan and Persia, lived at Kochanis, Turkey, five days travel from Urmia.

Now for the story of his wonderful discovery of the Ark. He said he had made three attempts to scale Mount Ararat before he succeeded. At last his toil was rewarded, and he stood overwhelmed and awed as he saw the old Ark there, wedged in between two rocks, and half filled with snow and ice. He got inside, where careful measurements coincided exactly with the account given in the sixth chapter of Genesis.

We invited him to give a lecture on his marvellous discovery in the College chapel, and missionaries, teachers, and students filled the place, and were deeply interested. He sincerely believed he had seen the Ark, and almost convinced others he had.

He had gone to Belgium and tried to organize a company to take it to Chicago, to the World's Fair, but they felt the risks of such a long journey were too great, in addition to the heavy costs of transporting it so far. He was much disappointed, for he knew it would be a great attraction, and that people from all over the world would go to see it. So there it lies![3]

[1] See John Henry Barrows, *A World Pilgrimage* (Chicago: A. C. McClung, 1897).
[2] Captain Russell Kelso Carter, *Alpha and Omega* (San Francisco: O.H. Elliott, 1894), pp. 461-62.
[3] Frederick B. Coan, *Yesterdays in Persia and Kurdistan* (Claremont: Saunders Studio Press, 1939), pp. 164-165.

9

Georgie Hagopian: 1908 to 1910

We have enumerated the various traditions found in the history of the Armenian people indicating that throughout the centuries since the Ark landed on Mt. Ararat many of that race actually made pilgrimages to the remains, and nearly all of the leaders knew generally where they were to be found. Evidently, after the 1840 earthquake when the Ark began to reappear, the Armenians were not at all surprised at either its existence or location.

When young Haji Yearam visited the Ark with the three skeptics, his father took them right to it. From all indications, it was not at all uncommon for an Armenian father, desiring to promote a proper spiritual attitude in his son, to take him up and show him the Ark.

At the end of World War I, the Armenians found themselves siding with the invading Russians, against their age-old enemies, the Turks. But, as the Russian Revolution broke out, patriotic Russians returned to their homeland, leaving the Armenians to suffer in the face of Turkish fury.

Those who could escaped. Most crossed the Aras River into what is now known as Soviet Armenia. Many escaped to various countries around the world, including America.

Today, no Armenians live on or near Ararat. Many live in Russia within sight of the mountain, but whatever traditions or memories they retain from previous trips to the remains of the Ark are generally inaccessible to Westerners. But, in all likelihood, elderly Armenian gentlemen, now living in Russia, were shown the Ark by their fathers before they were driven out.

In the last few years, Russia has relaxed its tourism restrictions somewhat and now allows visitors into this area. In two instances with which we are familiar, returning travelers had contacted people who seemed to have knowledge of the Ark's whereabouts but were unable to spend enough time with them to obtain meaningful information.

Upper reaches of the Ahora Gorge, showing the Abich II glacier. George claimed a sighting of the Ark in the general area.

One such meeting took place at the airport in Erivan, just thirty-six miles from Ararat. Dr. Nathan Meyer, Bible scholar and Ark enthusiast, on an international commercial flight which made an unscheduled landing for repairs, was whiling away the time by staring at Mt. Ararat. Police were everywhere, but an elderly Armenian stepped up to him, pointed to the mountain, and said, "That's Mt. Ararat. Noah's Ark is there." Before any more could be said, the old fellow was in the custody of several officers.

If the Armenians had retained their traditional home, the Ark would have long ago been revealed to the world, but such is not the case. Fortunately, not all Armenians fled to Russia; many came to America.

In 1970, a seventy-two-year-old Armenian immigrant became aware that expeditions were interested in the relocation of Noah's Ark. The story he told nearly overwhelmed the researchers, because, finally, here was an eyewitness, still alive, available for interviews, who twice had actually visited the Ark! First in 1908 and again in 1910, when he was just a boy, his uncle, a devout man, had taken him to see the relic.

Born before the turn of the century, Georgie Hagopian was only ten years old when he first saw the Ark. He grew up near Lake Van, to the south of Mt. Ararat. His grandfather was the minister of a large church there.

Georgie's uncle grazed his flocks on Mt. Ararat each summer and took Georgie along with him when he went. They approached the mountain from the south, went through the town now called Dogubeyazit, around the mountain, and began their climb from the north.

It had taken them seven days of hard walking to travel from Lake Van to the base of Mt. Ararat. A small donkey was borrowed for the young Georgie to ride until the trail became too steep. On the way up they passed a mound of rock that, according to traditions, was the burial place of a holy man. (This mound is mentioned numerous times in the literature. It was located near the monastery in the Ahora Gorge but was unaffected by the 1840 earthquake. Supposedly the burial place of St. Jacob, the holy man who miraculously obtained a piece of the Ark, it is still visible today.)

When forced to abandon the donkey, Georgie's uncle, a tall powerfully built man, hoisted the boy and the supplies on his shoulders for the roughest part of the ascent. Seemingly, his uncle knew exactly where the Ark was, because he went right to it. After exploring it for over two hours, they still had enough time to descend the mountain to the villages for the night.

There are many interesting points brought out by Georgie's testimony. The interviews were extensive and lasted over a period of a year and a half. Unfortunately, several things hindered the conversations. First, Georgie was an old man recalling an incident from his early childhood. Second, he was not fully conversant in English and frequently had trouble expressing himself, and his heavy accent disguised some of the words. Third, he had never studied maps of the area or of the mountain, and, although he claimed that if he was younger he could go right to the Ark, he was unable to pinpoint it on the maps.[1] He was, however, able to be quite specific on photographs.

Some of the more interesting aspects that he pointed out follow:

1. 1908 was a very hot year, with very little snowfall on the mountain, and followed a three year drought.
2. When they reached the Ark, it seemed to him to be "the top of the world." It was very cold and misty.
3. The Ark was resting on a huge rock, bluish-green in color, but one side was on the edge of a steep cliff. The mountain was impossible to climb from that side. When he looked over the edge, he could hardly see the bottom for the mist.
4. The Ark was very long and rectangular. Parts of the bottom were exposed and he could see that it was flat. The roof was nearly flat, except for a row of

windows, 50 or more, estimated size 18 inches x 30 inches, running from front to back covered by an overhanging roof. The front was also flat. The sides tipped out a little from bottom to top.

5. There were no holes in the sides or doors that he saw. The only hole was in the roof, and it was big and gaping. There was a small staircase or ladder running partway down from the top. He did not know if it was part of the original structure or added later by pilgrims.

6. When he first saw the structure, it looked as if it were made of stone. He didn't realize that it actually was the Ark. His childlike estimate of the size at the time was 1000 feet long, 600 feet wide and 40 feet high.

7. The wood appeared to be entirely petrified. Very hard. In fact, his uncle had a musket along and fired a few shots at the Ark. The pellets just dropped, hardly made a dent. The uncle was unable even to carve off a piece with his knife. The wood was smooth. Nowhere could he feel a place where the planks joined, although he could see the joints and the grain plainly. It seemed to be made out of one piece of petrified wood. There were no nails, but Georgie did notice wooden dowels.

8. A green moss covered the Ark, growing almost like grass. It made the Ark seem soft and moldy. When he brushed the light snow off, he found that the moss covered the entire top, but when he peeled the moss off, he exposed more of the petrified, dark brown, wood.

George Hagopian, the elderly Armenian who saw the Ark during his childhood, with Elfred Lee, artist and Ark researcher. (Photo by E. Lee)

Artist's conception of Noah's Ark from eyewitness description. The final drawing was approved by George, who saw the Ark when he was a boy.

9. His grandfather had told him that he would become a holy man, that visiting the "Holy Ark" was a good start. His uncle had piled up loose rock along the side of the Ark until he could lift Georgie up to the ladder. His uncle instructed him to remove his shoes in reverence to the holy relic. Once on top, Georgie knelt down and kissed the Ark, even though understandably frightened.

10. When he returned home, and told the story to his young friends, he found that many of them had also seen the Ark.

Georgie Hagopian returned to Turkey in 1922 to try to document his find. With him was an American photographer. Once in Turkey they found anti-Armenian sentiment running high, and heavy fighting broke out in the Izmir area as the Turks battled the Greeks and Armenians.

The Izmir Incident, as it is now called, demanded the attention of the travelers, and they documented it fully on film. Several years later Hagopian showed the movies and photographs to officials in Washington, only to have them confiscated, and the whole affair hushed up.

Georgie had had a long history of unfairness and persecution by several governments, and his suspicion grew to a desire to completely withdraw from the public eye. There he remained until 1970 when one of his few close friends responded to a piece of literature from SEARCH, Inc., a group interested in finding the Ark, and encouraged Georgie to tell his story.

The elderly gentleman was not at all interested in publicity. He even preferred to be referred to simply as "Georgie," afraid that either harm or inconvenience would come to him if he were known. He is dead now. He died in 1972 and had no living relatives, but his story lives on tape, on paper, and on canvas.

[1] As first reported by Elfred Lee, a former board member of Search, Inc., and confirmed by others who interviewed Georgie before his death.

10

Russian Expeditions: 1916, 1917

Tell us, when shall these things be? and what shall be the sign of thy coming, and of the end of the world?

And Jesus answered and said unto them,

Take heed that no man deceive you.

For many shall come in my name, saying, "I am Christ;" and shall deceive many.

And ye shall hear of wars and rumours of wars: see that ye be not troubled: for all these things must come to pass, but the end is not yet.

For nation shall rise against nation, and kingdom against kingdom: and there shall be famines, and pestilences, and earthquakes, in divers places.

All these are the beginning of sorrows.

(Matt. 24:3-8)

Never in the history of the world had there been a war like World War I. Nation rose up against nation until it truly seemed that the entire world was at war. Blood was shed at an unprecedented rate. Immediately after the war great portions of the globe were devastated by famine. Millions died of starvation. As always, accompanying the shortage of food, there were outbreaks of disease and pestilence. So severe were the aftershocks of the war that many years were required for stabilization, and many experts feel that the world never completely recovered. Even the food shortages of today can be traced to the early part of the twentieth century.

It is not our purpose to discuss the events of the end times, but suffice it to say that many students of biblical prophecy consider World War I to be the "beginning of sorrows," the beginning of the end.

It *is* our purpose to trace the history of Mt. Ararat and the search for Noah's Ark, and, as might be expected, Turkey's eastern frontier was subjected to graphic desolation during the war.

Mt. Ararat During World War I

Mt. Ararat occupies strategic territory. Present-day Ararat lies within the borders of Turkey, but at various times throughout history, and even during and shortly after World War I, Russia, Iran and Turkey all claimed the mountain as their own. However, for the most part, the Armenian people and Kurdish nomads dwelled there.

Prior to World War I, Turkey, formerly known as the Ottoman Empire, controlled vast areas throughout the Middle East, North Africa, and Europe. Siding with Germany during the war, the Empire soon found out that defending such a great amount of territory was impossible.

Czarist Russia was a constant threat to Turkish holdings along the eastern front. Fearing that the Armenian people would side with the Russians against their age-old enemies, the Turkish army moved in during April, 1915, and required nearly all of the Armenians to evacuate the area. They were to be taken, on foot, to the deserts of Saudi Arabia. Nearly one and a half million Armenians died on that march, and many thousands more died attempting to defend their homes.

When the Russians invaded, they found very few people in eastern Turkey at all. They occupied all of the territory around Erzerum and even as far south as Lake Van. Hundreds of thousands of beleaguered Armenians welcomed the Russians and fled across the Aras River at the base of Mt. Ararat into Russia for safety.

Meanwhile, in Russia proper, godless Bolshevism was beginning to vie for control of the government. Many of the Russian soldiers in eastern Turkey grew apprehensive for the welfare of their families and property back home. They deserted their posts in droves, not being able to see any reason to fight abroad while their own country was in turmoil. Those who remained for awhile left immediately in November, 1917, when the Russian Revolution broke out. Once more eastern Turkey belonged to the Turks.

The following two years saw almost the complete annihilation of the Armenian race. Left in a war-torn and desolate area with no crops to harvest and no government, the Armenians found themselves falling prey to a grim famine and tragic epidemics. Once again, great numbers died. They probably would all have died without U.S. and Red Cross aid, meager though it was. Finally, in 1919, the new Communist regime extended southward and incorporated much of the area into what is now called Soviet Armenia.[1]

But the situation of the Ararat region could hardly be called stabilized. World War I ended with Turkey in defeat. When the Armistice was signed in November, 1918, the Allies were in control of Istanbul, and all of the Allied countries were gathered like vultures to divide up Turkey. The quibbling went on for four years, during which time the Communists moved in once again and captured eastern Turkey.

Slowly, but with gathering momentum, a young Turkish army officer named Mustafa Kemal began to gain control of the military and win the support of the Turkish people and the battered remnant of the army. Finally, in 1922, he launched a revolt against all foreigners on Turkish soil and with surprising speed drove them all out. The Turkish troops, always known for their effective battle techniques, seemed almost in a frenzy as they mercilessly destroyed all non-Turks.

First, they drove out all of the occupation troops in Istanbul and other western cities, then the Armenian and Greek natives, and proceeded eastward. In violent clashes with the Russian troops, the Turks defeated them and completely drove them back across the Aras River and, by doing so, established the river as the border between the countries, a border which has lasted until this day.

Ataturk (Father of the Turks), as Kemal came to be known, wisely gave up all foreign holdings for borders he could defend. He moved the capital of Turkey to its present location at Ankara in the very center of the country and in 1923 established the Republic of Turkey.

For the first time, in any meaningful sense of the word, Mt. Ararat was the sole possession of Turkey. It had seen more than its share of blood, famine, and pestilence. Its populace had completely changed and its ownership had been transferred many times. The part the mountain had played so many years before in the preservation of mankind appeared in sharp contrast to the destruction all around.

With seeming irony, the Almighty used this time of turmoil and activity in eastern Turkey to once again reveal His Ark. In the face of rampant destruction and death, God allowed the Ark to bear silent witness to the fact that even in a time of far greater destruction He had provided a way of salvation to those who believed, rewarding them with life in a world free from strife and wickedness.

Anyone who has even the slightest prior knowledge of the possible existence of the Ark will have seen the story which follows, concerning a Russian sighting of the Ark both from the air and with a ground search in the summer of 1917. The Russians held control over the area after the Armenians had been evacuated. It is included here for completeness and

Searching for Noah's Ark on the ice cap of Mt. Ararat.

because some may not be familiar with it. But keep in mind as you read that the story did not appear until long after the event took place.

Noah's Ark Found
by Vladimir Roskovitsky

It was in the days just before the Russian revolution that this story really began. A group of us Russian aviators were stationed at a lonely temporary air outpost about twenty-five miles northeast of Mount Ararat. The day was dry and terribly hot, as August days so often are in this semi-desert land.

Even the lizzards were flattened out under the shady sides of rocks or twigs, their mouths open and tongues lashing out as if each panting breath would be their last. Only occasionally would a tiny wisp of air rattle the parched vegetation and stir up a choking cloudlet of dust.

Far up on the side of the mountain we could see a thunder shower, while still farther up we could see the white snow cap of Mount Ararat, which has snow all the year around because of its great height. How we longed for some of that snow!

Then the miracle happened. The captain walked in and announced that plane number seven had its new supercharger installed and was ready for high altitude tests, and ordered my buddy and me to make the test. At last we could escape the heat!

Needless to say, we wasted no time getting on our parachutes, strapping on our oxygen cans and doing all the half dozen other things that have to be done before "going up."

Then a climb into the cockpits, safety belts fastened, a mechanic gives the prop a flip and yells, "Contact!" and in less time than it takes to tell it, we were in the air. No use wasting time warming up the engine when the sun already had it nearly red hot.

We circled the field several times until we hit the fourteen thousand foot mark and then stopped climbing for a few minutes to get used to the altitude.

I looked over to the right at that beautiful snowcapped peak, now just a little above us, and for some reason I can't explain, turned and headed the plane straight toward it.

My buddy turned around and looked at me with question marks in his eyes, but there was too much noise for him to ask questions. After all, twenty-five miles doesn't mean much at a hundred miles an hour.

As I looked down at the great stone battlements surrounding the lower part of this mountain, I remembered having heard that it had never been climbed since the year seven hundred before Christ, when some pilgrims were supposed to have gone up there to scrape tar off an old shipwreck to make good luck emblems to wear around their necks to prevent their crops being destroyed by excessive rainfall. The legend said they had left in haste after a bolt of lightning struck near them and had never returned. Silly ancients. Who ever heard of looking for a shipwreck on a mountain top?

A couple of circles around the snow-capped dome and then a long, swift glide down the side and then we suddenly came upon a perfect little gem of a lake; blue as an emerald, but still frozen over on the shady side. We circled around and returned for another look at it. Suddenly my companion whirled around and yelled something, and excitedly pointed down at the overflow end of the lake. I looked and nearly fainted!

A submarine! No, it wasn't, for it had stubby masts, but the top was rounded over with only a flat catwalk about five feet across down the length of it. What a strange craft, built as though the designer had expected the waves to roll over the top most of the time, and had engineered it to wallow in the sea like a log, with those stubby masts carrying only enough sail to keep it facing the waves. (Years later in the Great Lakes I saw the famous "whaleback" ore carriers with this same kind of rounded deck.)

We flew down as close as safety permitted and took several circles around it. We were surprised when we got close to it at the immense size of the thing, for it was as long as a city block and would compare very favorably in size to the modern battleships of today. It was grounded on the shore of the lake with about one-fourth of the rear end still running out into the water, and its extreme rear was three-fourths under water. It had been partly dismantled on one side near the front, and on the other side there was a great door nearly twenty feet square, but with the door gone. This seemed quite out of proportion, as even today ships seldom have doors even half that large.

After seeing all we could from the air, we broke all speed records back down to the airport.

When we related our find, the laughter was loud and long. Some accused us of getting drunk on too much oxygen, and there were many other remarks too numerous to relate.

The captain, however, was serious. He asked several questions and ended by saying, "Take me up there, I want a look at it."

We made the trip without incident and returned to the airport. "What do you make of it?" I asked, as we climbed out of the plane. "Astounding," he replied. "Do you know what ship that is?" "Of course not, sir." "Ever hear of Noah's Ark?" "Yes, sir. But I don't understand what the legend of Noah's Ark has to do with us finding this strange thing fourteen thousand feet up on a mountain top."

"This strange craft," explained the captain, "is Noah's Ark. It has been sitting up there for nearly five thousand years. Being frozen up for nine or ten months of the year it couldn't rot, and has been on cold storage, as it were, all this time. You have made the most amazing discovery of the age."

When the captain sent his report to the Russian government, it aroused considerable interest, and the Czar sent two special companies of soldiers to climb the mountain. One group of fifty men attacked one side and the other group of one hundred men attacked the mountain from the other side.

Two weeks of hard work were required to chop out a trail along the cliffs of the lower part of the mountain, and it was nearly a month before the Ark was reached.

Two border outposts—one Turkish, the other Russian—overlook the Aras River at the base of Mt. Ararat.

Complete measurements were taken and plans drawn of it as well as many photographs, all of which were sent to the Czar of Russia.

The Ark was found to contain hundreds of small rooms and some very large with high ceilings. The large rooms usually had a fence of great timbers across them, some of which were two feet thick, as though designed to hold beasts ten times as large as elephants. Other rooms were lined with tiers of cages somewhat like one sees today at a poultry show, only instead of chicken wire they had rows of tiny wrought iron bars along the fronts.

Everything was heavily painted with a wax-like paint resembling shellac, and the workmanship of the craft showed all the signs of a high type of civilization.

The wood used throughout was oleander, which belongs to the cypress family, and never rots, which, of course, coupled with the facts of it being painted and it being frozen most of the time accounted for its perfect preservation.

The expedition found on the peak of the mountain above the ship, the burned remains of the timbers which were missing out of the one side of the ship. It seems that these timbers had been hauled up to the top of the peak and used to build a tiny one-room shrine, inside of which was a rough stone hearth like the altars the Hebrews used for sacrifices, and it had either caught fire from the altar or had been struck by lightning as the timbers were considerably burned and charred over and the roof was completely burned off.

A few days after this expedition sent its report to the Czar, the government was overthrown and Godless Bolshevism took over, so that the records were never made public and probably were destroyed in the zeal of the Bolshevics to discredit all religion and belief in the truth of the Bible.

We White Russians of the air fleet escaped through Armenia, and four of us came to America, where we could be free to live according to the "Good Old Book," which we had seen for ourselves to be absolutely true, even to as fantastic sounding a thing as a world flood.

The Source of the Story

The preceding story was first published in 1940 in *The New Eden*, a Los Angeles magazine, Floyd Gurley, Editor. Within days the newspapers as well as religious publications across the country had reproduced it until the story fairly saturated the nation.

Mr. Benjamin F. Allen, retired lawyer, amateur geologist, and Director of the Society for the Study of Creation, the Deluge, and Related Science, had long been interested in biblical catastrophism, or Flood geology. For years he had gathered information which would tend to support the biblical accounts of the Creation and the Flood of Noah. His quest for such data soon included researching the possibility of the survival of the Ark.

As might be expected, literally thousands of inquiries poured in to Mr. Gurley from all over the world. Gurley, in turn, passed everything on to Mr. Allen, for, as it turned out, Mr. Gurley had received the basic facts for his story from Mr. Allen.

Dr. Henry M. Morris, now well-known author and advocate of scientific creationism, was in the process of publishing his first book on the Bible and Science in June 1945 when he wrote to his friend Allen, desiring more information on the Roskovitsky story. After discussing some other matters, Allen replied:

> The Society for the Study of
> Creation, The Deluge, and
> Related Science
> 219 N. Grand Avenue
> Los Angeles 12, Calif.
>
> June 1, 1945
>
> Prof. Henry M. Morris
> Houston, Texas
> Dear Friend:
>
> I recognize at once the "story" you enclose on Noah's Ark. It was originally put out by an off-center man here whom I know very well. It is about 95% fiction, the one real part being some vague reports by two Russian soldiers in the World War I, which reports are being circulated by some of their relatives, they (the soldiers) having died several years ago. I have letters from them.
>
> As for my neighbor with the exaggerated "imagination," I told him about the letters I have and I told him the facts I have gathered about the history of glaciation and the snow line on Mt. Ararat. He later abused my confidence and "stole" the data, and worked it all up into a *perfect* deception. The character "Roskovitsky" sprang "full blown" from the brow of this eccentric mind of my neighbor, along with about 99% of the rest of it.
>
> This was published far and wide like "wild fire" (which it really is). I managed for several years to keep it down, but, when I got too busy to write and repudiate it so much, it sprang up again. For more than a year I have been ignoring it.
>
> Sincerely,
> B. F. Allen

The letters from the relatives that Allen mentioned seemingly are no longer available, but once the "New Eden" article was published, and Allen was swamped with inquiries, he was forced to re-establish contact with his original informant. And, on April 4, 1940, Mr. James Frazier of Malotte, Washington, verified the information.[2]

Your letter, dated March 30, is at hand, in regard to the Ark of Noah. Yes, my father-in-law, John Schilleroff, told me at different times about the Ark of Noah, but he did not mention any landmarks, though he did mention the town he started from. I could not pronounce the name and have forgotten it. He was German and I do not speak German.

Mr. John Georgeson, a Dane, formerly my neighbor here, now also deceased, told me the same story, he also having served in the Russian Army in the Ararat region. They had never met, though their accounts fully agree. They belonged to different expeditions and went at different times. They were both sober and reliable men, and therefore I believe their story. The following is the story as they both told it to me.

While in the Russian Army, they were ordered to pack for a long tramp up into the Mountains of Ararat. A Russian aviator had sighted what looked to him like a huge wooden structure in a small lake. About two thirds of the way up, probably a little farther, they stopped on a high cliff, and in a small valley below them there was a dense swamp in which the object could be seen. It appeared to be a huge ship or barge with one end under water, and only one corner could be clearly seen from where these men stood. Some went closer, and especially the Captain. They could not get out to it because of the water and the many poisonous snakes and insects. The Captain told them of the details.

Several other letters from friends and relatives of expedition members reiterated the same story, and finally a public denial of the Roskovitsky account by Allen and a public apology to Allen by Gurley set the record straight.

219 North Grand Avenue
Los Angeles, California
October 17, 1945

To Whom It May Concern:

One of the most exaggerated accounts of the Ark was published in 1940 by Mr. Gurley in one of his booklets called "The New Eden" which he printed in that year.

In conversation with him I had given him the few details originating from two soldiers in the Czarist Russian Army during the First World War, deceased many years ago. The story by these soldiers came to me from their relatives of how a Russian aviator had sighted a suspicious looking structure in one of Ararat's obscure canyons. Infantrymen were sent on foot to investigate and their officers and they decided it must be Noah's Ark, with one end sunk in a small swamp. *These were the only details they gave.* Being a geologist worker, I had investigated and speculated on how the Ark could have been saved by glaciation till recent times in view of the sudden origin and subsequent history of glaciation. To Mr. Gurley I gave some of these ideas, very briefly. I had no idea he was publishing anything. I told him plainly that the story from the soldiers was by no means worthy of publication till it could be corroborated from other sources. But, *without my knowledge and consent,* he concocted a masterpiece of fiction and invention and published it as though it were true in every detail. About 95% is pure fiction, but the meager details from the former soldiers could be true. The name Roskovitsky and the *person* are pure fiction, *as are all parts but the few I have given here.* With the geological ideas I gave him, he could construct a very plausible story, which has "deluged" the credulous world.

I soon began to be deluged with letters asking about the reliability of this wild story (as it was generally known that I had been conducting research and publishing articles on the folklore and archaeology of the Deluge), and letters are still coming. The story has been constantly published by the radical religious press, and even by some of the secular papers, with a constant addition of "embellishments." However, much harm began to be done to me, and has increased, because word got out that what real data there was in it came from me, and I am being charged by some with the whole fabrication. Much harm has been done also to the religious press, and the cause of the Bible truth. At my request it has been widely repudiated by many religious papers.

The following is a letter from Mr. Gurley which he wrote at my request on October 17, 1945, but which he wished to date back to 1940 when the incidents occurred:

Los Angeles, Calif.
August 1, 1940

To Whom It May Concern:

This is to certify that I, Floyd Millard Gurley, did publish in the *New Eden Magazine* (of which I am the editor) an article about the finding of Noah's Ark on Mt. Ararat.

All of the basic material used in that article came from the researches of Mr. Benjamin Franklin Allen, and the article was written up in story form with the intent of making it more interesting to read.

Apologies are hereby offered to Mr. Allen for having used some of his material which he feels was not sufficiently corroborated and which he states he does not wish to release for publication at this date.

Floyd M. Gurley

So evidently the basic facts of the story are true. But the researcher recognizes the unsatisfactory nature of the data. At this point, he looks up from the records and books and old letters with an uneasy feeling in the pit of his stomach. He wishes there were a little more information with which to work, a living eyewitness, additional details not included in the Roskovitsky account, details that could only be supplied by one who has ascended Ararat. And if more data had not come to light, this chapter would not be included in this book, except to repudiate the Roskovitsky account.

Telephoto of peak of Mt. Ararat.

But more data has appeared; data which substantiates the original research of Ben Allen, and multiplies our knowledge of the Russian expeditions many times. To Eryl Cummings, ardent Ararat researcher, went the privilege of uncovering most of this powerful evidence.

The Rosseya Report

Sparked by a lengthy and detailed article in the White-Russian publication *Rosseya* on October 6, 1945, on the Russian discovery of 1916, Cummings determined to finally uncover the essential truths in the story. His search finally led him to an elderly gentleman, formerly a Four-Star Russian General, Alexander Jacob Elshin, and in turn Colonel Alexander A. Koor, also formerly a Russian officer. Koor, the ghostwriter of the *Rosseya* article, had been stationed at the base of Ararat for several years before the Bolshevik Revolution. Both men had actively opposed the Communists' takeover, but, when the resistance troops were defeated, they escaped with their families to Manchuria, eventually migrating to America. They had not known each other until coming to this country.

Koor passed a wealth of information on to Cummings concerning not only the 1916 discoveries but the results of his own personal investigations of many significant archaeological sites in the Ararat region.

March 1, 1946

Here are some data which should help our research, from the official records of the Russian Caucasian Army, 1914-1917, by General E. B. Mavlovsky.

The headquarters of the 14th Railroad Battalion was at Bayazit, just southwest of Greater Ararat, with Brigade Headquarters at Maku, southeast of Lesser Ararat, commanded by Col. Sverczkoff. The 14th Battalion came to the front in the summer of 1916, from Russia. I understand that the discovery of Noah's Ark was in the end of 1916, with the scouting parties having to wait until the summer of 1917.

I know that Sergeant Boris V. Rujansky belonged to the 14th Battalion. I understand, and it is logical, that the first and second parties of the expedition to Mount Ararat were formed from the local force of the 14th Battalion of #-D Zamorsky Brigade, by order from the local Brigade Headquarters. Sergeant B. V. Rujansky was sent to join the party because he was a specialist. Before the war he worked in the Technological Institute of Peter the Great, and attended the Imperial Institute of Archaeology in St. Petersburg. In 1916 the 3-D Caucasian Aviation Detachment, under the command of 1st Lt. Zabolotsky, served air duty over the region at Mount Ararat, Lake Van, and Lake Urmia. This aviation detachment served the 4th Caucasian Corps, and the Army Aviation Inspector was Captain Koorbatoff. I hope 1st Lt. Zabolotsky is the man you are looking for, for he, from an airplane, sighted the Ark and started the investigation. Captain Koorbatoff was his supervisor. . . .

I was in the Ararat region in November, 1915, during the war between Turkey and Russia. The general headquarters of the Caucasian Army sent me and other officers in command of emergency forces from Barzem and Pytergorsky for protection of the Araratasky Pass, just northwest of the peak of Greater Ararat and Zorsky Pass a few miles northwest, from the imminent Turkish attack. In June and July, the 3rd Turkish Army had broken through our forces very close to Aghri Dagh, and also the region of Mount Ararat.

It was during this military service that I learned of the several undeciphered inscriptions, and investigated archaeological sites in that region.

Alexander A. Koor

March 21, 1946

To Whom It May Concern:

This is to certify that I, Alexander A. Koor, former Colonel and Chief-in-Command, of the 19th Petropaulovsky regiment, heard the following concerning the discovery of Noah's Ark:

(1) 1st Lt. Paul Vasilivich Rujansky of the 156th Elisavetpolsky regiment, Caucasian Army. I knew all of Rujansky's family for years. I met them in the city of Kazan, Russia, where I attended the government Military Academy. 1st Lt. Rujansky was wounded in Erzerum when his regiment took Chaban Dede, central fort of the Erzerum fortifications. He was relieved from active duty and sent to work in the Commandant's office, in the city of Irkustsk, Siberia. After the Bolsheviks made an uprising he moved to the city of Harbin, Manchuria, where I found him in 1921.

(2) Lt. Peter Nicolovich Leslin of the 261st Ahilchinsky regiment, also of the Caucasian Army. During the Bolshevik uprising he was arrested, but escaped from them, and in December, 1918, he joined my Petropaulovsky regiment.

(3) About July or August, 1921, I and Lt. Leslin met 1st Lt. Rujansky in Harbin. During one of our conversations, 1st Lt. Rujansky told me about the discovery of Noah's Ark. He (1st Lt. Rujansky) didn't know about the details because he was wounded and sent to Russia, but he knew because his brother, Boris Vasilivich Rujansky, sergeant of the military railroad battalion, was a member of the investigation party, which was sent to Mt. Ararat to corrorborate the discovery of Noah's Ark.

Lt. Leslin admitted he had also heard about the discovery of Noah's Ark, not as a rumor, but as news, from the Senior Adjutant of his Division, who had told him that Noah's Ark was found in the saddle of two peaks of Mount Ararat.

That is all I heard from these two officers, and I am sure both told me the truth.

Col. Alexander A. Koor

Further corroborating evidence has surfaced in the last few years. Mrs. Gladys Evans, of the San Diego area, tells of her excitement when she met three ex-Russian airmen in the summer of 1941 as they travelled through her home town of San Bernardino. Her father, who lived alone, had invited these men to stay with him for a few days. They related the same general story of their participation in the Russian expedition. When the news spread through the community, the details were written down and reproduced for any who were interested.

Their story was much more detailed and much less prosaic than the Roskovitsky account, although substantially the same. When Mrs. Evans, now in her seventies, read the Roskovitsky tale, she was positive that the other was more authoritative. It cannot be proved that one record was not derived from the other, but which came first? Perhaps once a copy of that account comes to light we will know, but until then, the research continues.

Conflicting Evidence

The discriminating reader will at once notice a discrepancy here. According to Mr. James Frazier, the expedition saw the Ark about two-thirds the way up as they looked over a huge cliff. It was in a small lake in a small valley and a dense swamp. Col. Koor affirms that Lt. Leslin locates it in the saddle between the two peaks of Mt. Ararat. Both of these statements seem to disagree with other accounts by Haji Yearam, George Hagopian and the Turkish investigators, as well as other accounts which will be discussed later, all placing the vessel in a most inaccessible region around the fringes of the Ahora Gorge.

Perhaps the details can be clarified somewhat by the testimony of Mr. Jacob Radtke, himself an infantryman in the Russian Army, stationed in the Ararat area as the Russian Revolution broke out. During the blistering summer of 1917, he and 500 of his fellow soldiers were ordered to march east around the northern edge of Mt. Ararat to the saddle area where they were to gather wheat to help feed the troops below. For the steepest part of their trek between the peaks, they boarded a narrow-gauge railway (which, to the authors' knowledge, is no longer in existence) spanning the distance between the lower slopes on each side of the saddle.

Twice, once on the way to the southern side and once on the way back, the officer stopped the train and pointed out to the 500 soldiers a strange barge-like structure some distance away on the upper slopes, near the edge of the glacier. According to Mr. Radtke it appeared to be in a rather flat area near a rugged cliff. The soldiers were not allowed to venture nearer, but the sighting provided material for endless conversations and speculation. All were in agreement that the structure was the remains of Noah's Ark, even though the news of the aerial discovery and the coming Czarist expedition had not reached them.

Mr. Radtke, despite a lack of much higher education, speaks German, Russian, and Polish fluently. His English is quite good, but at times he has trouble expressing himself in that language, and, unfortunately, most of the researchers have been American. It was not until we sat down with photographs and slides of the mountain that his story began to make sense and harmonize with other sightings, for he and the others had seemingly seen the Ark in the gorge area, but from the saddle. In all likelihood, Lt. Leslin had been speaking of the same sighting. Perhaps other minor discrepancies can also be better understood within the framework of imprecise word usage as these reports from eyewitnesses from other countries are studied.

As we have seen, the Roskovitsky article was based on at least a kernel of truth that, in time, was substantiated by authoritative witnesses. However, the fictional version has played an important role in this drama, for undoubtedly it remains the most widely circulated Ark story of all. Unfortunately, the ficticious part has led many to mistrust the accuracy of the event. Countless millions have read the article, and even today, thirty years later, religious publications reprint it as if it were true. Scores of companies have produced and continue to produce tracts entitled "Noah's Ark Found" by Vladimir Roskovitsky, even though it has been repudiated many times. It is our contention that the stories of the past relocations and present search are exciting and meaningful enough, and Christian publications should not have to resort to fictional accounts. This is not to suggest that the publishers know they are dealing with fiction, but more research is recommended.

But, getting back to the issue at hand, Koor makes reference in his March 1, 1946, letter to some "undeciphered inscriptions" and "archaeological sites" in the Ararat area. An amateur archaeologist, Koor located many important sites, discovered an ancient inscription, and listed many other areas of interest to the historian which should be investigated.

On the northwestern slopes of Ararat, he discovered an ancient carving on which were pictorial and cuneiform inscriptions. He traced the characters and translated them. His very exciting translation has been verified by experts and lends credence to the theory of the antiquity of the area and the possibility of Mount Ararat as the possible landing site of the Ark. His translation follows:

God sowed the seeds of the word into the waters. . . . the waters filled the earth, descending from above. . . . His children came to rest on the mountain or peak.

or alternate translation:

When the heavens were filled with waters, and the waters covered the earth, God the Word sowed the seeds of the word into the waters, and the seeds came to rest in the tops of the mountains.

Specialists in ancient languages feel that this inscription may well be one of the first accounts of the Flood story every recorded.

Since the Flood of Noah is a historic event and since Mt. Ararat was the landing place of the Ark, then it follows that the first civilizations,

Ancient writing found on Mt. Ararat by Institute for Creation Research in 1972. This was originally thought to be the same as Alexander Koor's discovery of cuneiform inscription in 1915, but was found to be even older.

and, therefore, the most ancient archaeological sites, are located in the general Ararat region and radiate outward to all other parts of the world.

It is interesting to note that Mt. Ararat sits in a very unique place on the globe. As will be discussed later, computer science has found that the center of the geographical land masses of the world is very near Ararat. Furthermore, there are no geographical formations that would hinder migration from Ararat. No oceans, deserts or mountain ranges which would prohibit easy access to Europe, the Middle East and Africa, Asia, and the Far East. No place on earth is so uniquely situated to encourage the descendants of Noah to "replenish the earth" as is Mt. Ararat.

Just as the geology of Ararat screams out the testimony of the Deluge, so the archaeology of Ararat and the surrounding area cries out for investigation. And we encourage it. In fact, we challenge universities and researchers to study and interpret the ruins in Eastern Turkey. If the Bible is indeed God's Word, and, if it is true, as we certainly believe it is, then it ought to stand the test of scrutiny. Under close examination of the scientific and historical data, we are confident that biblical revelation will be vindicated.

Additional References

LaHaye, Tim F. *The Beginning of the End*. Wheaton, Ill.: Tyndale House Publishers, 1972.

Michael J. Arlen. "Passage to Ararat." In *The New Yorker*. New York. Issues February 3, 10, 17, 1975.

Mikusch, Dagobert von. *Mustapha Kemal: Between Europe and Asia*. Trans. John Linton. Garden City, N.Y.: Doubleday, Doran & Co., 1931.

Papajian, Sarkis. *A Brief History of Armenia*. Fresno, Cal.: Armenian Evangelical Union, 1974.

Tarhassian, H. A. *Ezurum (Garin): Its Armenian History and Traditions*. Trans. N. Schahgaldian. Ed. K. Miridjianian (La Jolla, Calif.: The Garin Compatriotic Union of the United States, 1975).

Yalman, Ahmed Emin. *Turkey in the World War*. New Haven: Yale University Press, 1930.

Yalman, Ahmed Emin. *Turkey in My Time*. Norman, Okla.: University of Oklahoma Press, 1956.

[1] Melville Chater, "The Land of the Stalking Death," *National Geographic Magazine*, vol. 36, no. 5, (November, 1919), pp. 393-420.

[2] See A. J. Smith, *The Reported Discovery of Noah's Ark* (Orlando: Christ for the World Publishers, 1949).

11

Turkish Soldiers: 1916

Further substantiation (if any is needed) that the Ark lay exposed in the summer of 1916 came from Turkey many years later. It seems that six Turkish soldiers, returning home at the end of World War I after serving in the Baghdad area (approximately 450 miles south of Ararat), had climbed the mountain and spotted the Ark.

Not much is known about these men because by the time their story was told they were no longer living. All the information that we have was passed on by a friend of the soldiers, a learned man to whom they went to record their journey.

It seems that none of the soldiers could read or write, but somehow, in 1946, they heard that American explorers were organizing a trip to Mt. Ararat to try to relocate Noah's Ark. One of the soldiers, still considering himself fit to climb, desired to guide this expedition to the Ark. In order to offer his services he enlisted the aid of his friend, Duran Ayranci of Adana, Turkey, to write a letter detailing his offer. Not knowing the address of the American group, he simply sent the letter to the U.S. Embassy with instructions to pass it along to the Americans when they arrived.

The plan was simple enough and should have worked. However, the American expedition failed to materialize. For many years, the potential guide waited for the Americans, knowing that he possessed information that was valuable, even vital, to the world. Eventually he died, and the knowledge of the whereabouts of the Ark died with him.

The letter remained in the files of one of the Embassy diplomats who had been instructed to deliver the letter when the expedition arrived. But the expedition didn't arrive until 1966, twenty years later! Finally at the request of Mr. Eryl Cummings, a member of both groups, the letter was relinquished.

"When returning from World War I, I and five or six of my friends passed by the Ararat. We saw Noah's Ark leaning against the mountain. I

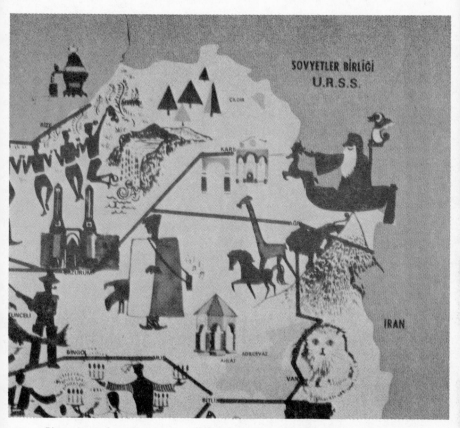

Pictoral map from Turkish travel brochure. Mt. Ararat is shown with Noah and the Ark on its summit. (Courtesy Turkish Bureau of Tourism and Information)

measured the length of the boat. It was 150 paces long. It had three stories. I read in the papers that an American group is looking for this boat. I wish to inform you that I shall personally show this boat and I request your intervention so that I may show the boat," . . . read the letter.

Some rather frantic correspondence ensued, but, much to the dismay of the researchers, the only remaining witness was the penman, Ayranci. He, of course, had not seen the Ark but had only heard the story from his now deceased friends.

In the letters that followed, Ayranci recalled his friends' descriptions of the Ark lying in a north-south direction on the west side of the hill and resting on a rock. Wooden pegs held it together. Portions were decayed and broken, he remembered, but most of it was preserved in the glacial ice.

Corroborating this, additional evidence came to light recently when two American military personnel living in Turkey testified that they had talked to some of the men involved. Both were stationed at the U.S. Air Force Base in Adana, but neither of them knew the other, and indeed their paths were not likely to cross.

One man, Elmer Rund of Gainesville, Florida, who participated in the 1973 ICR expedition, a dedicated, warm Christian, frequently talked to the Turks about their need for a personal relationship with Jesus Christ. One day he met a man who, shortly before his death, claimed to have seen the Ark at the end of World War I.

The second, an Air Force officer, made a habit of visiting one particular Turkish bar for his evening's entertainment, swapping stories with the Turks over the "bira" or "raki" or other more powerful Turkish drinks. One man, who owned a barrel shop, always told of his discovery of the Ark. The usually drunken officer never thought it necessary to gather details, and even though he is now a Christian and currently restationed in Adana, he has been unable to relocate the old man.

Many of the Turkish people, including most of the government officials, contend that Mt. Ararat was the resting place of the Ark and that the remains are still there. The travel brochures put out by the Turkish Bureau of Tourism and Information reflect this idea. In fact, on the pictorial map of the country, printed in many languages, Mt. Ararat is always shown with Noah, the Ark, and pairs of animals descending. The following excerpt from such a brochure should prove interesting:

One can make the ascension of Mt. Ararat, departing from Dogubeyazit, Igdir, or Aralik. The highest point in Turkey (5165 meters) is an ancient volcano which was the site of numerous expeditions, certain ones of which have had the purpose of retrieving the remains of Noah's Ark, which touched earth in this spot after the deluge. It is not probable that you yourself can find traces of this ante-diluvian vessel, but to discover there the nomadic population of the region and their artworks constitutes without a doubt marvelous souvenirs of the voyage.

12

Carveth Wells: 1933

Travelers in a foreign country frequently run into insurmountable problems, especially if they do not know the language of the country. Expeditions to Mt. Ararat are no exception, even when they have received the official sanction and protection of the government.

In 1933, Carveth Wells, a Los Angeles radio commentator, experienced situations that make even veteran travelers shudder. Wells, bent on searching Mt. Ararat for the remains of Noah's Ark, attempted to approach the mountain through Soviet Armenia. The harassment heaped on him by Communist officials is ably described in his humorous but factual diary *Kapoot*, published on his return. The Russians hindered his progress throughout his stay in Russia and forbade him to cross the border into Turkey to climb the mountain.

However, he was successful in visiting the monastery in Echmiazin, reported to possess the wood brought down by the monk Jacob. Excerpts from chapter fourteen of his delightful book follow.

"We have heard about your expedition to Mount Ararat, but I am afraid you will not receive permission to cross the border!"

"What would happen if we walked across the border to Ararat and then came straight back?" inquired Zetta. "Would we be stopped?"

"You would be shot by the sentries!" he answered.

"How about going to this place called Echmiazin?" I inquired.

"Echmiazin!" he exclaimed with enthusiasm. "That is very easy. We can drive there in an hour easily. You will find it one of the most interesting places in Armenia."

Echmiazin claims to have the oldest monastery in the world, whose monks have spent their lives from time immemorial trying to climb Mount Ararat in search of Noah's Ark. For many centuries, Echmiazin has been the seat of the Katholikos, or Armenian Patriarch, who is the spiritual head of all true Armenians, whether they live in Armenia or in Chicago's Loop.

View of Mt. Ararat from the monastery of Echmiadzen from *Journey to Ararat* by Parrot.

The name Echmiazin means, "the Only-Begotten descended." The church is surrounded by an ancient wall over a mile long, and within the walls are the monastery, library and other monastic buildings.

The library contains many priceless manuscripts, some of which have never been translated or published. On the library wall is a magnificent oil painting showing Noah descending with his family from Ararat, followed by a long line of animals!

"Please do not mistake us for tourists," I begged. "We have come all the way from Chicago on purpose to visit Echmiazin. We are looking for Noah's Ark or what is left of it!" I continued with a smile.

The old man's eyes twinkled. "We have the remains of the Ark here in the church!"

If he thought we were crazy, he didn't show it when we all three actually jumped with joy and excitement.

"May we see it?" we all said eagerly.

"That I cannot say, until I have consulted the brothers," he answered. "I must explain to you, that it is the most prized possession of the monastery, and no other church in the world possesses or even claims to possess such a thing."

The Archbishop then told us that, although he himself would have no objection to our seeing and photographing the portion of the Ark which had been in the church for centuries, it had never been shown to a layman.

"Good news!" he said. "They have decided to show you through the treasury and

The most prized possession of the monastery of Echmiadzen is a piece of wood reportedly from Noah's Ark and is kept in the golden casket shown here by Archbishop Mesrop. From *Kapoot* by Carveth Wells.

allow you to take whatever pictures you wish.'' Then he added: ''The church must always be cleaned thoroughly before the portion of the Ark is touched, and certain ritual must be gone through. That is what you hear, and the reason they are sweeping the floor.''

I opened the last casket, which looked very much like an ordinary ikon from the outside, but on opening the two doors of the casket, instead of finding the usual painting of Jesus or the Holy Family, there was a piece of reddish-colored petrified wood, measuring about twelve inches by nine and about an inch thick.

''You may examine it as much as you like,'' said the Archbishop. ''This is the portion of Noah's Ark which was brought down from Ararat by one of our monks named Jacob, St. Jacob.''

It was obviously petrified wood, as the grain was clearly visible, but having expected to see a piece of wood that was curved like the side of a boat, I remarked that I was surprised to find it was flat.

Archbishop Mesrop had a sense of humor. He instantly remarked, ''You have forgotten the rudder, Mr. Wells!''

So this was the piece of wood I had come so far to see, and the thing that so many other travelers, including Lord Bryce, had been unsuccessful in seeing.[1]

Again, Mr. Wells:

We had just said good-bye to the Archbishop when a young fellow in the costume of an aviator approached. Having heard we wished to reach Mount Ararat, he told us that he was willing to fly us to the mountain and back!

Forgetting for the moment what might be the consequence of even flying over the border without permission, I inquired how much the trip would cost.

''Three hundred rubles an hour, and I can make it in a couple of hours,'' he replied.

''Three hundred rubles!'' I exclaimed. ''Why, we can get a sight-seeing ride in America for three dollars an hour!''

Shrugging his shoulders, the aviator remarked: ''C'est la même chose! Trois cent rubles, trois dollars!''

Evidently rubles were of less value in Armenia than in Moscow, and I was almost tempted to accept his offer to take me for a joy ride around Ararat, even though three hundred rubles meant one hundred fifty dollars to me and only three to the Russian, but on thinking the matter over, I decided that a secret flight across the border might result in the confiscation of all my films and would give the Soviet authorities a legitimate excuse to arrest me. I gave up the idea and returned to Erivan.[2]

Although Carveth Wells never admitted crossing the border, there has been some speculation that he did. For his friends maintain that on certain occasions he showed a piece of reddish colored wood that he brought back from Russia.

I am very interested in the ark and about 30 years ago Carveth Wells was at the ark and smuggled a piece of it out and I examined it and it is of very hard wood. The piece he brought out was by bribing a Government inspector. The piece was about 2 feet long and 8 inches wide and 1½ inch thick.

I hope the snow does not come on the ark deep enough to hide it like it does some years. When Wells was up there, the shepherds had been up there and found the snow partly melted away from one end of the ark.[3]

Whether or not Wells ascended the mountain, bought the wood from a shepherd, or simply left Russia as stated is not really known. At any rate, the name of Carveth Wells can be added to the growing list of names of curious men who have ventured agonizingly close to the giant archaeological treasure. Far enough away to be frustrated by unforeseen obstacles, yet close enough to see evidences that inspired him to say, "It is there without a doubt."

---

[1] Evidently the piece of wood is not as hard to see now. To the authors' knowledge, one American family was allowed to see it in 1974 and another American traveler in 1975.
[2] Carveth Wells, *Kapoot* (London: Jarrold Publishers, 1934), pp. 215-234.
[3] From the personal files of Eryl and Violet Cummings.

13

Hardwicke Knight: 1936

Just as any foreign traveler can sympathize with the trials of Carveth Wells in Russia, so any former Ararat investigator can sympathize with the lengthy nightmare that confronted the young archaeologist Hardwicke Knight in 1936. Like all who have spent any length of time in the vicinity of and on Mt. Ararat, Knight was doubly exposed to the fury of the magnificent mountain as well as the whims of the nearby inhabitants.

Only the grace of God preserved and protected him on his journey which culminated in the accidental discovery of a framework of huge timbers extending out of the glacial ice and moraine at the 14,000-foot level on the northern slopes.

Knight's experience began on a hot summer afternoon in August of 1936. In the general Ararat area on business, he was answering the urge to explore and attempt to locate some of the archaeological sites on Ararat that he had heard and read about, particularly the ruins of the Armenian monastery near the village of Ahora.

With his sleeping bag, provisions, and a knapsack, he set out on foot, approaching Mt. Ararat from the east. As nightfall approached, Knight entered a Kurdish village expecting to be the grateful recipient of the famous Kurdish hospitality. Much to his surprise, a band of armed horsemen intercepted him, and, before he could really understand the situation, he had, in effect, been kidnapped.

He was given a horse and forced at gunpoint to ride with the men, who seemingly spoke neither Turkish nor Russian. They rode through the night up the lower slopes of the mountain, around the north, heading toward the saddle between the two peaks.

Much later, they arrived at their headquarters, where Knight was held prisoner for two days in a filthy cellar. No explanation was given for this treatment, indeed no attempt to communicate was made at all.

Evidently, the group was unwilling for the location of their hideout to be known, so on the third day of his imprisonment Knight was again

Some of the "not always so friendly" Kurds of the Ararat region.

taken on horseback for some distance away from the camp toward the greater Ararat and was suddenly abandoned, never to know who his abductors were or why they had detained him.

Alone again, Knight decided to continue on with his original plan. Already at a fairly high elevation, he considered his best course of action would be to circle Mt. Ararat, maintaining a fairly high contour, and approach Ahora from the west. Without a map of Mt. Ararat and without any prior knowledge of the mountain, Knight was never really able to get his bearings, especially since haze had shrouded any landmarks or reference points in the valley below and heavy clouds had covered the summit.

It would have been much easier to have proceeded counterclockwise, approaching Ahora from the east, but in his confusion and indecision he chose the other alternative.

Knight ascended as he circled to just below the ice cap. But Ararat is no small mountain, and the circumference, even at 14,000 feet, is staggering. It has been calculated that, even at periods of extensive glacial melt, the ice cap covers an area of 17½ square miles! And so, two days later, the weary traveler made it to the northern face of the mountain.

During that time he was exposed to severe weather conditions. He had experienced the infamous afternoon thunder and lightning storms that so frequently strike Mt. Ararat in the later summer, and hail, strong winds, and snow hampered his progress.

Within a few hundred yards of the western face of the Ahora Gorge, Knight made his discovery. Mentally and physically he was nearing exhaustion, and at first the existence of a framework of huge hand-hewn timbers protruding out of the ice and glacial moraine made no impression. But as he hurried on toward his destination, his archaeological curioity prevailed and he returned to investigate.

Knight did not at the time associate his discovery with possible remains of the Ark. What he saw seemed to him as the remains of a gun carriage or a heavy wagon. Rectangular timbers approximately 9 inches to a foot square were protruding several feet out of the snow. Crossbeams formed a rectangular pattern. The wood was very dark in color but extremely soft and soggy as if it had been submerged in water for a long period of time. The small piece of soggy wood that Knight broke off and carried away deteriorated rapidly.

Years later, after studying the subject in depth, Knight became convinced that his discovery might have something to do with Noah's Ark. He returned to point out the area to investigators in 1967, but an unusual amount of snow blanketed the area.

As a traditional archaeologist, Knight does not hold the opinion that the world was once covered by a global water catastrophe. Nor does he feel that the story of Noah's Flood and Noah's Ark in the Bible is to be taken literally, even though he does feel that Noah was a historical person and that the Flood, although quite localized, indeed occurred.[1]

In a recent conversation (summer of 1973) he expressed the view that the shepherd Noah, aware that the Flood was imminent, might have hauled great timbers up Mt. Ararat and built a shelter for his family and animals. Thus, he survived the Flood which inundated all the world that he could see, except for the top of Mt. Ararat.

The authors respect Mr. Knight's opinion but must point out that it cannot be supported biblically, except by taking extreme liberties with the account given in Genesis. Neither does it harmonize with the vast amount of scientific data which have come to light in recent years in support of global catastrophe.

Knight, however, remains anxious to relocate his find and possibly even the superstructure of Noah's "barn." In a letter dated February 12, 1974, he supplied the following information:

What I feel is more significant than the area of my previous find is the area directly above, i.e., the area which would feed the glacial flow. This we found a most inaccessible part of the mountain (in 1967). The area itself, however, is a beautiful platform at circa 14,000 feet with a steady slope right down to the plain, so in a way I am torn between regarding the site as the original or as a redeposited one.

[1]See Hardwick Knight, "Ararat and the Ark: Fact or Fiction?" *The Otaga Daily Times* (October 14, 1967), p. 19.

14

American Aviators: 1943

The next time you travel in an airplane look down at the ground below from your cruising altitude of, say, 25,000 feet. You will find the landmarks are barely distinguishable. Two-lane highways appear as a string twisting through the foothills. Occasionally, the glare of the sun on a car's windshield calls it to your attention. Farmhouses with vegetable gardens dot the landscape.

Mountain ranges seem grossly misshapen. The contours are more pronounced than they appear from the ground. The ridges are sharp and erosional features are easy to see.

As you drink in the distant scene, allow your mind to picture a huge glacier-topped mountain below. Picture, Mt. Ararat, 17,000 feet in height, reaching halfway up to your commercial jet. Notice the stark characteristics of the lava beds and the glacial morasses and contrast them to the dazzling whiteness of the ice cap. Let your mind's eye be drawn to the hideous chasm on the mountain's northern slopes.

The plane seems to be flying very near this mountain, startlingly near, in fact, in comparison with the flat arid desert and foothills that you have been flying over for the last few hours. So magnificent is the sight that all eyes are riveted on the mountain as you pass. And there is plenty of time for all the passengers to have a turn at the window, for Ararat is huge, and, even at this speed, it is in sight for many minutes.

Being aware that investigators are searching for the remains of Noah's Ark, your eyes dart back and forth looking for some sign of its existence. You cannot help but notice the flocks of sheep grazing on the grassy lower slopes. And, yes, that must be the village of Ahora, and, although the mud huts are hard to see, the tin-roofed school building stands out in a conspicuous fashion. On the other side of the stream issuing from the Ahora Gorge, you might even see several parked trucks, a minibus, a land rover, and you rightly assume that an expedition is on the mountain right now and has made Ahora its base camp. Surely if the Ark was exposed, you would be able to see it. A structure 450 feet long and 75 feet wide must be somewhere visible.

Today (back in the real world), Mt. Ararat lies in a heavily restricted zone. Because of its close proximity to the Russian border it is the location of several military outposts. On the opposite side of the Aras River, in Russia, several more military bases are to be seen. Consequently, no commercial flights are allowed into the area. Occasionally, flights from Tehran, Iran, to Ankara, Turkey, fly within sight of the mountain, as do flights connecting Erivan, Russia, with points south. But on each flight, Ararat is carefully skirted. The chances for a visual sighting from the air are minimal.

Furthermore, because of the area's sensitive nature and to honor agreements made with Russia for mutual security, Turkey does not allow researchers to explore the mountain from the air.

But there was a time when frequent flights were made over Ararat by military cargo and fighter planes. Mt. Ararat lay directly in the path of flights from the U.S. Air Base in Tunisia and the Soviet Air Base in Erivan during World War II. The United States alone was in a position to keep the Russian troops supplied with much-needed provisions, and many hundreds of flights were logged between the two bases.

If the Ark of Noah ever lay exposed during World War II, it would have been seen. To think otherwise would be to defy human nature. As in our imaginary journey above, every observer would find his eyes riveted to the mountain, just to observe its awesome characteristics, if not to actively search for the vessel. Consequently, it is not shocking to find that many claimed to have seen either the Ark or pictures of the Ark during this period.

The account that created the greatest impression on more people than any other appeared in the Tunisian edition of the U.S. Armed Forces paper *Stars and Stripes* in 1943. According to the article, two pilots saw the Ark on several of their flights and finally invited a professional photographer to accompany them to document their claims. The account was not particularly lengthy, but a photograph of the Ark joined it on the front page of the paper.

Each military area publishes its own *Stars and Stripes*, partially using major articles supplied by the main office. Local news, such as the discovery, was not reprinted in other papers around the world. Unfortunately, during those war-torn years, complete files of the papers were not kept, and the article has not been relocated.

Many veterans alive today remember the story. Some even kept the

Recent map of the Ararat area.

clipping for years before eventually discarding it. But the number of witnesses is astonishing and growing. Many are educated men, and their reputations are beyond reproach.

A retired Navy chaplain (at the time a California legislator from San Diego), when confronted with the research, remembered the story well. He initiated a search for the article that continued for some time but produced nothing except more men who remembered it.

Evidently, at least two other sightings occurred during that same time

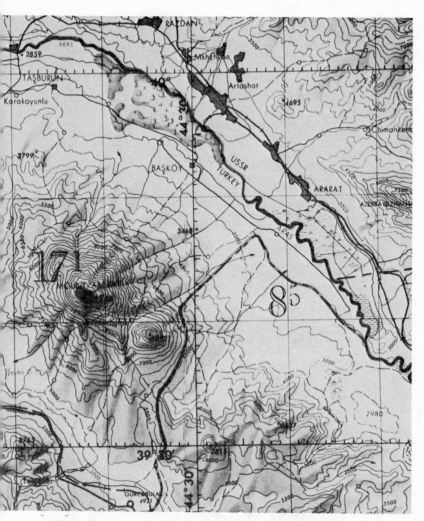

period. Dr. A. J. Smith, in his booklet *The Reported Discovery of Noah's Ark,* tells of attempting in vain to find two U.S. Army Air Corps men recently discharged after service in the Near East. According to many witnesses at a large statewide gathering at Birmingham, Alabama, in 1946, these two soldiers produced many photographs of the Ark and claimed to have personally seen it. They were traced to the Burma-Philippine area but never found.[1]

At about this same time two Australian airmen showed up in an English pub with aerial photographs of Mt. Ararat, clearly showing the Ark in a cleft of the mountain. They also claimed to have taken the pictures.

Mt. Ararat from the south, showing an exceptional amount of glacial melt.

But there's more. Ben Allen, the veteran researcher mentioned above, received a report from a World War II veteran living in Tallahassee, Florida, who claimed to have seen movies of Mt. Ararat and the Ark taken from a U.S.A.F. plane in the private possession of a mysterious man. Allen immediately flew to Tallahassee but was unable to contact the man. A sworn statement from the witness, though hardly sufficient as proof, revealed that a large portion of the Ark was clearly seen.

Many people (and the list constantly grows) also claim to have seen movies of the Ark in a "March of Time" newsreel taken from a plane or helicopter. These newsreels were shown as fillers between features at movie theaters for years all over the country. Again, the Ark was plainly visible.

Most baffling of all reported showings of such films was reported by a high school student in the Los Angeles area in 1973. He was quite certain that while living in the Philadelphia area in 1969 he, too, had seen movies of the Ark taken from a helicopter. His Sunday school teacher had shown the movies for his class of ten or twelve boys on the campus of Faith Theological Seminary in Philadelphia. He remembers details not found in other accounts, recalling the films taken from the air show the Ark partially protruding from a rubble-covered snow field. The planking was clearly visible, and several men were exploring it!

Needless to say, none of these stories has yet been verified, and consequently the accounts are weak. Recognizing that better proof of the existence of the Ark has been presented, and even better proof remains, these are presented both for completeness and for reader interest. It is also hoped that more names will be added to the ever-growing list of known viewers. And perhaps this inclusion will spark the revelation of the proof. Again the reader is encouraged to search for any possible record of these and other sightings.

[1]A. J. Smith, *The Reported Discovery of Noah's Ark* (Orlando: Christ for the World Publishers, 1949), p. 43.

15

Russian Aviators: 1943

Evidently American flyers were not the only ones to make such a discovery in World War II. As reported in the magazine *Navy, the Magazine of Sea Power* in January of 1961, by Raymond Schuessler in "Hark, Hark . . . the Ark!!" Russian interest also existed, perhaps sparked by the phony Roskovitsky account published in 1940. According to Major Jasper Maskelyn, wartime chief of Russian camouflage, "One of my men flew over Mt. Ararat in a reconnaissance aircraft in an attempt to check a story that the Ark had been sighted there by Russian airmen in the First World War. He reported that he saw a partly submerged vessel in an ice lake. Arctic climbers investigated the lake, which was partly thawed, and found the remains of an Ark, very rotted, over 400 feet long, composed of a fossilized wood looking almost like coal."

From time to time, reports have filtered out from behind the Iron Curtain indicating that the Russians maintain a considerable file on the existence of the Ark but are reluctant to reveal it, recognizing that the Ark contradicts their basic assumptions of atheistic evolution. More than that, the possibility of a global catastrophe is entirely incompatible with such assumptions.

By rediscovering the biblical Ark of Noah and by proving its authenticity, the Flood of Noah's day must also be regarded as a historical event, and Flood geology or catastrophism would be upheld. As mentioned previously, the evolutionary model rests entirely on the assumption of uniformitarianism, which is the converse of catastrophism. Without uniformity, evolution becomes mere folly.

Proof that godless Communism relies on evolution is found in the observation that Karl Marx, in laying down the ground rules in *Das Kapital*, desired to dedicate his work to Charles Darwin. Marx recognized that evolution provided him with the supposed scientific basis for Communism, that man was the impersonal product of random processes operating in a godless universe. Even today, the comprehensive Soviet

Encyclopedia terms the story of Noah's Ark as "a legend harmful to science."

Obviously we can expect no help from the Communist Party in our quest. Whether or not Russia actively engages in the refusal of permits to proposed expeditions and the sabotage of groups once the permits are granted is open to question. Certainly the tension between Turkey and Russia contributes to the problem, as does the fact that Mt. Ararat occupies such a strategic piece of real estate, overlooking Russian and Turkish military installations.

It does appear that, within the Soviet Union, information on the past discoveries of the Ark lies suppressed, far from the prying eyes of the world. Consider the following interview between Dr. Donald M. Liedmann, M.D., Ph.D., and James M. Lee, father of Elfred Lee, both long-time Ark researchers and former members of SEARCH, Inc., recorded in 1969:

> *LEE*: Doctor Liedmann, we first met at the Hilton Hotel in Chicago at the International Convention of the Full Gospel Business Men's Fellowship International. Demos Shakarian, the International President, had asked me to attend the Convention and show the pieces of wood found on Mount Ararat in 1969 by the SEARCH Foundation Team, and the movie film of that expedition. You will recall that I was standing at a table showing interested persons the print of an original painting of the mountain, when you walked up to the table, pointed to the picture and said, "The Ark is there!" You seemed to be so positive in your remark that we entered into a discussion of the subject, and then learned that you had had a very remarkable experience which you partially revealed to those standing there. Doctor Liedmann, will you please tell us about some of the background of your family, your experiences in Sweden, and how it is that you are so confident in your own mind that Noah's Ark still remains high up on the upper slopes of Mount Ararat?
>
> *LIEDMANN*: Yes, I will be happy to do so, Mr. Lee. I was born in Sweden of Orthodox Jewish parents who had migrated from the Russian Ukraine. From them I learned the Russian language. As a Jew I also learned the Hebrew and Aramaic languages. I have been interested in many different archaeological discoveries around the world—especially those connected with Old Testament history. My experience concerning Mount Ararat was a remarkable experience in itself, as you will see, and I still marvel at it myself. I have never related this story of my experience to anyone since it happened in 1947 and 1948. I received my medical degree in Upsala, Sweden, where I also studied and received my specialty in neurosurgery. I should mention here that I had been studying medicine for approximately five years when I quit my studies and volunteered for the RAF for a

Mt. Ararat as seen from Russia.

six-month tour of active duty. I fought against the Germans, and was shot down twice by them and was injured in my back. After my recovery I went back to medical school again and began studying hematology at Heidelberg. It was on one of my trips down there that I became acquainted with a Russian Air Force major. This was in Hamburg. As everyone knows, the Russians, the English, and the Americans were all fighting together as the common enemies of Germany. This Air Force major and I found that we had many things in common: we were both squadron leaders during the last portion of World War II; we had both been flying since early manhood; we both spoke the same Russian dialect; and he was born in the Ukraine and my ancestors came from there. Thus we had many common interests to discuss socially. On several occasions when we met by appointment, I would invite him for dinner and social entertainment. It was on these occasions that he described to me different happenings, which, naturally, no one in his position should have mentioned to anyone in the Western world.

LEE: What was the nature of the happenings which he revealed to you?

LIEDMANN: This Air Force major had been a squadron leader in the Russian Air Force and was in command of a group of three planes which had taken part in a number of special missions over Mount Ararat. To my understanding, they were going there at very specific times each year, because, as this major explained to me, there are only 30 to 38 days during the year that the glaciers in that area are melted enough to make it favorable for taking pictures. Which day of the month it was I cannot recall, but nevertheless the first time I met him in 1947 he showed me at that time three distinct pictures taken on Mount Ararat. They were marked at the 13-14,000 foot elevation, or 4,500 meters approximately. These pictures also showed a Russian aircraft with their insignia on the wings. Each of these pictures showed a boat-like structure which he pointed out to me to be what is mentioned in the Bible as Noah's Ark. I asked him a number of times why they were so interested in taking those pictures. He just laughed with a little grin and didn't answer my question. One of those pictures showed the ship protruding out of the ice approximately 80 to 90 feet and it was tilted slightly downwards. In the bottom of that area was a little melted pond or lake. The glacier was shown with the mountain summit in the upper right of that picture and the other pictures were taken at a similar angle. To me it appeared that they were taken on the north side. He wouldn't give too many of his own explanations of this, because, as he pointed out time and again, those photographs were the property of the USSR.

LEE: Were any photographs taken other than in 1938?

LIEDMANN: Yes, I met the same man a year later in 1948, also in Hamburg, Germany. At that time he showed me another set of pictures. Let me mention this. Those first pictures which I mentioned before were taken in 1938 at approximately the 14,000 foot elevation. Those other pictures which were shown me in 1948 were taken more recently. Just how recently, I don't know. He only mentioned that "these have been taken since I saw you." How this happened, I can't explain. To me it had no significance at the time for the simple reason that I was not a Christian, but a Jew. I did not pay too much attention, other than that I believed absolutely that Noah's Ark was there. I know the Old Testament very well, and so knew the Ark must still be there.

LEE: How much of the Ark was exposed to view?

LIEDMANN: This is what can be explained about those pictures that were taken the last time. On this occasion he showed me almost a dozen pictures. The Ark was covered up much more than the first time with maybe only 12 or 15 feet of the vessel showing. Only a tip of it was showing. Some sections could be seen through the glassy-clear ice. These were the pictures that were shown me on those two different occasions. The first one was shown to me in 1947, and the second one in 1948. All of these photographs were concerning Noah's Ark on Mt. Ararat, and there always appeared a Russian aircraft in the picture. I asked him for a copy of these pictures, but he said, "These are the property of the Russian government and I cannot give them out, nor give any more information regarding these pictures." Regarding the mountain—he described it as a high, rocky, volcanic mountain and that since it belonged to Turkey they could not do any research on it. This I could understand.

LEE: Did you meet this Air Force Major other than on these two occasions?

LIEDMANN: The third time I met that same Major he was with a number of his companions and when I asked him about his expedition he wouldn't talk or mention anything about them. He completely ignored the subject. In fact, he told me, "I don't know what you are talking about." That was on the third occasion that I met this same Russian Air Force Major.

LEE: How many planes were involved in the flights over Ararat?

LIEDMANN: I should mention that each time they made a mission, or flight, for taking these pictures, there were always three different planes involved. [1]

Little doubt remains of Russian knowledge on the subject and their continued suppression of the evidence. One very interesting article was published in the summer of 1974 in *The National Enquirer* and, as a sidelight, is reproduced below. The story reportedly emitted from a Russian source.

Christian-Hating Communists Dig Up Noah's Ark and Burn It!

The Russians are reported to have found Noah's Ark and burned it.

According to reliable Moscow sources, the Communists dug the ancient ship out of a glacier high atop Mt. Ararat just across the Russian border in Turkey.

Teams of Russian explorers dismantled the ancient ship and took it back to the capitol where they burned the pieces.

They also are reported to have found about thirty animals frozen aboard the ship in its hold.

Mt. Ararat is very near the Russian-Turkish border and each time a foreign expedition was planned to find the Ark, the Communists complained it was a spying expedition. At last, reports say the Communists sent their own party to find the Ark and destroy it.

"The anti-Christian feelings of the Reds had as much to do with it as anything," a Moscow source confided. The Communist search party, which reportedly numbered about 25 scientists and aides, found the Ark in less than 30 days.

They sent for help and dug the ship from its icy grave. The frozen animals were found on board. After dismantling the ship, they took the remains back to Russia and burned them, NEWS EXTRA sources reported.

Of course, the account consists of nothing more than the fabrications of a glory-seeking reporter under the pseudonym Igor Pavlovitch. Or does it? Such an event could not have occurred without the knowledge of the world for American intelligence is quite extensive, as is tourist travel in Moscow. The Turkish government would not have allowed the artifact to be removed, and it could not have been done without both Turkish and American knowledge. Furthermore, the claim of the discovery of frozen animals on board can only be viewed as the efforts of an uninformed reporter to try to make his falsified account more believable. Obviously, if the only living land animals were on the Ark at the time of its use, then they could no longer be there, or else we would have no animals today.

But the question remains. Why was such a fictitious account written in the first place? There are no answers as yet, but could it be that officials in Russia feel that researchers are getting too close? Was this a poor effort to discourage further exploration? Or an effort to discredit any future find?

Already the article has had an effect. The Turkish government takes a dim view of efforts to remove any item of archaeological significance from the country, and this article has certainly not encouraged them to support further foreign research.

Pictures of the Ark

This might be as good a time as any in our continuing study of the evidence to briefly discuss reports of pictures of the Ark seen in several countries. It is not uncommon for a lecturer on the subject to be approached after a meeting by one who claims to have seen such pictures. These pictures all seem to have uncertain origins but share a common fate. Some of the more important claims are listed below.

In Holtville, California, around 1940, a children's Bible class teacher produced pictures of Noah's Ark whenever she taught her students the story. According to several witnesses, Sister Bertha Davis had quite a portfolio of pictures covering Bible stories, but the ones of Mt. Ararat clearly showed the vessel from a distance, partially protruding from a debris-covered snow field. It looked like a barge with a catwalk along the top and the planking was clearly visible. An attached photograph showed a small stone bench with a partially burned wooden roof.

A woman in Los Angeles, granddaughter of an oldtime traveling evangelist, distinctly remembers seeing similar pictures of the Ark in her grandfather's possession. Others of her relatives remember the same pictures.

In a New York State public school a geography book used in grade school around 1950 contained a picture with the caption "Noah's Ark on Mt. Ararat," as several students recall. Again, the planking on the sides seemed quite visible.

Turkish military outpost—one of many guarding the border and access to Mt. Ararat (background).

A Lieutenant in the Turkish Air Force, a fighter pilot, remembers seeing a picture of the Ark a few years ago on a calendar, perhaps published by Turkish Airlines (THY).

The list could go on, but the amazing fact is that none of these photographs can be relocated. Nobody knows where any of them came from or how their owners obtained them, and in each case the pictures have disappeared.

A clue may be found in the following quote from a letter written by Mrs. J. R. Verbrycke, of Maryland, to the magazine *Pathfinder* and published in their July 3, 1944 issue. Mrs. Verbrycke evidently responded to a reprint of the Roskovitsky article when she wrote:

I was greatly interested in the article "Is Noah's Ark Found?" I have a photo taken by John Joseph Nouri on the top of one of the peaks with the Ark plainly shown. We knew him well and had perfect confidence in all his statements.[2]

More likely, however, these accounts stem from varied sets of photographs, because the descriptions are not the same. This book will no doubt jog the memory of a few readers and they will recall similar instances. It is our hope that this book will also jog a few pictures loose from their longtime hiding places.

[1] Used by permission of James Lee.
[2] As cited by A.J. Smith in *The Reported Discovery of Noah's Ark* (Orlando: Christ for the World Publishers, 1949).

16

Resit:
1948

Every now and then, the diligent Ark researcher reaps a reward for his efforts by uncovering a completely new piece of data. But at that point the work begins, for he must get to the root of the matter, weeding out all of the embellishments that attach themselves when the true facts are contaminated by contact with humans.

Imagine his delight when a new eyewitness appears on his own and reveals his story. Imagine also his frustration when the eyewitness disappears.

Such was the case on November 13, 1948. On that day, Edwin Greenwald, Associated Press correspondent, announced to the world, in a story from his office in Istanbul, that a Kurdish nomad named Resit had seen the Ark.

The petrified remains of an object which peasants insist resembles a ship has been found high up on Mt. Ararat, biblical landing place of Noah's Ark.

Apparently hidden for centuries, it came to light last summer when unusually warm weather melted away an ancient mantle of ice and snow.

While various persons from time to time have reported objects resembling a "house" or a "ship" on the mountain, Turks who have seen this new find profess it to be the only known object which could actually be taken as the remains of a ship.

Shukru Asena, a 69-year-old farmer who owns large acreage in that far-off Eastern frontier district, told about the discovery in an unheralded visit to the Associated Press Bureau here. This is his story:

Early in September a Kurdish farmer named Resit was about two-thirds of the way up the 16,000 ft. peak when he came upon an object he had never seen before, although he had been up the mountain many times. He moved around it and then climbed higher to examine it from above.

There, Resit said, was the prow of a ship protruding into a canyon down which tons of melting ice and snow had been rushing for more than two months. The prow was almost entirely revealed, but the rest of the object still was covered.

The contour of the earth, Resit said, indicated the invisible part of the object was shaped like a ship. The prow, he added, was about the size of a house.

Resit climbed down to it and with his dagger tried to break off a piece of the prow. It was so hard it would not break. It was blackened with age. Resit insisted it was not a simple rock formation.

"I know a ship when I see one," he said. "This is a ship."

He spread the word among little villages at the base of the mountain and peasants began climbing up its northern slope to see the weird thing he had found. Each who came back said it was a ship.

There is no folklore there about the Ark, Shukru Bey said, and persons who saw Resit's find came away in great surprise. There are no cameras out in the wild, isolated country where Turkey, Russia, and Iran meet, hence no one came away with a picture. The snows have been falling again, and perhaps have covered it again by now.

The story of this exciting find, of course, stimulated much interest in religious circles around the world. Among those determined and dedicated researchers eager to corroborate the Istanbul report was the Reverend Aaron J. Smith, retired missionary from China, and Dean of North Carolina's People's Bible College, who fervently wished to go along.

The Reverend Smith had also collected a formidable array of reports dealing with Mt. Ararat and the Ark, beginning with Josephus in A.D. 93, on up to the latest press releases in 1948.

News of this discovery sparked increased interest in the search around the world. Hurriedly, veteran researcher A. J. Smith organized an expedition to verify and document Resit's claims. The details of Smith's heartbreaking search will follow, but the reason most responsible for their failure is that they were unable to locate Resit. Without a guide and without prior knowledge of the mountain, they encountered innumerable hardships and returned dejected.

To understand why Resit did not respond to their appeals, one must understand the mistrust that exists between Moslem and Christian in that part of the world. To understand that takes a great deal of study in the history of the area and the peoples who have lived there.

Much has already been said about the Armenian people who had lived in the Ararat region throughout history until World War I. The Armenian people trace their origins back to a grandson of Noah and had always maintained a traditional sort of worship of the one true God. When, in the third century A.D., they were told of the person and work of Jesus Christ by Saint Gregory the Illuminator, they became the first nation on earth to

Even though ownership of Mt. Ararat has changed many times, the Kurdish people have always lived there and are the only inhabitants of the mountain now.

Moslem mosque. An interesting blend of the modern and the traditional. Near Adapazari, Turkey.

embrace Christianity as a national religion. They maintained a strong faith in God throughout the centuries in the face of seemingly unbearable persecution at the hands of the conquering followers of Mohammed three hundred years later and at the hands of various invaders and pagan nations.

In the nineteenth century the strongly Catholic Russia gained strength, and racial hatred grew between the Russians and the Moslem Turks and Kurds. Bitter fighting broke out frequently in the name of religion. The Armenians, having a similar form of worship, usually sided with the Russians. Indeed almost every conqueror or ambitious nation has marched through the Ararat area, and ownership has changed many times. All in all, this area has probably seen more bloodshed than any other part of the world, most of it in the name of various religions.

The result of all this is that a deep-rooted hatred and mistrust exists even today among the people of this region. Consequently, when the Kurdish Moslem Resit heard that an American Christian expedition was looking for him in order to prove the biblical account, he did not come forward and, even though a small reward was offered for any information, he was not to be found.

The Shukru Asena story indicated that others also visited the site. The Smith group scoured the countryside for any witnesses but could find none.

The present generation of Kurds who live on Mt. Ararat respond quite favorably to visitors to the mountain, so long as the visitors mind their manners. Due to the lack of formal education and their nomadic tendencies, these people only vaguely remember the Armenian people and the many wars fought in the area. The hatred does not so often come out as it did twenty-five years ago. But when it comes to revealing information concerning the whereabouts of the Ark, they clam up. All of them seem to know that it is up there, somewhere near the top, under the snow, but that's all they will say. No one has any specifics, as you think they surely would. They hide this knowledge well, but it becomes quite obvious that they know more than they are willing to tell.

17

A. J. Smith:
1949

Responding favorably to Resit's discovery, Dr. Aaron J. Smith, Dean of the People's Bible College in Greensboro, North Carolina, retired missionary to China, and avid Ark-researcher, organized the first Western expedition to Mt. Ararat in postwar years, with the specific and declared purpose of relocating the remains of Noah's Ark. Incorporating under the name Oriental Archaeological Research Expedition, Smith planned to first contact Resit, who would lead them right to the Ark; second to document the find; and third, to reveal the find to the world.

Dr. Smith, a devout Christian, recognized the prophetic and evangelical implications of locating the Ark. His deep abiding faith had already led him to compile a massive collection of documents, all of which had some bearing on the research. In order to gain financing for his expedition, Smith published a small booklet entitled *The Reported Discovery of Noah's Ark*[1] in 1949, which quickly went through several printings. But the expedition that finally reached Turkey was woefully underfinanced and poorly planned. This is not a reflection on the foresight of Dr. Smith, but rather a comment on the lack of foreknowledge.

Mt. Ararat is a formidable foe, not to be taken lightly. It would be safe to say that no expedition has ever challenged Mt. Ararat to give up her secret that has not run into problems so severe that in the end they were forced to return empty-handed. Problems arise of many different sorts. Financing is always a problem. Monetary backing for such a venture eludes the would-be team. Indeed, Smith admittedly ventured out on faith, expecting the Lord to supply the money as it was needed.

Official permission from the Turkish government must be secured, and in this area every expedition has had its problems. Smith's group was forced to remain in a hotel in Istanbul for nearly two months of prime searching time waiting for clearance to be obtained. By the time it was granted, they were almost out of money and time.

A proper team must be chosen. Smith, a man of deep faith and desire,

Dr. Aaron J. Smith, Ph.D., D.D., Dean of People's Bible College, led an expedition to Mt. Ararat in 1950.

was not surrounded by men of like conviction. In the face of adversity, their courage and desire abandoned them, reducing their effectiveness as a team. Personality conflicts crop up between individuals who are not totally committed to God and to the discovery of the Ark when they are marooned in a foreign country and finally exposed to severe hardships and physical strain.

It should be noted that another man, well known for his interest in the research, also entertained notions of a trip to Ararat that summer. Eryl Cummings, by this time a close personal friend of Dr. Smith, was invited to lead the Smith expedition but declined, dismayed at the lack of advance planning and financial backing, and it seems his caution was justified.

The weather on Mt. Ararat can change drastically within minutes. Storms of such intensity can strike, seemingly with a vengeance, that injury and death to climbers becomes a distinct possibility. Although not the tallest, Mt. Ararat may be the most massive mountain in existence. It covers an area of approximately 5,000 square miles, and without knowledge of the whereabouts of the remains of the vessel, an expedition holds no chance of success. Smith's group covered great portions of the mountain but found nothing.

Mt. Ararat is not a mountain for amateurs. The official "scouting report" on the mountain is summed up in the following quote from the 1971 *Encyclopedia Britannica:* "From a mountaineering point of view, the ascent is said not to be difficult, requiring only considerable endurance." But professional mountaineers know when and where to climb. In planning a summit climb, guides and porters can establish a base camp at 10,000 feet, and on the proper day, with only minimal survival gear, they can attain the summit. Not so when searching for the Ark. Once the safety of base camp is abandoned, the searcher must carry on his back everything he needs to survive for the duration of his stay on the glacier. To be effectively mobile, sometimes a pack of seventy-five pounds or more must be carried by each participant. Once committed to the upper reaches of the mountain, the climber is at the mercy of the moody Ararat, and without proper training and knowledge of mountains (which even today most Ararat expedition teams lack), he can hold no hope for success.

The people living on the mountain can be most helpful or they can be devastating to the hopes of potential explorers. A personal knowledge of the Turkish language is invaluable and a professional interpreter is advised. One should never attempt to search Mt. Ararat without proper protection and cooperation of the Turkish military. Smith's group was provided protection by the military, but communication was a problem.

Finally, unless God Himself sees fit to melt the snow and ice cover which covers the Ark each winter, there is no chance of success. A glacier several hundred feet thick, being a product of powerful natural forces, can only be removed by forces beyond the capabilities of man. We do not know exactly where the snow line was in the summer of 1949, since until that time very little information was available for comparison; but at any rate, no discovery was made.

Smith and his men were truly pioneers on Mt. Ararat, and, in retrospect, we can see that they accomplished a great deal. Today, several books are available on the subject of the search for the Ark, as well as books on the geology and geography, meteorology, glaciology, and the people of Mt. Ararat. Even though Smith did not have this luxury, to his credit he produced information which still aids today's researcher.

On his return, Dr. Smith himself wrote a book, and through it the reader can share the intense zeal of the man for the discovery of the Ark.

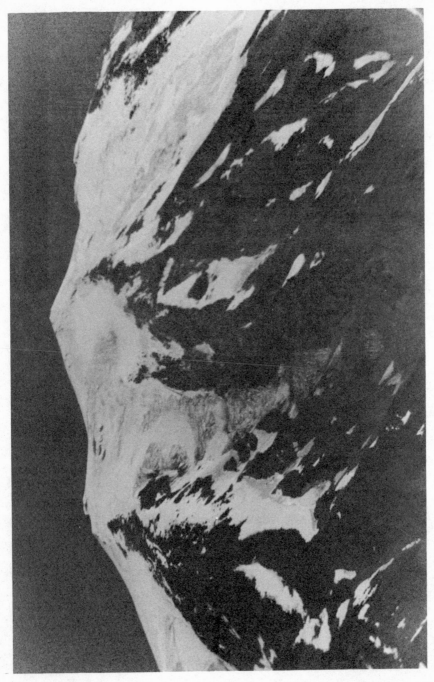

The summit of massive Mt. Ararat. (Photo by Ikenberry)

But the reader cannot help but be moved with sympathy as his heartbreaking tale is told.

Another Sighting

One of the many positive results of the investigation was the uncovering of another reported sighting. In his book, Smith recalls, "A report came last night from an elderly woman who declared that ten years ago some people went up on the top of Mt. Ararat and found the Ark there."[2]

A good summation of the expedition came from Edwin Greenwald, a member of the group and the Associated Press correspondent who had first announced Resit's discovery. His dejected feelings flowed through his typewriter in his release to the press, immediately after leaving the mountain.

September 28, 1949

The Ark of Noah, if it ever landed on Mount Ararat, is lost eternally to the ages. It will never be found.

Some of the Americans who have just completed a grueling search of the great Ararat chain still hope confidently that it will be uncovered some day.

But use of cold logic makes it certain that it will not. Either it rests forever beneath deep and perpetual ice and snow at the peak of the 17,000 ft. mountain, or else it has been destroyed and its fragments buried in this volcanic wilderness.

The four-man expedition, first formally organized searching party in Turkish record, explored every crevice and every clue. It scouted through the villages for 100 miles around, seeking anyone who might know anything.

Nothing, absolutely nothing, was uncovered.

In the mountains we climbed laboriously across dead volcanoes and burned-out stone. We scrambled over small plateaus lifeless and black with biting volcanic ash. In the villages, the old men and the young had heard the legend that a great boat once rested in the snow way up there.

But no one had ever seen it, and they knew of no one who had.

For all its futility, there was good in the results of the expedition's search. This was reflected in a statement to me by Necati Dolunay, 36-year-old departmental director of antiquities and museums for Turkey. He said:

"It has disproved the all-too-frequent claims that it is on a mountain plateau that reaches between small Ararat and big Ararat. Many persons, including Russians, have held to this contention. I do not believe that anyone, Russians or others, ever saw the Ark on the mountain."

Dr. Aaron J. Smith headed the expedition.

Dogubeyazit, a town near Mt. Ararat. Inhabited almost entirely by Kurds, it is the most frequent starting place for Ararat expeditions.

A pious, white-haired man whose 61 years kept him at base camps rather than going up Ararat, he still is not reconciled that the Ark is not there. He came with an abiding faith that it would be found; he left with an abiding faith that it will be found one day.

"We have made an attempt but failure of it does not imply the ultimate failure of the Ark's recovery," he said.

The mountain towers above the triangle where Turkey, Russia, and Iran come together. From the mountain we looked down on the three countries and a heavy detachment of police and gendarmes kept us under exceptionally heavy guard to prevent any incident. The Russian press already had complained that the expedition was a group of spies rather than searchers after the Ark.

But probably of greater concern to Turkish security forces was the possibility of the group clashing with smugglers and Kurdish bandits who slip into Turkey from Iran in the area under exploration. Lt. Halil Borck, 25-year-old commander of gendarme field forces, came along personally. His men carried machine guns and kept scouts far ahead.

An even better summation of the Smith expedition is recorded in the introduction of the book written upon his return. It graphically describes some of the situations that expedition leaders try to avoid but invariably must cope with.

I wish to register my protest here concerning some erroneous reports made by an unqualified, unscrupulous person concerning the expedition. A great work remains to be done. To telescope into twelve or fifteen days a work that ordinarily would consume from four to six weeks is unreasonable. That such a monumental project should be accomplished in so brief a time, is an insult to human intelligence.

The fact that we did not have sufficient time was merely one of the reasons why we did not undertake further explorations, there was a change in the weather for the worse also; however, the principal cause was rebellion on the part of some of the members of the expeditionary group against pooling their money to help finance Mr. Resit, who claimed to have seen the ark in the fall of '48, to have him come and point out to us the object of our quest. Another barrier was the fact that members of the expedition did not cooperate fully with me in the execution of the work. The insatiable craving on the part of some for publicity, when the matter of making releases to the press was the prerogative of the head of the expedition. Such contemptuous conduct future expeditions must guard against and render their repetition impossible. I wish to state, too, that I received by far superior treatment and consideration from the Turks than from members of my own group.[3]

[1] A. J. Smith, *The Reported Discovery of Noah's Ark* (Orlando: Christ for the World Publishers, 1949).
[2] A. J. Smith, *On the Mountains of Ararat in Quest for Noah's Ark* (Apollo, Pennsylvania: West, 1950), p. 121.
[3] Ibid., p. 7.

18

Fernand Navarra: 1952 to 1955

In 1937 I served in the French military forces in the Middle East. During my days off, I took long walks in the hills above Damascus, accompanied by an Armenian friend, Alim. One day, hiking farther than usual, we started climbing up Mount Hermon. About 1,300 feet from the top, Alim sank to his knees exhausted. I trudged on by myself until I reached the top, an altitude of over 9,000 feet. There I stayed for half an hour viewing the sea of haze and clouds stretching before me under the blue sky and a burning sun. On my way down, I rejoined my companion, and as we walked, he began to tell me his own life story.

"I was born in 1907 on the island in Lake Van," he said. "As a child, I lived there happy with my mother, father, and sister, until 1920. Then my parents moved to Damascus. Before I left Armenia, I went to visit my grandfather in the town of Bayazid, at the foot of Mount Ararat. The old man assured me that Noah's Ark was still on the mountain. 'When I was young.' he told me, 'I once tried to reach it. But I wasn't strong enough in the high altitude and had to give up. I never found it!' "

"I promised granddad that I would try, too," continued Alim. "But *you* are the one who should go, Navarra. Mountain climbing does not wear you out the way it does me. I am sure you would bring back a fragment of the Ark."[1]

Thus began a most interesting story. A story of dedication, of perseverance, sacrifice, failure, and finally success, followed inevitably by ridicule but eventual vindication. It is the story of Fernand Navarra and his discovery of hand-tooled timber on Mt. Ararat.

The initial information passed on to Navarra by his Armenian friend was never to leave his mind. For the next fifteen years he collected bits of data—reported sightings of others, ancient traditions and folklore from around the world—becoming more and more convinced that the relic had survived the thousands of years since its landing.

First Expedition

Not until 1952 did Navarra have his first chance to tackle the mountain. When he did, he and his four companions, de Riquier, Kirshner, Zubiri, and Vailland, met with the same obstacles that every Ararat expedition before or since that time has experienced. His efforts were ably summed up in a delightful book called *The Forbidden Mountain* in its English translation, necessary reading for all who are deeply interested.

Before fulfilling a promise made to the Turkish government to document the summit climb of a group of Turkish soldiers on movie film, Navarra and de Riquier returned to the town of Igdir on the northwest side of Mt. Ararat to make preparations for their search. Relaxing in a small cafe one evening, they were approached by an elderly man who had heard of their exploits and had sought them out, for he had some very important information to transmit. Navarra writes:

And we listened to him, our chins in our hands, our eyes turned toward the Holy Mountain. Thus, on August 11th, 1952, Akki Usta, the historian of Igdir, spoke to us:

"Young men of France, you have come to explore Noah's mountain, and you think to find the Ark there. Well, this is what I have to say to you:

"You know the legend, the beautiful legend of the vessel which God the Father brought to land on Ararat with its cargo of men and animals. And it was as a result of that loving kindness of God that the Earth was repeopled after the Flood had satisfied His wrath. While Noah, his family, and the animals were able to descend from Ararat and to go in the direction of Ahora and Erivan, the Ark stayed on the mountain. You know that.

"And now listen to what I am going to say. The Ark is still there! This I was told by the greybeards, and they were told it equally by those who were old during their youth. And all of us here believe it. All the people of Igdir, of Bayazid, of Erivan, to the last shepherd on the twin mountains, all believe it. And we shall hand on that belief to our children, with the bounden duty of passing it on to their descendants."

"What are your grounds for stating this with so much conviction?" we asked him.

"Are there not enough signs? Do you believe that the monasteries of Ahora, of Koran and of Etchmaidzin could have arisen if these historic facts were not true? . . . Know ye that to reach it (the Ark) one must be as pure as a new-born child. . . . "[2]

Navarra and de Riquier spent a few days alone on the ice cap exploring

Upper portion of Parrot glacier, site of Navarra's discovery in 1955. Crevasses denote ice movement.

likely hiding places for the Ark in the vicinity of the Ahora Gorge. After a confrontation with a family of surprised bears, the two men walked westward from the edge of the gorge.

Alone . . . on this immense sheet of ice which dazzled our eyes. The air was brilliantly clear. All around us was bare and forebidding. Our pursuit of a dream continued. . . . Below us an eagle wheeled in the sky. Borne on the wind, it let itself glide steadily in regular circles, imparting a silent rhythm to the solitude.

In front of us was always the deep transparent ice. A few more paces and suddenly, as if there were an eclipse of the sun, the ice became strangely dark. Yet the sun was still there and above us the eagle still circled. We were surrounded by whiteness, stretching into the distance, yet beneath our eyes was this astonishing patch of blackness within the ice, its outlines sharply defined.

Fascinated and intrigued, we began straightway to trace out its shape, mapping its limits foot by foot: two progressively incurving lines were revealed, which were clearly defined for a distance of three hundred cubits, before meeting in the heart of the glacier. The shape was unmistakably that of a ship's hull; on either side the edges of the patch curved like the gunwales of a great boat. As for the central part, it merged into a black mass, the details of which were not discernible.

Conviction burned in our eyes: no more than a few yards of ice separated us from the extraordinary discovery which the world no longer believed possible. We had just found the Ark![3]

No documentation or further exploration of their find was possible without the proper equipment, and the two men descended the mountain. Recognizing that their find was not provable, they did not disclose any of their ideas for some time.

Second Expedition

In planning a follow-up expedition for the summer of 1953, de Riquier released to the press the following information on March 29, 1953:

Just before I left the region, I talked with a venerable Turk who swore to me that in youth he heard a party of hunters report that they had come across timbers of a ship in a small valley near the pinnacle of one of the peaks in the Ararat group. I hope that we will be able to find that valley.

Navarra did return alone to Mt. Ararat in 1953, but unusual weather conditions and a severe case of "mountain sickness" prohibited him from reaching the spot.

Third Expedition

The summer of 1955 finally yielded positive results. For Navarra, many years of investigation culminated when his icy fingers gripped a hand-hewn beam far beneath the ice cap. Accompanied only by his eleven-year-old son, Raphael, Navarra explored this time without the official sanction of the government. Returning with a section of wood, he was very fortunate to escape arrest and confiscation of his artifact. Again we will allow Navarra to tell his own story.

By three in the afternoon we had reached the everlasting snowfields 13,750 feet high.

Climbing up a moraine which hung a hundred yards above our camping site, I saw, on my left, a sea of clouds. Eventually, it dissolved, revealing a mass of ice, the one I had discovered in 1952. The landscape had changed, for at least one third of the ice had thawed. But this was the spot.

When the mist disappeared, I recognized a wide basin on the other side of the icy mass. In this crater, the glacier's branch ended. The branch, frequently called a stagnant glacier, had receded at least one hundred yards, barely flowing into the area where the remains of the Ark rested. The valley bottom was still covered with mist, and I could not distinguish a thing.

The stagnant icy mass was caught between two steep rock walls three or four hundred yards high. Opposite, the glacier's branch formed a smooth wall of ice fifty yards high. Between the branch and the mountain of ice was a funneled hollow covered with mist. Since the glacier had receded, there could be a lake there, where the wood from the Ark would be out of the ice.

The mountain of ice which from the top of the moraine had not seemed so formidable, now loomed sixty yards above us. Though imposing, it was dangerously fragile with its crevasses and ice-bridges.

The other side ended in a sheer wall, and we could not see what lay at its foot. If I walked too close to the edge, I feared the ice would break under my feet. How could we have a look into this hollow without falling into it?

Raphael found the solution. "Take good hold of me with the rope. I'll get close to the edge and try to see what's at the bottom."

I hesitated a moment, then agreed. I braced myself carefully and propped my back against the rock. He leaned over.

"A little bit more," he called. "More,—a bit more—."

I played out a bit more rope.

"There, I can see now. Yes, the boat is there, papa. I can see it distinctly."

Once on the edge of the crevasse, I lowered the equipment on a rope. Then I secured the ladder and climbed down myself, assuring Raphael I would not be long.

Attacking the ice shell with my pickaxe, I could feel something hard. When I had dug a hole one and one half feet square by eight inches deep, I broke through a vaulted ceiling, and cleared off as much icy dust as possible.

There, immersed in water, I saw a black piece of wood!

My throat felt tight. I felt like crying and kneeling there to thank God. After the cruelest disappointment, the greatest joy! I checked my tears of happiness to shout to Raphael, "I've found wood!"

"Hurry up and come back—I'm cold," he answered.

I tried to pull out the whole beam, but couldn't. It must have been very long, and perhaps still attached to other parts of the ship's framework. I could only cut along the grain until I split off a piece about five feet long. Obviously, it had been hand-hewn. The wood, once out of the water, proved surprisingly heavy. Its density was remarkable after its long stay in the water, and the fibers had not distended as much as one might expect.

It was 7:00 A.M., July 6, 1955.[4]

Needless to say reports of this find have been heralded around the

Fernand Navarra holding hand-tooled lumber found at the 14,000–foot elevation on Mt. Ararat.

world. Although Navarra himself has never claimed a discovery of the superstructure of the Ark, many thousands of people with only a superficial knowledge of the discovery contend that the Ark has indeed been found and do not understand why the search continues.

Navarra's Wood

The wood has not been universally accepted as a piece of the Ark. Almost as many opinions of its age and origin exist as there are people who have expressed an opinion. Navarra makes a good observation in his book. "What else could it be?" he asks. "In all likelihood, these are the remains of the flat hull of the Biblical vessel intact through the years, protected by nature itself."[5]

The wood has been studied, tested, and dated by many laboratories around the world. Some of the results have been confusing, others have been contradictory. About all that can be said with any degree of certainty is that the wood is probably from some kind of large white oak tree, is of considerable age, has been hand-tooled, and is partially fossilized (not petrified).

The ages of samples of the wood returned by several experts reveal only the unreliability of the dating methods. The best possible clue to the age of the wood is found in its degree of lignitization (a step in the fossilization process). Its high percentage of lignite suggests a rather old age. But the rate of this process is subject to change. The fact that Navarra found his specimen submerged in ice water and damp soil relegates any estimate of age to the realm of speculation.

The Carbon-14 method of dating age has likewise been applied to the wood, and again the range of values given far exceeds a proper percentage of error. Most researchers today recognize the serious limitations of the C-14 method and never claim that the C-14 apparent age equals the true age of the specimen. In fact, the theory has drawn so much criticism in the last five years that few archaeologists accept its results, and never accept the C-14 age when it contradicts historical dates.

It is not our purpose here to discuss the C-14 dating method. Many books and papers have appeared recently covering the subject in depth. However, to list a few of the inherent problems in dating Navarra's wood might be in order.

1. The wood was handled by many people for several years before testing. All samples should be gathered under sterile conditions.

2. The wood was subjected, before its discovery, to water action, and the possibility of either leaching out or adding to parent element or daughter product exists.

3. Since C-14 atoms are formed by the bombardment of Nitrogen atoms by cosmic radiation from outer space, the fact that it was found at a high elevation where the concentration of such rays is higher than at sea level presents serious problems.

4. Cosmic radiations can vary widely, due to many factors, such as magnitude of the earth's magnetic field (which is known to be deteriorating rapidly); amount of water vapor in the atmosphere (consider the pre-Flood water canopy in the upper atmosphere); solar and stellar activity; volcanic or even industrial addition of carbon dioxide into the air; electrical activity; and many others. All factors are subject to change and give indications of different conditions in the past.

The C-14 method, with its precise measurements and short half-life appeals to the professional researcher in theory, but its results are no longer taken seriously by objective scientists. The other radioactive dating methods used to date inorganic materials and even the earth are all under close scrutiny; all are based on several unlikely and unprovable assumptions. For more detailed discussions, the interested reader is referred to books such as *The Genesis Flood*[6] by Whitcomb and Morris, *A Critique of Radioactive Dating Methods*[7] by Slusher, and *Prehistory and Earth Models*[8] by Cook.

The Jury Is Still Out

But there are other reasons to withhold final judgment on the wood, for there are certain discrepancies in Navarra's account which cast grave shadows over its authenticity. In all of his published writings, Navarra has displayed a disturbing tendency to describe his location at any time in such vague and even contradictory terms that even Ararat veterans cannot pinpoint and trace his steps. This overt trait is so obvious that it must have been intended. It seems as though Navarra has tried to cover his tracks, and he has a perfect right to do so, to insure the uniqueness of his find. His siting of a dark spot in the ice in 1952 seemed to be above the Ahora Gorge, and a picture in his book indicates the same thing. In 1953 and 1955 his claim seems to center around the Parrot glacier above Lake Kop, but even that is unclear. Several years later he pointed to a place near the lower end of the ice cap near the gorge as the place of discovery, but in 1968 and 1969, while serving as a guide for SEARCH Foundation, he showed them on different instances three separate locations. Maps that he has provided for other expeditions have not fit the landscape.

In Navarra's defense, it must be said that the mountain continually changes its appearance, and directions are easily confused or lost. But certain landmarks such as the Ahora Gorge can hardly be misinterpreted.

J. A. de Riquier, Navarra's friend and climbing partner in 1952, has accused Navarra of attempting to purchase a piece of timber from a very ancient structure in a nearby city in 1952, intimating that the wood was not found on Ararat at all. This accusation either resulted from or caused a serious and deep-seated rift between Navarra and de Riquier which still exists.

In 1969, SEARCH, Inc., again discovered wood on Ararat under the guiding hand of Navarra. But once again cries of fraud went up from the expedition's team members, which will be discussed later.

A very serious accusation, if it can be believed (and there is much room for doubt), comes from Navarra's climbing partner in 1952, Turkish Lt. Sahap Atalay. Navarra does not mention climbing with Atalay in 1955, but the following quote from Atalay, which reached the press shortly after the 1969 expedition, indicates that he did.

We climbed to the top with Navarra who offered me the job of his guide, but he decided to return just when we started our search. On our way back, he said, "Sahap, we have found Noah's Ark!" I was taken aback. In fact, I found out later that Navarra had given his son a piece of wood and had taken pictures and movies of him. With these photographs and films, the crafty Frenchman announced to the whole world that he had found Noah's Ark and sold these pictures to a lot of magazines for thousands of dollars, but also sold three million copies of his book dealing with the subject and made his fortune.[9]

It must be emphasized that some of the details of this quote are inaccurate, casting a shadow over the rest of it. The opinion of the authors is that the Navarra wood in neither case was planted, as has been suggested. Navarra may even be correct when he claims great amounts of wood are still buried far beneath the surface of the ice. Only further research will tell.

However, enough evidence has been presented which shows rather conclusively that Navarra did not find the Ark as described by so many witnesses. He may indeed have found wood from the Ark that has broken off and been separated from the rest by the movement of the glacier. But somewhere on that vast mountain, the superstructure of the Ark remains, substantially intact, patiently waiting for the impatient explorers to stumble across it.

[1] Fernand Navarra, *Noah's Ark: I Touched It* (Plainfield: Logos, 1974), pp. xiii, xiv.

[2] Fernand Navarra, *The Forbidden Mountain,* trans. Michael Legat (London: MacDonald, 1956), p. 130.

[3] Ibid., pp. 165, 166.

[4] Navarra, *Noah's Ark,* pp. 51-63.

[5] Ibid., p. x.

[6] John C. Whitcomb and Henry M. Morris, *The Genesis Flood* (Philadelphia: Presbyterian and Reformed Publishing Co., 1961).

[7] Harold S. Slusher, *A Critique of Radiometric Dating* (San Diego: Institute for Creation Research, 1973).

[8] Melvin A. Cook, *Prehistory and Earth Models* (London: Max Parishan & Co., Ltd., 1966).

[9] *Gunaydin* (Istanbul), October 1969.

19

George Greene: 1953

In 1953, Navarra climbed to within a few hundred feet of the dark shadow under the ice that he and de Riquier had spotted the year before. Unfortunately, a severe case of altitude sickness attacked him, driving him from the mountain's slopes. But another explorer visited Mt. Ararat that summer, also searching for something valuable, and discovered to his astonishment that Mt. Ararat had been used as a landing place by a huge vessel.

Navarra centered his brief attention to the area above Lake Kop. Unfortunately he did not explore greater portions of the upper elevations of the mountain as he had the year before, because he was thoroughly prepared to document the accidental discovery of George Greene.

Greene was prepared for documentation also, but he did not have the ear of the world press as did the wealthy French industrialist Navarra. Greene, an oil and pipeline engineer and mining geologist working in eastern Turkey as a representative of an oil company, had a helicopter at his disposal to use as he searched for mineral and oil deposits.

Perhaps aware that Smith and others had revealed their interest in Mt. Ararat as the possible site of the remains of Noah's Ark, he detoured from his major area of interest on the northern flank of the mountain to the high elevations above the Ahora Gorge.

The family and friends of the late geologist report that in the latter part of the summer of 1953 Greene did indeed spot the Ark in an almost inaccessible region at the 13,000- to 14,000-foot level on Mt. Ararat. While his pilot hovered as close as possible, Greene captured the vessel on film and located it on his geologic maps.

According to these reports, Greene described the Ark as lying generally in a north-south direction, situated seemingly on a large rock bench or shelf on the side of a vertical rock cliff. Protruding from the end of a melting snow field or glacier, only about one-third was visible. The rest was covered not only by snow, but by rock debris and mud. The bottom,

The upper portions of the Ahora Gorge. Greene claims that he saw the Ark in this general area from a helicopter in 1953.

submerged in ice and mud, was not visible. Distinct planking appeared on the side of the craft, running parallel to its roof.

Recognizing the overwhelming nature of his discovery, Greene enlarged the photographs, and once he returned to America presented the material to his business associates. Over and over again he approached individuals and groups of businessmen with his claims, trying to drum up interest in the project and raise money to form an expedition to return to Mt. Ararat and study the craft completely from the ground. Even though the photographs never failed to impress those who saw them, no one was inclined to support a ground search.

Greene's mining interests kept him on the road. In 1954, he was in Utah; in 1955, Nova Scotia. More often he was in the southern states, and frequently home in Texas. During this time, he showed the pictures to dozens, maybe hundreds of people, but each time he was disappointed. No one seemed to realize the importance of the discovery as he did.

Weary of the continued heartbreak the pictures caused him, Greene finally left them with his good friend Frank Neff in Texas. Neff had often seen and admired the pictures and agreed to keep them until they were needed, which he did for several years until 1961, when Greene came for them.

Greene's mining and prospecting spirit again gripped him. After he had stored most of his belongings in storehouses and garages in several cities, he traveled to British Guiana to assist in gold mining operations. Whether he took the photos with him or packed them with the rest of his belongings is not known, for they have not been seen since.

What is known is that on December 27, 1962, George Jefferson Greene was found face down in the swimming pool at his hotel in Georgetown, apparently having been hurled from his room several floors up.

The police investigations of the tragedy turned up no clues that would solve the mystery. Rumor had it that Greene was murdered for his gold, but the fact is that Greene's room had not been ransacked as would be expected. The only item disturbed was his briefcase—his empty briefcase. The contents were missing. Were the precious photos, so important to Greene, in that briefcase? Or, are they still filed in a storeroom in Texas?

A systematic search of the files was undertaken by researchers, assisted by the family of the late George Greene and by his friend, Frank Neff. Mountains of material on Greene's work had been left behind and much of it had been destroyed by vandals. The search has never been completed even though many hours were spent pouring over the long inactive files.

Much time and energy have also been spent in an attempt to identify and locate the helicopter pilot who was with Greene in 1953. The records show only that the U.S. government issued a passport to Greene in 1952 with a Turkish visa, and that Turkish government had issued a helicopter permit to Greene for the Ararat region in 1953 and 1954. But nothing about the pilot can be found, although that search continues.

In the process of trying to locate Greene and his evidence, Ark researchers have located and interviewed at least thirty people alive today who remember seeing those amazing photos. With so many witnesses, the fact that the pictures existed cannot be questioned. The question of their subject does remain, but each of the witnesses testify that George Jefferson Greene, an honest and intelligent man, thoroughly believed the picures to be of Noah's Ark on Mt. Ararat in eastern Turkey.

20

John Libi:
1954 to 1969

People always want to know why the Ark is so hard to find. Why can't an expedition simply climb the mountain, search the areas under investigation, and find out if it is there or not? Why have hundreds of men, traipsing all over the mountain for twenty-five years, not been able to find it? There are many possible answers to these questions.

Consider the size alone of Mt. Ararat. Its base covers approximately 5,000 square miles. The ice cap covers nearly twenty square miles, varying from season to season. Its peak of 17,000 feet certainly does not rank among the world's highest, but the overall dimensions measured from bottom to top (12,000 feet on the south side and 14,000 feet on the north) make Mt. Ararat just about the largest mountain in the world. In terms of volume and surface area, Mt. Ararat may even be the largest mountain in the world.

The previous discussions of the earthquake tendencies of the area, as well as the volcanic nature of the mountain, bear out another difficulty. Add to that the fact that the shifting, flowing glaciers constantly erode the weak lava intermingled with sediments and weathered rock, and deposit loose boulders in moraines and on severe slopes, and you soon appreciate that climbing is understandably extremely hazardous and difficult. Avalanches, both rock and snow, are frequent occurrences, as are ice falls. The ice cap, riddled with hidden crevices and sub-surface lakes, has claimed many lives.

The evaporation from the semiarid flatlands around the base of Ararat condenses daily on the summit, due to the vast temperature differential between the ice cap and the lower elevations. Even when good weather prevails and Mt. Ararat is crystal clear in the morning hours, haze, followed by clouds, appears in the early afternoon. The wind picks up and mounts steadily as the temperature drops until its fury is released in a storm, sometimes a violent one. In the summer these storms come and go, lasting literally any length of time from minutes to hours, and may move from one area to another. Generally they are accompanied by rain, sleet, snow, or hail (sometimes as large as baseballs). It has been known to snow ten feet within a few hours in August.

These storms are more often than not thunderstorms, complete with thunder and lightning. Ararat explorers are well aware that living at high elevations exposed to these elements is not conducive to long life, but realize that the exploring must be done. One has not truly lived until he has been in a thunder head, (not in a thunderstorm, but in the clouds), with lightning flashing and striking close by and with explosions of thunder on all sides.

In addition to the general suspicion and opposition of the lawless Kurds living on the mountain, other inhabitants can cause problems. Grizzly bears live in rock fissures and caves up to the ice line, as do mountain lions and wolves. Snakes infest the lower regions.

All of these discouraging factors must be confronted by even those who attempt the summit only or climb for purely personal or aesthetic reasons. But when a team of Christians, desiring to see the vindication of God's Word, disprove the godless theories of atheism and evolution, and call people back to a personal relationship with the true God and His Son Jesus Christ, sets foot on that ancient mountain, they can expect additional trouble from principalities and powers, rulers of the darkness of the world, spiritual wickedness in high places (Eph. 6:12).

Satan obviously knows what would be the effect of finding the Ark. He knows that the entire world would be confronted with overwhelming evidence that the Bible is true and that such evidence could not be overlooked; everyone would have to deal with it. He knows that many would not choose to reject it.

Therefore, he must try to stop the find. Each and every expedition member has felt the presence of supernatural forces on Mt. Ararat. Whether the opposition takes the form of unnatural or natural forces, coincidental events, or personality disagreements does not matter. The forces of evil are very evident on Mt. Ararat, and without God's supernatural care the loss of life would be staggering.

Consider the case of John Libi from San Francisco. Extremely capable and experienced mountain climber, fluent in Turkish and several other languages, knowledgeable leader and dedicated adventurer, Libi tried eight times in fifteen years to find the Ark. Although he nearly lost his life several times on the mountain and faced countless other dangers, he combed the mountain more thoroughly than many succeeding groups but never achieved his objective.

John Libi, who led numerous expeditions to Mt. Ararat to search for the remains of Noah's Ark.

1954—Thinking that the Ark was near the summit of the mountain, Libi engineered two ascents. On one of the ascents, Libi was attacked and chased by two huge bears up near the ice cap. The additional exertion required to outrun them, coupled with rarefied air and the cold, caused Libi to develop a serious illness and fever, from which it took a month to recuperate.

On the second climb, late in the summer, the weather turned bad even though it had been quite favorable, and further explorations were impractical.

The summer of 1954 was an extremely hot and dry one as members of the U.S. Air Force later testified. They had been photographing and mapping Mt. Ararat from high elevations in a joint security project for the Turkish and U.S. governments. But the Ark was not exposed that summer as it had been the previous one when George Greene photographed it, for members of the mapping team were aware of the search for the Ark and looked for it at some length, but did not see it either in person or on the photographs.

1955—Libi returned with his team of explorers, but due to unexpected political turmoil, permission to climb the mountain was rescinded. This was the same year that Navarra climbed without permission and claimed the discovery.

Storms can appear suddenly on the 17½ square mile ice cap of Mt. Ararat.

1958—This time leading a group of forty men, Libi, sixty-two years old, fell thirty feet to a rock ledge, and had to be carried off the mountain and hospitalized in a nearby town.

1960—The weather on Ararat won another battle, for again Libi required hospitalization, this time in Ankara, the capital of Turkey, for pneumonia.

1962—On May 9, while boarding a train in Italy en route to Ararat, Libi was robbed of all the expedition's finances.

1965—A horrible July thunderstorm and blizzard separated the team of ten into three groups. One group finally returned to camp suffering from advanced stages of fatigue and exposure after wandering on the mountain slopes in search of safety for three days. The storm washed away the entire food supply, and the dejected group returned to the states.

1967—In Libi's estimation, the worst weather he had ever seen on Mt. Ararat virtually attacked them. Great quantities of snow and extreme cold forced them off the mountain. The weather did claim the life of a Belgian climber who had joined Libi's party on the mountain. The freshly fallen snow and a recent earthquake had loosened the footing, and the youth slipped over the edge of a huge cliff to his death.

1969—Libi, defying his seventy-three years, and in spite of the fact that in 1967 he swore that he would not return, reached the summit and the spot where he believed the Ark to be. There he found a layer of water-borne fossils, but no Ark. His climbing companions were two Ararat veterans, Colonel Sahap Atalay and reporter Yucel Donmez. In a feature article shortly after the expedition, Donmez wrote:

At 1:00 P.M., we reached the peak. From the top we walked to the place where Noah's Ark rested according to John Libi's idea. Here there was a terrible crevasse, 30 meters deep. The Colonel and I descended into it. At the bottom we tore off three pieces which were stuck to the ice.[1]

These pieces turned out to be pieces of fragmentized lava which looked surprisingly like charcoal. Libi, who considered Navarra's claim to be fabricated, suspected that he might have found similar pieces.

Ever since his first expedition in 1954, Libi had been convinced that the Ark, locked in place by rock formations, was to be found about 500 feet below the summit, and he concentrated his efforts there. When little snow was present on the summit, he discovered three huge stone "corrals" there, high walls that appeared to him to have been used to house animals. Nothing in the past century has been built there and previous to that the inhabitants believed the summit to be impossible to reach. This find demands more investigation.

[1]*Gunaydin* (Istanbul), October 1969.

21

Life Photos:
1959 to 1960

Dynamite! What on earth could prompt archaeologists and researchers to use dynamite to search for an artifact? Better yet, what under the earth could prompt such action?

Even though the thought of such methods causes chills and shudders on the back of professional archaeologists, in this case the dynamite solved the problem confronting the determined men of the Archaeological Research Foundation in August of 1960.

The event is well known to all who have followed the search for Noah's Ark for the past few decades. Except for the widely circulated and fraudulent Roskovitsky account, no piece of information on the subject has reached so many millions of people.

Near the end of 1959, the story hit the papers. The Ark had been found! Not by explorers, not by elusive airmen, nor by local pilgrims or farmers. It had been found on stereo photographs by a mapping cartographer. The stereophotos had been taken on a routine survey on behalf of the Geodetic Institute of Turkey several months before.

The working press seized this exciting story and ran with it. Between the first release in October 1959 and the time an expedition actually investigated the site, many newspapers and magazines carried feature articles on it. Most of them were reprints in some form or another of the article which appeared first in the Turkish magazine *Hayat* on October 23 and was expanded in the following Associated Press release from Columbus, Ohio, on November 14.

If Noah's Ark is really at Mount Ararat in Turkey, then there is a discovery from a young Turk who is living in Columbus, Ohio. Sevket Kurtis has filtered stereographic airphotos in Turkey, from which maps can be produced, and he has made a curious discovery.

Even if it is not Noah's Ark, discovery will be something quite extraordinary.

The "discovery" has not yet been verified. However, Kurtis assumes that the curious form of the discovered object could be the Ark of Noah, which is described in the Bible and the Koran.

Discovered with stereoplanograph

The airphotos were taken a year ago on behalf of the Geodetic Institute of Turkey. But the curious object was just recently discovered in one of the photos. The "Ark" was not recognizable with the unaided eye. It was discovered when, in Ankara, Captain Ilhan Durupinar used a stereoplanograph in order to prepare maps. With this instrument this object was discovered, which could not have been created by nature itself but by human hands. Kurtis reports that Captain Durupinar has worked on thousands of square miles in this method for the preparation of maps, but has never seen a similar object in stereographic airphotos. Captain Durupinar is convinced, because of his topographic experience, that this discovery must be an object created by human hands. The size corresponds with the description of the Ark in the Bible and in the Koran. The object has the form of a boat, is 450 feet long, and 160 feet wide.

Expedition next spring

Kurtis said that at this time of year it is not possible to send out an expedition for the verification of the discovery, because the whole area around Mount Ararat is covered by snow. So one must wait until spring comes and the snow is melted.

The place on which, according to the airphoto, the discovery was made is about fifty miles south of Mount Ararat, close to the Russian border. This area is volcanic, mountainous, and uninhabited. It was never before topographically registered.

Kurtis said that the object, which could be the Ark, is sunk in a field of lava. Through heat the Ark might be preserved like Herculaneum and Pompeii. If it is really Noah's Ark, then it must be 7000 years old.

Dr. Arthur Brandenberger of the Geodetic Institute of Ohio State University said after he had seen the stereophotos he also is convinced that this discovery cannot be a "product of nature," but possibly a "petrified boat." He added that if it were really Noah's Ark it would be a sensational discovery.

In the last years several expeditions searched in vain for Noah's Ark near Mount Ararat. However, every time the mountain peak was scoured but not the fields of lava fifty miles south of the mountain. Nobody thought to search from the air.

Hurriedly, an organization was formed to investigate the artifact. Headed up by George Vandeman, well-known Adventist television preacher, and incorporated under the name Archaeological Research Foundation (ARF), this organization contacted both Sevket Kurtis and Captain Durupinar and incorporated them into their plans.

The Archaeological Research Foundation

The newly formed ARF's expectations soared when they found the

Turkish government more than willing to cooperate in an effort to determine exactly what this unusual artifact might be. There were, of course, a few problems to be overcome, but these involved only minor delays.

Soon the promise of permits was in the hands of the ARF. When the advance team entered the Turkish capital Ankara, they began to acquire the permits one after the other from each ministry involved, until only one signature was lacking.

But suddenly the cooperation of the governmental officials disappeared. Appointments were broken. Conferences were canceled. No one was available. Unable to understand the seeming reversal, the men of the ARF returned to their hotel. George Vandeman tells the story.

And then it happened. At three o'clock Friday morning the city shook with the tanks and gunfire of a revolting army. We looked out to see the hotel surrounded by artillery, the doors guarded by bayonets. The radio blared out messages that I could not understand.

This was the real thing. In three hours nearly all the ministers were arrested and the Menderes strong-arm regime was overthrown. By six o'clock the people were shouting their approval.[1]

The pre-revolution expedition permits were, of course, nullified. And all of the friendships and contacts cultivated were no longer of any use.

But, luckily, the new government appointed as foreign minister a diplomat who had already been a great deal of help to the ARF. Even though the new official had many more pressing matters to attend to, he was able to secure permission once again for the exploration of the mysterious shiplike formation. And finally, after seemingly insurmountable odds had been overcome, they were on their way.

Receiving full cooperation from the Jandarma officials in the city of Dougubeyazit at the base of the mountain, the expedition team proceeded with a minimum of difficulty to the lava flow southwest of Mt. Ararat, at about 7,000 feet. They were accompanied by a group of Turkish cavalrymen and foot soldiers.

From close range the formation looked more than ever like the outlines of a ship. The teardrop-shaped pattern seemed much too symmetrical to be merely carved by nature. It must have been caused by a shiplike structure far under the surface, buried by the accumulation of thousands of years of mud and silt.

So they began to dig. Directed by their archaeologists, they dug one hole after another in the most promising spots. Nothing of archaeological significance was found. Finally, the Turkish soldiers, who were doing all the digging, wearied of such a cumbersome method and raced off to get the dynamite. By this time the ARF men were so disillusioned they made no effort to stop them.

Soon the deepest shaft was extended by the blast. Several shafts received the same treatment. Nothing was found, nothing but soil, clay, and lava. Their bitter disappointment showed only in the silence as they packed their gear and left the area, never to return.

Life Magazine

The results of the expedition were also published far and wide, and probably read by more people than any other bit of Ark news. The most widely read, remembered, and saved article appeared in the September 5, 1960, issue of *Life* magazine. Portions of the short account are reproduced below.

From the air the ship-shaped outline lies in the center of a landslide on the slope of a mountain that is only 25 miles from the Russian border. The landslides are of recent origin and may have packed mud and stones around the strange form. The photo was shot by a Turkish aerial survey plane from 10,000 feet.

At 7,000 feet, in the midst of crevasses and landslide debris, the explorers found a clear, grassy area shaped like a ship and rimmed with steep, packed-earth sides. Its dimensions are close to those given in Genesis. A quick two-day survey revealed no sign that the object was man-made. Yet a scientist in the group says nothing in nature could create such a symmetrical shape. A thorough excavation may be made another year to solve the mystery.

Even though the results of their efforts were negative, the 1960 Archaeological Research Foundation expedition could claim one of the very few successes ever in the search for the Ark. Most other expeditions have not had such good fortune, for they have tackled the massive Ararat itself, not confining their investigations to the nearby foothills. The 1960 expedition had, by contrast, accomplished their objectives. They had come to study the strange formation in the Tenderick mountain range. After locating it in a very remote area, they determined that it was simply a "freak of nature," a "clay up-push in a lava flow" and not the anticipated remains of the Ark of Noah.

---

[1]George E. Vandeman, "The Riddle of Ararat" (unpublished manuscript), pp. 64-65. Used by permission.

22

Frustrating
Sixties

The keen disappointment of the 1960 trip soon wore off. The men of the Archaeological Research Foundation, with their appetites whetted, took a little better look at the vast amount of data compiled by Eryl Cummings and others. This data indicated, of course, that the Ark was trapped in the glacier high atop Mt. Ararat itself, not on a nearby mountain range.

And so, expeditionary plans were drawn up. Not much was known at that time of the upper reaches of the mountain, and, rather than launch a full-scale search of the mountain, the ARF decided first to complete an aerial reconnaissance of the area.

Photography: 1961

Dr. Lawrence Hewitt and Wilbur Bishop, in the summer of 1961, set out to study the glacial activity from the air, to observe melting patterns, and, hopefully, actually make the momentous discovery. First, they flew over and around Ararat in a plane provided by the Turkish Air Force and flown by a Turkish pilot. Later they were allowed to search from a private plane. Keeping their cameras busy, they obtained excellent movies of the ice cap as well as numerous color slides.

However, it seems that much of the information provided by the years of research had not sunk in. For, as had Smith, Libi, and others before them, the ARF simply assumed that the remains of the Ark would be found near the very summit of the 17,000 foot mountain. The full significance of the reported sightings had not been realized. If it had, the men would have concentrated their efforts on the northwest quadrant from the 13,000-foot to the 15,000-foot level, at the edge of the ice cap on one of the glacial fingers. In fact, it was not until 1966 that attention was focused in the more promising area.

But Bishop and Hewitt, photographing the summit from the air, happened to swoop down the northern face over the Ahora Gorge area.

Engraving of Mt. Ararat from *Letters from the Caucasus and Georgia*, by Freygang.

Out of range of the area that they were interested in, they temporarily rested their cameras while the pilot turned the plane around and regained altitude. Both of the men commented on a strange shiplike object protruding from a glacial finger, high in a crag, in the upper reaches of the Cehennem Dere Circ on the western face of the Ahora Gorge. They were only a few hundred feet away and noticed the appearance of ribs. But neither of them believed that this was where the Ark might be, and so, even though they thought it odd, no particular significance was attached to it, and no pictures were taken.

Several years later, when informed that the research indicated that the Cehennem Dere was the most likely area, both men sheepishly recalled the incident but unfortunately could not recall the exact location of the huge canyon. A frantic restudy of all of their photographs revealed no clue.

Navarra's Maps 1962

Early in 1962, the ARF members met in New York to discuss plans for another expedition. At their invitation, Fernand Navarra, who had found wood on Ararat in 1955 and had since written two books on the subject, was in attendance. He had flown from France to share his information and offer suggestions for further work.

Although he hoped to accompany the ARF group that summer, Navarra was afraid that his demolition business, which was undergoing serious financial strain, would not permit it. Instead, he drew several detailed maps which he claimed would lead them right to the spot of his discovery.

Armed with these hand-sketched maps, Navarra's written accounts in his books, and the photographs taken the year before, a team of nine men ventured to the area above Lake Kop on the northwestern slope. Led by three experienced climbers, Gordon Mansell, a Briton who had conquered Everest, Bill Dougal, and Bud Crawford, they felt that nothing could go wrong.

Once again, however, the tendency of Navarra to be rather vague about his directions surfaced. Day after day, the men sat around reading his book and studying the maps. Nothing seemed to fit. To make matters worse, a small Turkish plane flew overhead each day, and the pilot would lean out and make strange gestures at them.

Finally, after about two weeks of exasperation, they descended the mountain for rest and recuperation. Imagine their surprise when they chanced to meet the Turkish officer who, as it turned out, had accompanied Navarra to the summit in 1953 and had also accompanied John Libi on most of his expeditions. The officer, Sahap Atalay, revealed that he was the one who had been signaling them each day from his plane, hoping to divert them to the area where wood had been found.

Atalay was willing to point the area out to them if he could obtain permission from his superiors, but, before details could be worked out, the winter snows set in and all work had to be canceled.[1]

Frustrated in 1964

Spurred on by a growing case of "Ark fever," the ARF laid elaborate plans for an expedition in 1964. All in all, a total of twenty men participated in the effort. And effort is the right word, for very little was accomplished—but not for the lack of trying. Such a large group with planes, sensitive sonar gear, powerful photographic accessories, and mountains of mountain equipment invoked a great deal of mistrust among Turkish officials. To make matters worse, many of the scientists and photographers on the team were U.S. government officials and employees, and much of the equipment was furnished by the U.S. military.

Small wonder that permission to enter a sensitive military zone such as Mt. Ararat was hard to obtain. But eventually the problems were overcome, only to be followed by transportation and logistic problems. And after all that, once on Mt. Ararat the team had to abort the entire expedition due to a lack of cold weather survival gear.

Very little was accomplished, but a great deal was learned in 1964.

A Good Year—1966

Once again, the ARF backed off and took another run at the mountain. This time, in 1966, the expedition was less than half the size of the 1964 attempt. It was also better prepared for both searching and researching, for it included Dr. Clifford Burdick, one of the outstanding field geologists of our day, and Eryl Cummings, whose knowledge of the mountain from decades of stateside research was finally heeded and put into play on the mountain.

It was a very good year to search. The snow had melted back a great deal; in fact the summer was billed as the warmest in fifty years. And search they did. More was accomplished in a single year than in any

Mausoleum of Ataturk in Ankara, Turkey. A fitting tribute to the "Father of Turkey."

previous attempt. To begin with, Dr. Hewitt, a medical doctor whose hobby is botany, carried out a botanical study on the mountain. Dr. Burdick studied the geology of the area. Some of his conclusions were detailed in chapters 2 and 4 of this book. Nicholas Van Arkle of Holland received his doctorate by studying and recording the glaciation of the mountain.

Unfortunately, there was very little time left for looking for the Ark, although each team member kept his eyes peeled for any discovery.

One very positive piece of data was uncovered by Dr. Hewitt. He interviewed at great length an aged Kurd who claimed to have seen the Ark in his younger days. He offered to guide the men to the vessel, but his health simply would not permit it.

Since the entire mountain was scoured at least superficially by the various explorers, the Ark must not have been readily visible. The obvious conclusion must be made then that even the "hottest summer in fifty years" was not sufficient to expose the Ark. It is the opinion of the authors that several consecutive years of mild winters and hot, dry summers are required if the Ark is to be found protruding from the ice, as has been the case when sightings have been reported.

A much smaller group in 1967 found Mt. Ararat under a thick blanket of snow. A new member of the group was the New Zealand archaeologist Hardwicke Knight. Because of the unusual snow cover, Knight was unable to relocate the field of timbers he had stumbled across in 1936, as detailed in chapter 13.

By this time, the Archaeological Research Foundation was beginning to break up, crumbling due to internal disagreements and conflicts. The strong leadership that it had enjoyed since its inception had withdrawn, and the group split into two factions, divided mainly on the issues of the possible location of the Ark and the type of organizational effort it would take to find it. The rivalry between these bands became insurmountable in 1967.

One group consisted mainly of three men, Eryl Cummings, Dr. Burdick, and Dr. Hewitt. These dedicated Christian men all felt a need to operate within a framework of personal Christianity and felt that the remains of the Ark would most likely be found in the Ahora Gorge area.

The other group soon reincorporated under the name Scientific Exploration and Archaeological Research or SEARCH Foundation, Incorporated, and was under the leadership of Ralph Crawford, father of Bud Crawford, experienced Ararat climber. This group preferred to launch their probes from a completely secular and more technical stance.

They felt quite sure that the Ark had been found in 1955 by Navarra and only needed to be excavated and removed from the ice.

ARF Report

But the Archaeological Research Foundation had served its purpose. It had taken a very random situation and replaced it with order. By the end of 1967 the mountain was well known to a number of men fully capable of carrying on. To fully illustrate this point, the following sections taken from the combined geological reports of the 1964, 1966, and 1967 ARF expeditions are offered.

Greater Ararat is perpetually covered with an ice cap capping down to the 14,000 foot level in summer. This ice cap is hundreds of feet thick; and as it flows down the sides of the mountain, it divides into twelve fingers or glaciers, two of which are the Parrot and Abich glaciers, the latter of which tumbles down a vertical precipice thousands of feet into the Ahora Gulch, with a mighty roar that can be heard for miles. Both the ice cap and the resulting glaciers move over rough terrain, which breaks them into segments, separated with crevasses. Often new falls of snow drift over these crevasses, thus hiding them from view. Climbers often fall into these crevasses.

The comparatively high snow-line is due to the light precipitation and the upward rush of dry air from the Aras plain. This plain is a veritable bread basket for both Turkey and Russia. Although the upper and lower zones on the mountain are sterile, the middle zone, from 5,000 to 11,500 feet, is covered with good pasture, which the Kurdish sheep and goat herders make good use of.

The dangers are many. Storms and winds of 100 miles an hour and temperatures of below zero made life disagreeable for our glaciologists. At one time during the expedition our geologists were caught out on the mountain in a thunderstorm that brought with it pelting sleet and rain. After the storm an ensuing fog developed, making it difficult for them to find their way back to camp. They arrived late at night, soaking wet, cold, and exhausted. Without a good sense of direction and a flashlight they might have been new victims of Ararat.

The largest stream flowing down the mountain of Ararat comes down the Ahora Gulch and joins the Aras River. One wonders why there are not more streams, until it is realized that the surface of Ararat is very rough and porous and the youthful morphology of the mountain explains why fine sediment has not yet filled the interstices. For that reason the water from the melting snow sinks deep into the rock cover and may come to the surface down in the valley as springs or artesian wells.

Jacob's Well, in Ahora Gulch, where camp was made, at the 7,500 ft. elevation on the N-E side of the mountain, is fed by seepage down the mountainside in an

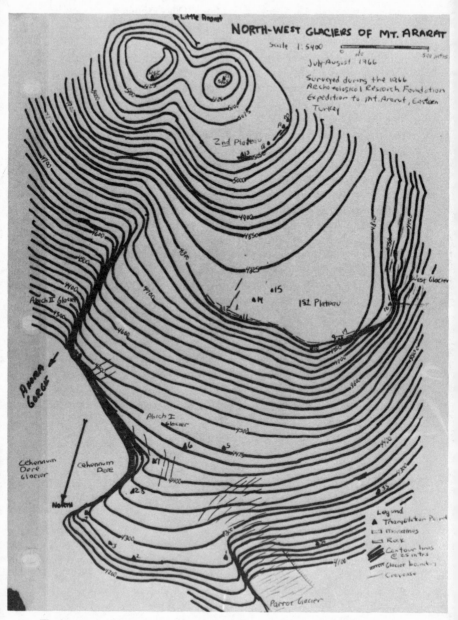

The best map of the northwest glaciers of Mt. Ararat from the Archaeological Research Foundation surveys.

aquifer of tuff sandwiched between lava flows. Other exposures also show beds of tuff covered with lava flows, indicating that the volcanic explosion was not the first nor the final tectonic event at Ararat.

Instead of Ararat forming a drainage pattern radiating from the mountain, the water shed drainage flows to the Aras and Tigris and Euphrates apparently as if it did not know that Ararat existed, thus suggesting a more recent birthday for Ararat. The original drainage system may have been established from the days of Creation. Everything about Ararat suggests youth.

The sunken ring or moat around the mountain calls for an explanation. Ararat apparently followed the same pattern as other volcanoes. As it grew it domed the surrounding rock strata to make room for the rising magma. After the volcano reached its ultimate height and maturity, it gradually reached the old age phase, and the lava began to drop back the lava conduits into the bowels of the earth, forming what is known as a caldera. As the molten magma drained back into the lower crust, it left a void or hollow; and the weight of the cover rocks caused the crust to collapse and fill the voids, thus leaving a sunken ring around the mountain, now occupied by poorly drained swampy land.

From 2 July 1966 until 3 August 1966 I was on Mt. Ararat. The actual time spent on the ice cap was from 17 July until 3 August, so 17 days. In this time 26 stakes were put into the ice and were triangulated. In addition field sketches and photographs from triangulated points were made. Only one third of the ice cap could be covered. Lack of time, dangerous climbing and bad weather were the cause that not more area could be covered. Temperature measurements could not be done as no ice-drill was available. Thickness and heaviness of the wooden stakes were also a cause that not more could be done. . . .

The first week of our stay on the ice cap was marked by bad weather conditions. We got much hail, with hailstones of ± 5 mm. and some thunderstorms. Also it could be very misty. Often the fogs came up out of the Ahora Valley. Needless to say we could not work during such weather and had to stay in our tents.

The second week we had much better weather. The temperature was higher, and there was much more melting on the glaciers. However, in the afternoon we got in general fogs and wind. On Tuesday 26th July we had a very bad storm during the whole day. I measured a wind velocity of up to 23 mtrs/sec. The wind came from the South, directly over the summit of the Mountain. Some stakes on the ice were blown down. Also the next day there still was much wind (± 10 mts/sec.). However, on Thursday the weather was beautiful and we could work again.

The best time to be on Mt. Ararat is probably in August when ablation is most intensive, and the crevasses are clearly visible. In 1964 I was in the middle of August on Mt. Ararat.

Our base camp was near Lake Kop at a height of ± 3500 mtrs. Starting at Lake Kop, one can reach point 1 in a 4-hour climb.[2] First, one enters a flat area, the

Lake Kop plain, which is completely covered with black moraines from the Parrot Glacier.

A small rivulet coming from the Parrot crosses the plain. The snout of the Parrot glacier is to the right and completely covered with moraines, stones and grey-black dust.

From the Lake Kop plain one can climb straight to point 33, and to point 1 along grassy slopes, keeping the Parrot at our right. During the expedition we had two small tents near point 1, some meters away from the ice. From point 1, one sees the sharp edge of the first plateau. To the right, bare rocks come up to this edge. One cannot see the summit (point 21) from here. Close to the right, one has the crevasses of the Parrot glacier. To the left, there is a small wall of edge moraines leading to point 4. On these moraines there is plenty of plant life, mostly succulent plants.

From point 1 to the summit (point 21) takes three hours' climbing. One has to cross several crevassed areas and has to be roped. In 1½ hours one reaches the first plateau. First, one goes to points 5 or 6 and from there one gets a slope of ± 30° to the first plateau. It is best to head for a point somewhat left of point 12, as most of the edge of the first plateau is covered with deep snow (± 1 mtr.), while the flatter areas between points 1 and 5, and on the first and second plateaus have much less snow. Here one can meet bare ice. Especially during the afternoon the surfaces of these flat areas are melting and water pools get formed. During the night they freeze again. Also at the summit I found a snow temperature which was close to the melting temperature. At a depth of 10 cm. I measured a temperature of 0.1° c., and at a depth of 80 cm. 0.05° c.

From the first plateau one can go straight to the second plateau (point 13). From there to the summit (point 21) is only a small climb. I noticed that much snow had accumulated on the summit since my visit 2 years ago, seen by complete covering of a military badge. From the summit one gets an uninterrupted slope down southwards to the Turkish plain. To the east one sees Little Ararat.

Not far away, and easy to reach, is a second summit, point 22, only 13 meters beneath point 21. Standing at point 22 one gets a beautiful view of the Abich glaciers and the Ahora Valley. Point 22 belongs to a small plateau, bordered by edge moraines at the south-east side. The mountain slope into the direction of Little Ararat is not covered by snow here. We noticed here a smell of sulphur. Also, Blumenthal writes about this smell.

From point 1, it is easy to reach point 4, where one gets a wonderful view into the Cehenem Dere, and of the Cehenem Dere glacier.

From point 4, Little Ararat is just visible over the north-east ridge of the mountain. Also, the summit is visible. The Ahora Valley cuts deep into the mountain and is here hundreds of meters deep. We have not been into the valley nor have we been on the Cehenum Dere glacier. The sharp break off of the Abich

I glacier is in the middle ± 60 meters high, which we measured with our ropes.

Point 8 was a stake we had on a rock overhanging the Cehennem Dere. From here we could see deep into the Ahora cut. The area around point 8 was covered with moraines. Thirty meters further, one can see onto the Abich II glacier which is badly crevassed here and looks like an icefall. We did not dare to plant any stakes on the glacier. That is why the contour lines of the Abich II glacier on the map are merely guessed.

---

[1]George E. Vandeman, "The Riddle of Ararat" (unpublished manuscript). Used by permission.
[2]For identification of points mentioned, see A.R.F. map, "Northwest Glaciers of Mt. Ararat."

23

SEARCH, Inc.: 1969

Actually, the official last gasp of the Archaeological Research Foundation was drawn on Ararat in August of 1968. But this small expedition was ARF in name only. Organizationally and functionally it was SEARCH all the way.

Under the influence of Ralph Crawford, Fernand Navarra was finally enticed to return to the mountain to point out the location of his 1955 find. This time there should be no mistake. No contradictory statements. They expected to just walk up to the place where wood had been found.

Navarra Injured: 1968

But nothing on Ararat is easy. The year 1968 proved to be no exception. To begin with, a lot of snow had fallen the previous winter, and the summer of 1968 was not sufficiently warm to melt it. Furthermore, the team, operating on minimal permits, was not really equipped to stay on the mountain for any length of time.

Navarra, instead of solving all of the problems, actually seemed to spark a few more. One of them involved Bill Dougal, also a veteran Ararat climber, who had participated in some of the ARF expeditions. It seems that since the permits they had been given were only good for about a week and not wishing to waste any time, Dougal and Navarra were sent up alone to the area in question. It was Saturday, and the others, including Bud Crawford, being Seventh-Day Adventists, were unwilling to work that day.

Both Crawford and Dougal were somewhat familiar with the area, but Navarra took Dougal to a completely different site than had ever been considered before. Nevertheless, the next day, when they attempted to set up camp, Navarra disappeared. That evening a search was instigated and eventually Navarra was found. He had been searching for the new campsite on his own and had slipped and broken his foot, effectively ending the activities.

More Wood: 1969

Navarra once again agreed to guide the SEARCH team in 1969. This time he was more successful, for, probing around under the ice near the supposed location of Navarra's find in 1955, the SEARCH explorers recovered several small pieces of wood identical to Navarra's wood.

But even this find was not untainted by suspicion and mystery. When the Frenchman pointed out the spot to Bud Crawford, it was obviously at a completely different spot than the year before. At Navarra's insistence, drilling and digging was begun, and before long wood was found.

Once again the public was to be deluged with press reports. Covered were details of the find, results of efforts to date the wood, plans for future work, and speculations as to the origin of the wood. Not covered was the fact that the wood was not found in the same place that Navarra had indicated to Dougal in 1968.

When asked about the contradiction, Navarra explained that he had not trusted or liked Dougal and refused to share his secret with him. He had injured his foot before he could set the record straight.[1]

Parrot glacier from above. Glacier moves from right to left, alongside rock cliff.

These inconsistencies, while they do somewhat mar the impact of the find, in no way mask the fact that wood of obvious antiquity has been found very high up the slopes of Mt. Ararat, a mountain on which there are no native trees. This hand-tooled wood should not be there. Natural forces that we are familiar with could not have placed it there. What else could it be?

Searching through records kept in archives and libraries, no mention of a wooden structure built on Ararat is found. Likewise, no structure has been built there in modern times. Furthermore, the thought of hauling huge timbers up Mt. Ararat is inconceivable. It is hard enough to climb without any extra weight.

Whether the wood found by Knight, Atalay, Navarra, SEARCH, and others has anything to do with Noah's Ark is still open to question. Whatever it is, it warrants further study. Even if it is from a more recent era, it would constitute the archaeological significant remains of a heretofore unknown structure.

Questions About Navarra

Of course, there are those who feel that the find was totally fabricated. They claim that Navarra purchased the ancient wood and falsely reported the 1955 find.

These claims were lent credence when the 1969 SEARCH team revealed that Navarra had resorted once again to his hazy directions. On one day he pointed out the site to Bud Crawford, but it was a different site than the one pointed out to Dougal the year before. The next day Navarra completely disappeared, returning at nightfall exhausted. On the following day, he led the group to a completely new site, and told the men to start digging, for Noah's Ark was just below them, and sure enough, they found small pieces of wood.

John Libi, who in August of 1969 had just completed his last expedition to Ararat, leveled a sharp blast at Navarra in the Turkish press. In two personal letters, dated August 25, 1974, and January 20, 1975, he reiterated:

Colonel Sahap Atalay (who was with Libi in 1969) and the Frenchman got together, and the Frenchman asked the Colonel to help him with the Noah's Ark story, because Navarra's wife is a writer and the two of them wanted to write a story that Navarra discovered the Ark.

Colonel Atalay, at the time, had a vacation of six weeks coming to him and he wanted to go to France with Navarra to spend his vacation there. They planned to sell the story to publishers while there. But Atalay and I always spent two weeks of his vacation right at Mount Ararat.

After two weeks in the mountains, Colonel Atalay consulted with me. He asked for a loan of $500 to go to France with Navarra. I obliged him immediately.

While in Ankara, I discovered that Atalay and Navarra planned to make a big fabrication that Navarra had found some remnants of Noah's Ark. They wanted to make a lot of money by selling this big lie story.

I reported this information to the Turkish press. When Navarra read about this, he and his family left Istanbul at once and flew out of the country. They left Colonel Atalay to hold the bag.

And:

. . . Navarra, who claims he found pieces of wood on Mount Ararat. This kind of news is a total lie. I happen to know Navarra himself and his son. Navarra has been carrying his wood from France to Ararat and bragging that these pieces are from the Ark. He tried hard to convince the Turkish press, but I exposed him to the press on my last expedition in 1969.

To the authors these accusations do not appear conclusive. The 1969 find indicates that. The wood was found by several different men whose honesty is above question. It could not have been easily faked. The 1955 discovery, frankly, was in quite a bit of doubt until then. Navarra, in his writings, in his personal accounts, in his map drawing, and in his personal directions has too often exhibited his tendency to be misleading, as if purposefully attempting to throw off the trail those who would try to follow, and he has consequently earned the reputation of being unreliable. Even though his reputation has not changed, his find has seemingly been verified.

With the recent discovery under their belt, as well as massive doses of worldwide publicity, SEARCH began making plans to excavate and remove the supposed artifact trapped in the ice. Trying to proceed with some measure of organization, SEARCH figured that the summer of 1970 should be spent in determining exactly what must be done to remove the ice cover. The summers of 1971 and 1972 would then be used to do the actual excavation.

However, nobody really asked the Turks what should be done. True, several governmental officials were contacted, but such a project cannot be carried out without governmental sanction and participation. Perhaps that was the reason permits were not reissued to the SEARCH group in 1970. Even though scientists, photographers, and explorers were poised

The stationary ice pack adjacent to the Parrot glacier where the SEARCH, Inc. expedition found several small pieces of wood in 1969.

in Turkey, at great expense, ready to swing into action, they were not allowed to return to the site.

Three researchers from the Arctic Institute of North America, part of the 1970 SEARCH team, did spend several days on the mountain before the larger group was turned away, and they were forced to descend. No new sighting was recorded, but perhaps an excerpt from the preliminary geologic report to SEARCH by geologist Dr. William R. Farrand might prove interesting.

Our preliminary observations are of two sorts. First, the altitude of the base camp and of the "artifact area" were repeatedly measured with a Thommens altimeter. The base camp lies within 100 feet vertically of 12,100 feet above sea level, and the "artifact area" is close to 12,760 feet, not "at the 13,000 to 14,000 foot level" commonly cited. The top of the high ice fall above the "artifact area" is about 13,500 feet above sea level.

The second type of observation concerns the Parrot Glacier itself and its moraines. The glacier is a rather complex system consisting of several streams of ice that move down valley, side by side, but not all at the same velocity. The ice stream that flows through the "artifact area" (and in which wood is reported to have been found) seems to be moving much more slowly at the present time than the two more powerful streams to its left. However this situation may have been different in the past, if one can judge from the large masses of stagnant ice and morainic deposits immediately downstream from the artifact-bearing ice. Both the large masses of stagnant ice that constitute the lower part of the Parrot Glacier and the huge lateral moraines along the left margin of the glacier (in the area of base camp) suggest that the Parrot Glacier was much more active in the recent past than it is now.

A final observation concerns the activity of the Parrot Glacier in the "artifact area." Several boreholes made by SEARCH Foundation in 1969 were identified, and it was clearly seen that these holes, which were originally circular in cross section, have been deformed into ellipses by the continuing movement of the ice. While the total movement of the glacier in the "artifact area" cannot be determined from these observations, they do show that the ice is still active in that area. Within very rough limits it is judged that the total ice movement must lie between one and ten meters per year.

These geologic investigators were summoned off the mountain unexpectedly when the main SEARCH party below ran into problems with the Turkish government at the negotiation table. To further widen the breach, frustrated SEARCH board members insulted the Turkish government publicly for their actions. Perhaps it is no accident that SEARCH, Inc., has not been allowed to return to the mountain to this day.

It does not take a great deal of research to postulate the reasons for Turkish refusal of SEARCH permits, for all of the publicity and official information issuing from the organization has been filled with highly unrealistic claims and plans.

Bulldozers and drilling machinery, even if they could have been somehow brought up the mountain, could not have been used to any degree of efficiency. That's bad enough, but these claims are followed by plans to pulverize the ice by using sonic vibrations and blowing the ice chips away. But then it was planned simply to paint the glacier black, and let the sun melt it. Even plans to cart huge chemical-burning rods to drill holes in the ice, chip off sections, and let gravity slide them down off the mountain were mere child's play to the plans that followed. SEARCH began raising money to build a plastic dome over the mountain, melt the glacier by turning Mt. Ararat into a huge greenhouse, protect it from all bad weather and build a sixteen-mile ski lift up to the site. Visionary plans were conceived to build an airport at the base of the mountain, along with enough elite hotels to rival Miami Beach. Tourists by the millions were going to flock to Ararat. The list could go on.

Keep in mind that this is Mt. Ararat that we are talking about, perhaps the largest mountain in the world, and certainly one of the most treacherous. The area is so remote that few roads go into it. The Kurdish tribesmen who live on the mountain are in many cases thieves and smugglers. In fact, the area just below the "Navarra site" is widely acclaimed as a haven for renegades, fugitives from justice. Any Kurdish outlaw can go there to live and have no fear of the Turkish police.

Apparently no thought was given to the effects of disturbing a mighty moving glacier, currently in equilibruim. Removing any part of the lower ice would cause immediate and violent avalanches. By melting the glacier, or any large part of it, the ecology of the area would be altered drastically. The Kurds of the mountain who depend on the normal rainfall and runoff would be subjected to floods and droughts and would need to change their life-style.

Furthermore, since the Russian border is so close, the area is a restricted zone. Around the base of the mountain and just across the border are military installations. No one is permitted into the area without written permission and, as we have seen, that permission does not come easily. No doubt Russian eyebrows were raised by all this talk of such sophisticated gear.

Several of the SEARCH officials were sincere Christian men. Some, however, were wealthy enthusiasts who were not primarily interested in the possible spiritual benefit of the Ark's relocation. In fact, SEARCH as an organization has stated emphatically and repeatedly that it is a non-religious group seeking to promote good will and to produce a relic that would be meaningful to all religions of the world.

The SEARCH goal of launching a carefully planned, staffed, and financed expedition is admirable and should be followed by all groups. However, it is the authors' opinion that too much was planned and publicized on the basis of finding several pieces of wood of uncertain origin, in an area where none of those who claimed to see the Ark had been, and without Turkish governmental participation.

[1]See Rene Noorbergen, *The Ark File* (Omaha: Pacific Press, 1974).

24

1969, 1970, 1971

The name Eryl Cummings is not unfamiliar to those who are interested in the search for Noah's Ark. His name has already been mentioned many times in these pages, as it has in all other recent works detailing the events of the search and research.

Eryl Cummings has long been known as the dean of "arkaeologists." He and members of his family have uncovered an amazing amount of information relative to the existence of the Ark.

Cummings was the first president of the Sacred History Research Expedition in 1945, aborted due to lack of funds. As a member of the Oriental Archaeological Research Expedition in 1949, Cummings was asked by Dr. A. J. Smith to lead the exploration efforts, but he declined, recognizing that the proposed trip was woefully underfinanced and poorly planned. When the Archaeological Research Foundation was organized in 1960, Cummings was among its charter members and participated in the expeditions in 1966 and 1967. More recently he has led expeditions under the auspices of International Expeditions and Trans-World Foundation of Washington D.C., sponsored in part by the Bible Science Association of Caldwell, Idaho.

As the Archaeological Research Foundation began to break up in 1968, Cummings and his two long-time friends, Dr. Clifford Burdick and Dr. Lawrence Hewitt, found themselves realizing that if the superstructure of Noah's Ark was still extant on Mt. Ararat, its remains were to be found on the northwest to northeast quadrant of the mountain near Ahora Gorge, as indicated by the many reported sightings. The area of Navarra's discovery in 1955 and the SEARCH discovery in 1969 might well contain displaced pieces of a partially destroyed Ark, but they felt that the major part of the vessel, substantially intact, was still to be found approximately one-half mile away.

Small Group: 1969

Shunning grandiose plans for bulldozers and sonic ice crushers, the three men and Dr. Hewitt's wife ventured to Mt. Ararat in 1969 with short-term permits. After reaching base camp, Mrs. Hewitt asked to be taken back down, and Dr. Hewitt did not return until their limited time was up. Meanwhile, Cummings was thrown from a horse on the upper slopes and suffered badly torn ligaments, displaced vertebrae, and a chipped bone in his hip. Burdick contracted a violent case of the dreaded "mountain sickness" and was incapacitated for days. Despite his weakened condition, Cummings pulled off a solitary climb to the 14,000-foot level where he spent a torturous night with minimal equipment. It almost seems that Mt. Ararat recognized the fact that all four expedition partici-

Eryl Cummings (left foreground), at base near entrance to the Ahora Gorge. Cummings is properly termed the "Dean of Arkeologists" for his thirty years of work in the field.

pants were in their sixties, was merciful, and dealt none of them a fatal blow; but it made sure that only minor progress was made in the actual search for Noah's Ark.

Just as their allotted time on the mountain was running out, Cummings and Hewitt set off on foot to attempt to relocate and photograph the ancient cuneiform inscriptions discovered by Col. Alexander Koor in the early 1900s. Koor had given them only general directions. They only had a few hours in which to reach their objective and return before nightfall. Thus the stage was set for a most amazing discovery.

On the little hill, known as Karada to Col. Koor (more properly Kara Daḡ, or Black Mountain) decades ago but now referred to as Korhan by the Kurds and Turks, Cummings and Hewitt chanced upon the ruins of a civilization that can only be described, even in conservative terms, as dating to the remotest antiquity.

These remains will be discussed in greater detail in a later chapter, for many more trips to the area have transpired, more items discovered, and greater insight gained. Unfortunately, as of this writing, no qualified archaeologists have been allowed to explore and evaluate the find.

Discovered in 1969 were ruins of a magnificent shrine, the walls of which are in places ten feet thick; a huge altar thirty feet high, made of hand-hewn lava; an ancient graveyard with carvings and inscriptions on the tombstones; one major tombstone sporting eight striking crosses of seemingly Sumerian origin; several stone buildings; a grinding wheel five feet in diameter, and similar structures, all in an area so remote that even the mountain people seldom venture there and an outsider would not consider it. Very little time remained for Cummings and Hewitt to study their new-found relics. In the twilight, photographs were taken to study at a later time, and for use in planning future work.

Quite a few valuable lessons were learned that summer. To begin with, Cummings realized that younger men were needed to handle the rigors of climbing. And so, in 1970, several experienced climbers were included, and in general the proposed search was better organized, planned, and financed.

Due partly to the increased awareness of Cummings' work and partly to the vast amount of publicity that the SEARCH, Inc., group received as a result of their 1969 discovery, millions of people grew interested in the search for Noah's Ark, church leaders included. Two well-known religious authors cooperated with Cummings in his work.

Huge, ancient altar at peak of Mt. Ararat foothill known as "Korhan." Notice crosses carved into rock at the foot of the altar.

Interest Grows: 1970

One, Dr. Tim LaHaye, co-author of this book and author of several popular Christian books, intended to accompany the 1970 team as scribe and chaplain. Two, Dr. John Montgomery, then Contributing Editor for

Christianity Today, planned to join the team once it was on the mountain. Plans were straightforward and workable.

However, when the relocation of the remains of Noah's Ark is the goal of the project, one tried and true principle (Murphy's Law) can always be applied, "If anything can go wrong, it will." International Expedition '70 proved to be no exception. Dr. Hewitt decided to journey to Ararat completely on his own to continue his study of wild flowers which grow there in such abundance. Dr. Burdick's health forced him to withdraw. Dr. LaHaye, involved with the founding of Christian Heritage College of San Diego and its scientific research institute, could not continue his involvement. Dr. Montgomery arrived at Mt. Ararat a week after the pre-arranged rendezvous. To top it off, the permits which had been promised fell through.

Very little was left of the well-planned search when Cummings, an American climber, and a Turkish guide reached Mt. Ararat. Cummings was able to secure simple tourist permission to climb, and the three intended to do what they could. But even their minimal efforts were foiled. The remnant of the team sponsored by SEARCH, Inc., frustrated by the fact that they had been unable to secure permission to climb, and irate at the fact that Cummings was on the mountain again, demanded approval of their application, citing Cummings's success as a precedent.

The net result, however, was an official statement from the Turkish government that SEARCH would never be allowed to return to Turkey, and a Jandarma troop was sent up the mountain to retrieve Cummings and his companions, only two days after their climb had begun, not enough time to accomplish anything. Indeed, Cummings, sixty-five years old, had spent another solitary night at 14,000 feet with no tent and minimal equipment.

When Dr. Montgomery arrived five days later with his eleven-year-old son, everyone was long gone. Refusing to be totally denied, Montgomery succeeded in gaining permission to climb to the summit of the mountain with the help of an approved guide and along the established tourist route.

Expedition Canceled: 1971

Each summer new hope wells up in the hearts of "Arkeologists." Plans were in full swing in anticipation of a major exploratory effort during 1971 with a Turkish governmental promise of full cooperation. Once again, the list included the familiar names of Cummings, Burdick,

Hewitt, and Montgomery. Other scientists and climbers included Mike Turnage and John Morris (co-author of this book), representing the newly formed Institute for Creation Research.

Unfortunately, this expedition ended in disappointment, for the permits were never granted. Many of the team spent weeks in Ankara, the capital city, attempting to encourage approval but without success. Burdick, Turnage, Morris, and Montgomery waited in America for word from Turkey. When word finally came, it was, "Do not come, the expedition is off." Weeks later, Montgomery took a quick trip to the mountain to get a few pictures of the north side.

By now the reader should be quite aware that there is no such thing as easy access to Mt. Ararat. Many factors influence the Turkish officials not to sanction such efforts; some are internal, dealing with the Turkish political, social, military, and economic situations, but most are international.[1] True, it must be said that in 1971 Turkey was experiencing major upheavals domestically. Student riots, fomented by Communist sympathizers, and civilian sabotage forced the entire country into martial law. The military took over the government, removing the prime minister from office. A potential full-scale war was imminent over the Island of Cyprus. Agricultural production was low and unemployment was high. These are reasons enough to deny foreigners access to a remote area.

But the real problem lies in the fact that Ararat sits in a most sensitive military zone. On its eastern side lies the country of Iran. At the base of its northern flank runs the Aras River, the border between Turkey and Russia. From the slopes of Ararat, one can easily see cities, towns, military installations, and the like in Russia. On a clear day, the flat terrain affords an unobstructed view for a hundred miles or so.

Whether or not Russia has any influence over Turkish decisions as to who is allowed to climb Mt. Ararat is open to question. It is well known that expeditions are branded in Russian newspapers as cover-ups for spying ventures. It is not known how much attention Turkey pays to these accusations. Surely they want to maintain as good a relationship with their neighbor as is ideologically possible. As a result, they have a standing agreement with Russia establishing a "buffer zone" on each side of the border, in which no air traffic and no military actions are allowed.

The main hindrance lies in the fact that Mt. Ararat provides an excellent location for military defenses. Such a vantage point has not been unnoticed or underestimated. Turkey holds long-standing member-

Tombstone at Korhan etched with eight Summarian crosses, bearing testimony to the antiquity of the civilizations of Ararat.

ship in NATO and CENTO, and its location is strategic for international stability; defenses must be installed to protect both Turkey and the free world.

In this world, so bent on self-destruction, more sophisticated and more powerful defense-oriented items are being produced each day. Because of their very nature, the function and location of such installations must remain a secret. It is unrealistic to believe that permits to climb Mt. Ararat will be easier to obtain in the future. The fact is they will continue to be increasingly hard to get as time goes on. The summers of 1970 and 1971 provided only a glimpse into future difficulties.

One exception: Seemingly due to a fluke, a chance circumstance in the handling of a very complex problem, Mt. Ararat opened wide during the summer of 1972; in the space of one month, more was accomplished in a lasting sense toward the eventual relocation of Noah's Ark than in any previous comparable time period.

---

[1]*Area Handbook for the Republic of Turkey* (Washington: U.S. Government, 1973).

25

1972

The Turkish political scene has never been known to be a particularly stable one. However, it had enjoyed a period of comparative continuity from 1965 to 1971 under the leadership of Prime Minister Suleyman Demirel, Chairman of the Justice Party, and President Cevdet Sunay.

During this time, Turkey was going through radical changes. Seemingly yanked out of the Middle Ages only a few decades before, Turkey was maturing into a country with twentieth-century problems. The changes in many cases were so rapid and dramatic that growth pains were inevitable and hit the country in the late sixties.

Despite the fact that the Demirel administration had adopted a firm pro-West and anti-Communist attitude, the Communists made significant strides. Their influence was particularly felt on the university campuses. With a sense of conviction that bordered on willful martyrdom, the students openly rebelled against the system.

In the opinion of the Turkish military establishment, Prime Minister Demirel did not deal with this problem as decisively as he should have, and in March 1971 they stepped in and seized control of the government. The entire country was placed under martial law.

The elderly President Sunay, who had postponed his retirement until the crisis was over, now found it impossible to retire until a suitable successor was chosen. The Turkish Parliament, stripped of all its power, loudly protested the military take-over, but to no avail. Prime Minister Demirel was forced out of office. From all appearances Turkey had become a military dictatorship and chances of its return to a democratic state were minimal.

Over the next two years, however, the regime and its puppet civilian officials did deal effectively if not brutally with Communist sympathizers and anarchists. In riots that followed, many were shot or hanged or arrested and sentenced to death. It was not long before dissidents were relegated to a more subtle position. During all this turmoil, the 1971 Ararat explorations were promptly turned away.

Much to the surprise of most political analysts, the Turkish military structure began to turn control of the government back over to civilian officials as soon as the situation stabilized. Although they maintained virtual control of the executive branch until the spring of 1973, the spring of 1972 saw them begin slowly to remove the stifling martial law from many sections of the country.

Meanwhile, back in the United States, other winds of change were blowing. Due to the fact that permission to search Mt. Ararat was apparently unobtainable, an effort was made by John Bradley, newly elected president of SEARCH, Inc., to merge all the various groups interested in relocating Noah's Ark and to apply as a united interest for an expedition of major scale.

The concept of a joint expedition does possess many favorable qualities. One of the standard objections from the Turkish government has always been because of confusion of the groups and an indecision as to which group merits their support. The Turks, unaware of ideological differences among the groups who all appear to them as representatives of the Christian faith, tend to throw up their hands in frustration when presented with several similar requests and consequently refuse them all. A pooling of resources, contacts, and influence could, from one point of view, have the greatest potential.

Noah's Ark: Fact or Fable?

The factor which precipitated the consideration of a combined effort was a manuscript, in which almost everyone interested in the Ark was involved. Written at first by Mrs. Violet Cummings, wife of Eryl Cummings, it consisted primarily of a history of the Cummings family search and research. It was a fascinating book, detailing all of the accounts of past sightings, as well as recent expeditions. It included all the excitement and heartbreak of twenty-five years of dedication on their part.

As the book progressed, Dr. LaHaye agreed to co-author the unfinished work and ready it for publication. The book was written and re-written several times, but the final version was done solely by Mrs. Cummings. Quite a bit of valuable information was gathered from SEARCH archives to make the work complete. Dr. Henry Morris, Director of the Institute for Creation Research, wrote the foreword and edited the book, as did John Morris, Field Director of the ICR expeditions. The book was published immediately before the formation of the ICR by the organization which was the forerunner of the Institute, and the initial printing and advertising costs of the book were financed almost entirely by a personal loan from John Bradley, president of SEARCH.

The book was truly a result of the cooperation of all involved, and it was well worth it. For the first time, the details of the search were made accessible to all. Thousands upon thousands of concerned and dedicated Christians, now knowledgeable on the subject, became involved financially and through prayer support.

At the request of John Bradley, both Eryl Cummings and John Morris attended a meeting of the board of directors of SEARCH, Inc., in Washington, D.C., during April 1972. Even though each of the three groups was planning separate attempts that summer, a spirit of cooperation prevailed and a joint effort was considered. But even though all shared a common goal, it soon became obvious that differences were too great to be overcome. SEARCH was interested only in studying the so-called "Navarra site," while the other two were more inclined to search elsewhere. Vast differences were also noted in logistic methods, both financial and ethical. Ideologically, SEARCH was far removed from their two guests, and official connections were out of the question.

As the meeting broke up, it was understood that SEARCH would attempt to overcome their "persona non grata" status in Turkey and apply for permission to study in depth the "Navarra site." Cummings would attempt to gain official permission from the central government in Ankara, as he had done before, to search in the Ahora Gorge area; and the ICR team, with a small group of mountain climbers, would apply for tourist permission from the authorities at the base of the mountain. In this way, all possible avenues would be covered.

SEARCH had very little hope of success. Spring and early summer feelers revealed that the Turkish attitude toward them had not changed. But all hope vanished when a devastating article appeared in one of the many newsstand scandal sheets, *The National Tattler*. A cover article about the group and their activities entitled "Noah's Ark Found!!!"[1] rehashed much of the information which had appeared numerous times before, but it also contained inside material that could only have come from the highest level of SEARCH. Not all this material was favorable. The article insisted that the Russians were responsible for blocking progress. But it also mentioned names and dates, bribes and their amounts, and the officials who supposedly received them. Since it smacked so of an official SEARCH release, the government effectively slammed the door on future SEARCH efforts.

Turkey Under Martial Law

Since the military took over the government in March of 1971, martial law has existed in most areas of the country, including Mt. Ararat. The deposed Prime Minister Suleyman Demirel was succeeded by Nihat Erim and then by Suat Urguplu in April, 1972, and by Ferit Melen in May, 1972. Even more often the entire government had to be restructured. Turkey was going through a period of real political turmoil. The military structure, although in essence controlling the puppet governments, recognized that power had to be returned to elected officials as soon as the anarchical trend was reversed. Gradually, provinces of relative stability were released until only eleven of the sixty-seven remained under martial law.[2]

In the summer of 1972, Cummings and Hewitt were beginning their negotiations for official approval of their plans and the ICR team was en route to Ararat to apply for local permission. Then martial law was lifted from the province of Kars, which includes the north face of Ararat. But the south face of the mountain, in the province of Agri, remained under strict control. The decision, as far as is known, was thought to be totally unrelated to the proposed expedition plans but was no doubt a direct result of the prayers of many thousands of people who were deeply interested in the outcome.

A Spirit of Cooperation

The ICR team arrived on the mountain more than two weeks in advance of the other team. Although no official relationship was ever established between the two groups, they did work together, sharing information and at times the same camp site. Until both expeditions ended on rather dubious notes several weeks later, an effort was made to split up in order to cover more ground.

In this way, enormous amounts of work were accomplished. The Cummings-Hewitt-led group covered in detail the eastern edge of the Ahora Gorge, documenting fully the western face with telephotos. Violent storms hindered their attempts to cross from one side to the other between the gorge and the summit, and friction between the members of the group nearly cost them their lives. But even with the difficulties, Cummings, in a later statement, observed that it was the most profitable time he had ever spent on the mountain.

Base camp for ICR expedition, near village of Ahora, 5,000–foot elevation.

The ICR team ventured far into the Ahora Gorge, searching the vital western face from below. Later, they spent five days in the area above the Ahora Gorge and Cehennem Dere and on the Parrot Glacier. Again, internal friction limited the effectiveness of the team, but for the first time, excellent photographs of the upper reaches of the mountain became available in quantity.

Mysterious Ark-Shaped Object

Both teams were trying to relocate an object noticed in a strange picture taken either by Eryl Cummings or Bud Crawford in 1966. It was not spotted until two years later while the slides were being reviewed. This mysterious unidentified object appeared to look exactly like that of the eyewitness accounts and the reports of pictures of the Ark. It had the shape of a long, slender barge with a catwalk along the top. It was sitting in a most inaccessible area, with a high cliff on one side and a drop-off of thousands of feet on the other. One end of it appeared to be protruding from a grayish snow bank. Everything seemed to fit. Whether or not it was actually the Ark was open to question, but all agreed that the object must be relocated and photographed.

The "unidentified object." The picture was taken in 1966, but the "object" was noticed in 1968. Finally in 1974 the area was tentatively determined, but it awaits verification.

Unfortunately, overhanging clouds obscured much of the surrounding area in the picture, making identification of the location difficult. But the picture appeared to have been taken from a high position on the eastern face of the Ahora Gorge looking across the canyon at the western face of the Gorge and in all probability at the lower reaches of the hanging valley known as the Cehennem Dere.

The ICR team felt they had located the object from the bottom of the gorge, but they had been unable to reach it from below. From above they found exploration of the area almost inconceivable. Pictures taken revealed that what was thought to be the "unidentified object," turned out to be a rock formation, very uniform in shape, giving a finished appearance. Erosion had carved it out of intermittent layers of basalt and volcanic tuft, giving a definite appearance of a catwalk along the top. As of this writing, the "object" has not yet been relocated.

If the Ark remains on Mt. Ararat (and the evidence indicates that it does), it must be in an area where the glacier is stationary. A moving glacier moves with tremendous force and a wooden structure such as the

Ark could not survive in its path. Furthermore, a glacier moves unevenly due to friction forces applied at areas of contact with the rock below, generating shear forces which would grind to powder anything in its path. In order for the Ark to have been preserved since Noah's time, it must have been frozen almost constantly and must be in a quiet and stable area protected from these destructive forces.

While on the glacier, the ICR team studied and photographed several potential stationary ice-packs. They were unable to finish this preliminary study, however, because trigger-happy Kurdish thieves relieved them of most of their gear one evening.

Korhan: Mysteries Discovered

Both teams also visited the area of Korhan, site of discovery of many intriguing artifacts and structures in 1969. In that year, only mediocre pictures were taken in twilight conditions; but in 1972, even though the Cummings-Hewitt team lost most of their pictures due to a mishap with one of their pack animals, the ICR was able to document the entire area thoroughly.

An additional discovery was made, probably the most important one, to go along with the others. Very near the top of the foothill of Korhan a large rock was discovered. It was covered with both pictorial writing and an ancient style of cuneiform, more pictorial in form than Sumerian cuneiform and even more ancient. At first it was assumed to be the same rock that Col. Alexander Koor had found in 1915 which, when translated, told the story of the Flood. A more complete analysis by experts has shown that it is not the same inscription but a hitherto unknown one, one that has yet to be translated.

Photographs were sent, among other places, to Dr. Carl E. DeVries, an expert in ancient inscriptions at The Oriental Institute of the University of Chicago. In a letter dated September 11, 1974, he writes:

The photographs you sent were given to Professor I. J. Gelb, who received them gladly. He wrote the following comments: "Such primitive rock inscriptions do not represent real writing, but forerunners of writing. They are personal manifestations of magic or religion. They lack a consonantal system of signs." He also said that this is a rock inscription (petroglyph) such as were found by an expedition in Armenia in the late '20's. Only preliminary reports have appeared, so any addition is valuable. He said that these are the first photos he has seen. He is a specialist in this specific area and is one of the best in the field.

Many other structures and remains were located which seemingly had

Ruins of ancient shrine at Korhan on lower slopes of Mt. Ararat.

Undeciphered writing found at Korhan by ICR team in 1972.

not been noticed before. Surrounding the altar at the very summit of the hill were approximately twenty-five sacrificial pits, which were used perhaps by later civilizations or lesser personages than those who used the main, superbly constructed one. An ancient graveyard was located nearby with ornate carvings and crosses on the tombstones. Either a large washbasin or a key-base for a statue was nearby. Down at the foot of the hill was an Armenian graveyard with perhaps thirty to fifty ornate tombstones. Crosses and carvings were also discovered on the walls of the huge shrine at the base of the hill.

Undoubtedly, a great deal more awaits discovery on Korhan. Much of the remote hillside is covered by three to four feet of grass. Numerous times the ICR explorers stumbled across "shaped" boulders and rocks that they could not see. Perhaps even the remains of an entire city are waiting to be found.

Sketch: Environs of Korhan

1. Altar
2. Water Bowl
3. Washbasin or Statue Key
4. 3- to 5-foot high wall, thirty feet long
5. Stairs
6. Tombstone with eight Sumerian Crosses
7. Ancient Graveyard
8. Rock with Cuneiform Inscriptions
9. Armenian Graveyard
10. Circular Shrine
11. Grinding Wheel
12. Under High Grass—Shaped Rocks
13. Twenty-five Sacrificial Pits

A Brutal Snow Storm

All who had any experience with the amount of glacial melt on Mt. Ararat agreed that 1972 was indeed a good year to search, estimating a ten-year thaw (in other words, about once in every ten years the glacier melts back to this point). The research shows that at least a twenty-year thaw is needed for the Ark to be exposed.

However, glacial melt is not the only factor involved. Summer storms can also play an important part. Veteran climbers had rarely seen a year so violent on Mt. Ararat. As a result, the Cummings-Hewitt group had two narrow escapes due to the weather. The first occurred when the two leaders were separated from the rest of the group at the 10,000-foot elevation as nightfall approached. The temperature plummeted, and lacking sufficient survival gear they would not have been able to survive had not Gary Oliver, a member of their party, searched for several hours to find them in the dark.

Two weeks later, as Cummings and two professional Turkish climbers attempted to cross above the Ahora Gorge, they were caught in an electrical storm that prompted one of the guides, who had made thirty ascents of Mt. Ararat, to say that he had never seen such brutal weather on the mountain. The electrical storm caused an ice covering to blanket the area, forcing a cautious retreat, but not before Cummings had successfully engineered another of his unique solitary nights at the 14,000-foot level.

Probably the most exciting afternoon in the history of Mt. Ararat was spent by three men from the ICR team in the middle of a howling snow blizzard and electrical storm at 14,000 feet. The story is lengthy, but it must be told; and it is told best in the diary kept by the leader of the expedition, one of the authors of this book (Morris), later published in the book *Adventure on Ararat*.

The snow was falling harder. It was sliding down the slope, covering our knees at all times. The wind was blowing hard and it was difficult to see. We stopped under a big rock, providing us a little shelter from the wind and since the time was 1:00, we broke out our trail food. As we ate, Roger dropped his sun glasses, and they fell down a hole at his feet. As he reached his hand down after them, he discovered that the hole went forever. Come to find out, we were standing on a thin ice covering over a large crevasse where the rock and ice separated. Needless to say, we moved.

Since the snow was coming down in such torrents and we were on the steepest part of the glacier, we decided to rope up, cross the finger glacier to the other side, and continue our ascent on the rocky-side slope. The rocks were almost completely covered with freshly fallen snow and were much more stable than before.

We got the feeling that we were right in the middle of a war. It seemed that Satan was doing his best to destroy us, and God was protecting. Remember, I had felt that this day we would find the Ark. Satan must have felt the same thing and was desperately trying to stop us in time. He must also realize the tremendous impact such a discovery would have on the world. But we were filled with a real peace, knowing that no matter how tough the going got, the Lord was protecting and leading, and nothing could happen unless the Lord allowed it to happen. We were in His Will and on His mission and whatever happened we knew would be

Searching for Noah's Ark above the Cehenem Dere on the right flank of the Ahora Gorge. Three members of the ICR team were struck by lightning 100 feet below this plateau.

The ICR "high camp" at 14,000–foot elevation.

according to His purpose. How wonderful it is to be a Christian and know that you are right where God wants you.

The weather got worse. The temperature dropped, the wind blew harder and the snow got thicker. We were on a slope of about 45° only 100 feet below the ridge or shoulder of the mountain where we had planned to make camp, when thunder clapped all around us and lightning struck nearby. Lightning began striking all around. Every large rock in the area was struck repeatedly. This was the first time I was ever in a storm—I mean *in* a storm. We were actually in the clouds. Lightning was not striking in bolts, it was just collecting at one place or another. The thunder was deafening, all around us. Static electricity was evident everywhere. Our ice axes and crampons were singing, our hair was standing on end, and even J. B.'s beard and my moustache were sticking straight out. We could feel the electricity build up until it collected on some nearby rock.

In our training we had been taught to avoid electrical storms if at all possible, but if ever caught in one to try and stay away from large rocks. The storm had come up quickly, and we were surrounded by big rocks and just below the ridge of huge rocks. Our only hope of safety was to continue upwards over the ridge of rocks and onto the relatively flat glacier, staying close enough to big rocks so that we ourselves would not be struck directly.

Although we were in a most dangerous situation, I felt that we would not be struck. I knew that Satan was again trying to stop us, and that God was allowing the storm, but protecting us, and that if we kept our faith in Him, with His help we would overcome the situation.

Struck by Lightning

The wind and snow kept increasing as we neared the top. At one point, J. B. sat down beneath a large rock to rest and gain some relief from the blinding snow. I had seen lightning strike this rock several times and returned to warn him, but as all three of us stood or sat on this big rock, lightning struck it again, sending unbelievable jolts of electricity through us.

J. B. was frozen to the rock by his back. His arms and legs and head were extended out into the air. He was in no pain at that time even though he could feel electricity surging through his body. From that vantage point, however, he could see Roger and me thrown off the rock. The force of the lightning seemed to suspend us in the air and then dropped us far down the slope. At this point, J. B. succeeded in forcing one of his legs to the ground, completing the electrical circuit, and the force somersaulted him down the mountain, following Roger and me.

I had been standing on the rock (now known as "Zap Rock") when the lightning struck. Once again I had been thanking the Lord for protecting us, feeling that we would not be harmed. When the bolt struck, my whole body went numb, and I could not see or move, but never lost consciousness. I fell over backwards, still wearing my heavy pack. I expected an impact but it never came; it seemed like I was floating very slowly for several seconds. I was gently lain on the snow by unseen hands and began sliding down the steep slope. I knew I must stop, and, for an instant, my eyes and arms would not function. When they did, I spied and grabbed a rock in the snow, stopping my slide.

For a few seconds I lay there, not moving, aware only of intense pain. I reasoned that since the pain was so great, that I had received the full force of the bolt, and that the other two were unaffected. I tried to roll over and sit up, but, to my horror, found that both legs were paralyzed! There was no sensation of touch or life in them, just burning, searing pain!

I called to my friends for help, thinking they were unharmed, but the only answer was another call for help. Looking back up-hill, I saw J. B. sitting up in the snow, about ten feet away, obviously also in great pain, with one leg twisted underneath him. He also was paralyzed and thought one leg was broken.

We remained there for some minutes, crying out to God for relief from the pain and deliverance from the horrible death that surely was to be ours. Suddenly I missed Roger, and called to him frantically, looking around for him. J. B. spotted him, much farther down the mountain, lying face down in the snow, one side of his head covered with blood. We were unable to go to him, but prayed for him and called to him from above. Finally, he stood up, looked around and walked up to us. His face was at least as white as the snow, and his eyes were filled with confusion and fear. He did not come all the way to J. B. and me, but from a few feet away, bombarded us with questions. "Where are we? What are we doing here? Why don't we go sit under that big rock and get out of this snow?"J. B. patiently tried to explain to him that we were on Mt. Ararat, looking for Noah's Ark, and had just been struck by lightning under that big rock.

Roger was in shock and experiencing total amnesia. He didn't know who he was, who we were, he didn't know anything; furthermore, he didn't even like us. He wondered who these two nuts were sitting in the snow, freezing to death, when they could gain some shelter from the storm up among the rocks. J. B. convinced him to go get our ice axes, but that was the only thing he would do to help.

So J. B. and I, unable to help ourselves, had to rely totally upon God. We reasoned that Roger would slip into deep shock soon and would need medical attention. J. B. thought his leg was broken, and both of us were paralyzed, unable to move. We discussed the possible descent of the mountain, but ruled it out as impossible.

Our situation was, in short, critical. Unless we were able to get to some shelter, we would die within a few hours, freezing to death in the storm. And so, not being able to see any way to alter the situation, I prepared to die.

That's a weird feeling, rationally knowing that you are about to die. I never once doubted my salvation and did not fear death. In fact, I felt real peace, knowing that soon I was to be with my Saviour in Heaven. I had always envisioned meeting Jesus face to face as a rather exciting experience, but I now felt no excitement, just comfort. In fact, I wanted to get on with it—to die now, rather than slowly over a period of hours.

As I sat there, contemplating the horrible death in store, the Holy Spirit began to interject some of His thoughts into my mind. First, I was reminded of the hundreds of thousands of Christians who have suffered and died while following the Lord's leading, and how they considered it a privilege to suffer for Him. Then I was reminded of the marvelous way in which our group had been led in the past months and particularly the past weeks in Turkey. I was reminded of the miraculous acquisition of our VW minibus, of the Christian friends who had helped us, of the granting of the impossible permits, of all the many deadend streets down which we had wandered, only to find an open door at the end. I was reminded of the Christians back home who were praying for our safety and success. I was reminded of the job we had been called to do and its implications, importance, and urgency.

And then the conclusion! No, I wasn't going to die. God still had a purpose, a job for us to accomplish. He wasn't going to let us die up in that frozen wasteland. Somehow, He was going to remedy the situation, heal and strengthen our bodies, and allow us to continue the search for the Ark.

Miracle on Ararat

I was reminded of two passages of Scripture. James 5:15, which states that "the prayer of faith shall save him that is sick," and I John 5:14, 15, stating that "this is the confidence which we have in Him, that if we ask anything according to His will He listens to us. And since we know that He listens to us in whatever we ask, we also know that we have the request made of Him."

These thoughts were all whirling around in my head at dizzying speeds. I knew that I wasn't going to die. I knew that I was going to be healed. I knew that this was according to God's will. And since I knew these things, the realization came suddenly that I also had faith that these things would come to pass. And if I had that faith, then I could pray the prayer of faith. And so, with my heart pounding wildly, I prayed that prayer of faith, knowing that the Lord heard me and knowing that He would answer my request and heal my body.

Before the Holy Spirit had directed my thinking, I had prayed for relief from the pain and for healing. But it was a prayer of desperation, not of faith. This time I expected a miracle. I tried to move my legs—no response. Or did that toe move? Frantically I began massaging my legs and could feel the firmness return. There was no sensation of touch in them, just a burning numbness. Before when I had felt them, they resembled a balloon filled with water, shapeless and pliable. But now they were hard. I continued to massage, covering them with snow to ease the burning sensation. Their strength gradually returned, but still no feeling. Within thirty minutes my knees would bend! Within an hour, I could stand!

Using an ice axe as a cane, I hobbled over to J. B. and massaged his legs. He had been unable to reach his ankle and still thought it was broken. We determined that it was not broken, but both legs felt like jelly. He was quite calm and relaxed and felt that Roger needed attention more than he.

Roger was sitting on a nearby rock, obviously cold and still in shock. He didn't even have the sense to put on heavier clothing. So I retrieved his pack and re-dressed him—nylon pants, down parka, wind parka, and poncho. As I was tying his poncho up around his chin, a look of recognition crossed his face, and his memory began to return. When he asked why I was dressing him, I knew he was going to be all right. He did not fully recover for several hours, but in the meantime was able to heat some water for a hot drink. In doing so, we lost all of the coffee, cocoa, tea, soup, all hot drink material. It slid down the hill, along with some valuable equipment.

J. B. had been massaging and flexing his legs all this time. His right leg had recuperated somewhat, and he could move it. Roger and I helped him over to a rock where he was able to don warmer clothing and find shelter from the storm.

Finally, I began to dress myself. My legs were weak and shaky. I had walked up and down the slope, gathering gear, until exhausted; but together we huddled under the rock to gain shelter from the storm, drank a hot drink to ward off hyperthermia, and prayed to gain victory over the situation.

Earlier, the Holy Spirit had given me the knowledge that it was in the Lord's will for us to be healed and to survive the ordeal. Now we were partially healed and growing stronger each minute, but we still faced a cruel blizzard with little chance of survival. Lightning was still flashing everywhere, snow was still coming down in buckets, and gale winds were blowing. We knew we were going to survive, but that it wouldn't be easy.

We, as Christians, are expected to have faith, large amounts of it, in fact; but we must never expect our faith to be sufficient. Frequently the Lord requires hard work and then rewards our faith by blessing our efforts. Such was the case on the mountain. The only possible area of safety was on top of the ridge away from the big rocks. We needed a flat place to pitch the tent and gain shelter from the storm, so as soon as the lightning intensity lessened, Roger and I began searching for a way to the top.

The wind was blowing the snow so hard we could not see more than 10 feet maximum, but we located a path between several huge rocks and climbed it. It was nearly vertical and footing was treacherous. Once we reached the top, however, we found the weather worse. We were right on the edge of the Abich I Glacier, and the wind velocity doubled; but we picked out a flat place to camp and returned to J. B.

J. B. had been massaging and exercising his legs. His right leg had regained its strength, but no response from his left. He still could not move, so Roger and I climbed the slope with our packs and made plans to anchor the rope to a rock and assist J. B. in his ascent. I was nearly exhausted after this second climb. My legs were shaking like rubber, so I rested in the snow for several minutes. We descended once again to J. B., and much to our surprise found him standing up waiting for us. His legs still had no feeling, but their strength had returned enough to allow him to stand, so Roger carried his pack, and with little assistance from me, J. B. climbed that vertical slope on two numb weak legs!

Within minutes of the time we reached the top, the storm broke. I guess the Lord figured that we had had enough. The snow and wind stopped, and the clouds disappeared just as suddenly as they had appeared. In complete comfort and peace we were able to pitch our tent and eat a hot supper. In fact, that evening before the sun went down, it was rather warm and pleasant.

Throughout the day, you remember, I had felt that this would be the day we would find the Ark. This feeling was strengthened by the fact that Satan was so determined to stop us. It's not hard to imagine what I was doing and thinking as we pitched the tent and set up camp. As soon as time permitted, I wandered off to the edge of the Ahora Gorge, positive that the Ark was in full view. I did not approach any dangerous cliffs, but with binoculars searched in all directions from a safe vantage point. Much to my disappointment, I did not see the Ark; but the view of the Gorge from above was magnificent. The freshly fallen snow covered everything above elevation 9,000 feet, including, I suspected the Ark. So we had to settle for a comfortable place to sleep, hot food, and our lives that night. We were satisfied and gave thanks to God. Very few people have ever camped that high on Ararat, but I'm sure no one else has had such a wonderful time of prayer and singing hymns as we had that evening.[3]

[1]June 4, 1972.
[2]See *Area Handbook for the Republic of Turkey* (Washington: U.S. Government, 1973).
[3]John D. Morris, *Adventure on Ararat* (San Diego: Creation-Life Publishers, 1973), pp. 59-66.

26

1973

Just as the ICR team was leaving the Ararat area in 1972, the local military commander in charge of the most vital section of the mountain invited them to return the following year, assuring them full cooperation. While promising to make a bona fide attempt to capture and return the equipment stolen in the midnight robbery by Kurdish brigands, the young commander even indicated a desire to join the search himself.

The promise was reinforced several months later when nearly all of the equipment (about $3000 worth) was returned to ICR headquarters in San Diego. The thieves were safely in custody and an elaborate pilfering, smuggling, and fencing ring had been exposed. The area was much more inviting.

Ideal Weather Conditions

The situation was perfect. Permits to search Mt. Ararat with full cooperation of the local authorities were assured. There was no need to make adjustments in methods of operation, just a need to firm them up in anticipation of not only finding the Ark but also thoroughly documenting it. The Cummings group, committed to a more formal stance, seemed assured of governmental cooperation as well.

To top things off, the heat wave which had produced such extensive glacial melt in 1972 extended into 1973 and, coupled with a very mild winter with little precipitation, produced optimum conditions for the search. As the spring and early summer rolled around, however, the destructive heat wave and drought crippled major parts of Turkey as it did throughout Russia, the Middle East, and Northern Africa. Water and food shortages became the norm, and in many places disease epidemics broke out. Agricultural production in eastern Turkey tapered off, but the glacier on Mt. Ararat receded back farther than anyone could remember.

Unfortunately, the volatile political situation in Turkey did not subside, and the added pressure of an agricultural nation facing hard times did not help. The Army-controlled government seemed unable to cope with the problems but determined to hold on until the scheduled general election slated for October 14, 1973.

The Melen government, considered somewhat weak, was able to hang on until April of 1973, but only with direct help from the military on several occasions. To add to the fire, the term of President Sunay expired in March. It took fifteen ballots and even a brawl or two on the floor of the Parliament to elect his successor, Fahri Korutürk, whose first act of office was to instruct Naim Talu to set up another coalition government. [1]

Obviously these numerous and frequent alterations in the entire government of Turkey made it difficult for foreigners to maintain contact with favorable officials who survived the transitions, and to know just how to approach the newly appointed ones.

By the time the ICR team arrived in Ankara, the Cummings-Hewitt team, recently incorporated under the name of Trans-World Foundation of Washington, D.C., was already in trouble, having been denied after all the permission promised earlier in the spring. Negotiations were in full swing, but it looked like a long drawn-out process.

Ararat: "Off Limits"

Unbeknown to the travelers, some very sophisticated military construction was going on in the Ararat area. Absolutely no one was to be allowed in, pursuant to a directive from the new Talu government. The directive was in the form of an open letter to all military personnel and civilian officials in the entire Ararat area. Briefly, it stated that no one of any nationality was to approach the mountain. The only ones who were allowed to leave the roads surrounding the mountain at its base and head toward the mountain were the Kurdish nomads who could prove that they lived there. Villagers were authorized to arrest any illegal trespasser and to return him to Jandarma headquarters for a reward, dead or alive!

The unsuspecting ICR team arrived at the mountain in July, confident of local permission to climb. They found the atmosphere quite coopera- tive among their contacts there; but the officials were apologetic, unable to issue the necessary papers. The subject was not open to question, they no longer had the authority to help. The team of Institute explorers had to retreat to Ankara to join the Trans-World group attempting to overcome the general prohibition of access to the mountain.

Several other lesser groups, also interested in searching for the Ark, were in exactly the same situation. Dr. John Montgomery, attempting to launch an expedition on his own, was "in abject despair" (according to an Ankara newspaper reporter) at his inability to coerce the Turks into giving him special permission. A Swedish expedition under the direction of Gunnar Smars was also turned down. (Smars related the rumor that a combined group of foreigners and Turks were engaged in secret but sanctioned excavations on the western slopes of the mountain. It was told him by local Ararat officials. ICR had also heard the rumor from a less official source, but was unable to verify it.)

The Wrong Way to Search

There was one American group, however, who did succeed in entering forbidden territory. The Holy Ground Mission Changing Center from Palestine, Texas, a small, amalgamated cult featuring "revealed" doctrines gathered from almost every other cult and Eastern philosophy, claimed God's special permission and directive to search Mt. Ararat. They spent several days in the area of Korhan, photographing and studying the ruins there. After discovering a large cave going into the center of Korhan, they themselves were discovered and promptly removed, further tightening the security of the area.

This group, led primarily by Tom Crotser, had also visited the mountain in 1971 and 1972. The first year ended when their baggage was lost and they were temporarily arrested in the town of Dogubeyazit. When finally released, they attempted a climb of the mountain itself without any kind of permission from the authorities, resulting in a near calamity.

They first visited Korhan briefly in September of 1972, again making no major discoveries, before hiking up to Lake Kop—the area below SEARCH's 1969 find. The weather had completely closed the area, and survival was difficult. Hopelessly underfinanced, underequipped, and unprepared, the Holy Ground group was fortunate to have lived through their experience.

Some Archaeological Progress

The ICR group refused to be entirely stymied by the events of the summer, and, while awaiting a decision on their application for official permits, returned to Ararat to launch a detailed study of another important archaeological site in the area.

In the upturned strata east of Dogubeyazit rests one of the most

An engraving of Old Bayazit, from *Penashkharhik Pararan*. The pre-Hittite cave is to the right of the dome in the foreground. Old Bayazit is in ruins now.

inspiring castle ruins in Turkey, Isak Pasa. Its beautiful and ornately carved pink stone attracts tourists from all over the world. It was originally built for an insane Persian ruler by a luckless Armenian architect whose hands were amputated as soon as work was completed so that the Persian ruler could glory in its unique splendor. It sits in ruins now, demolished by an earthquake and two wars in the 1820s.

Within sight of this well-known attraction is another more important area that has not drawn so much attention. High on a vertical rock face one can see the entrance to a hand-carved cave, framed on each side by relief carvings of priests and on the top by an animal in a sacrificial position.

This cave has been noted by several authors throughout the last few centuries. In fact, more detail on the facade was noted before in a section which now has been purposely chipped away. As far as is known the cave has never been excavated and until the ICR team first entered and explored it in 1972 no documentation of any quality existed.

There is considerable disagreement as to the exact origin of the cave; but all agree the cave stems from a very ancient civilization. In his scholarly dictionary written on Armenian people, places, and events, Father Eprikian gives a sketch of the cave and discusses it:

Near the jail near the mountain of stones, there is a famous site carved into the

An old sketch (artist unknown) of the entrance to the ancient cave. More of the carving was visible then, and the entrance was sealed.

rock face. As you can see from the picture, there are two priests with Armenian headdresses who are sacrificing a deer. One of the priests is without a beard and has a cane. The other is elderly and is praying with his hands raised.

This cave needs many archaeological investigations to determine what is inside.[2]

We could not agree more.

In *The Ancient Faith of Armenia,* by Alishian, the same sketch bears the following caption.

Relief found at Bayazid. A priestess and a priest with a Phrygian hood, in the act of worship and of offering a lamb as a sacrifice. The tail of the animal indicates a variety now extinct. The figure of the deity seems to have disappeared.[3]

The next comment comes from the Archaeological Institute of North America. None of these appear to have entered the cave, and indeed the sketch shows the opening blocked.

In Bayazid (the ancient Bagravand) an old Armenian relief was found with an altar upon which a strange animal stands and, on each side, a man clothed in a long tunic. One is beardless and carries a heavy club. The other has a beard. Their headgear, Phrygian in character, differs in detail. Both have their hands raised in the attitude of worship.[4]

Dr. Burdick had seen the cave in 1969, when a Swedish archaeologist showed it to him. This European scholar had indicated that the carvings on the outside definitely placed its origin with the original inhabitants of the area, antedating the Phoenicians and the Hittites.[5]

The following descriptions of the explorations of the cave are taken from the official diaries of the 1972 and 1973 ICR expeditions kept by the field director, John Morris.

July 30, 1972.

We found it with no trouble, but climbing to it was another matter. It is carved into the face of a sheer rock cliff. We climbed up the steep slopes to the base of the cliff easily. J. B. did not hesitate—he climbed up the vertical face like an experienced rock climber. I didn't follow since it is a very small cave. (At least that was my excuse.) Roger later joined J. B. J. B. took many flash pictures inside the cave, the first ever taken, to my knowledge.

The entrance to the cave is a square hole, probably three feet square. Inside are two small rooms, and in one of them there are the remains of what appears to be a sarcophagus, or coffin, carved out of the mountain stone. The walls of the rooms and the sides of the coffin are extremely smooth; someone spent a lot of time carving this thing.

A stairway, apparently to several lower rooms, has been silted up, and is impassable. We did not have the time or tools to dig, but someone certainly should.

Surrounding the entrance to the cave, the carvers had carved a scene; by studying this scene, archaeologists have determined the civilization responsible for it. The carving shows two robed figures, one on each side of the entrance, each wearing a turban and carrying a staff. Between them, above the entrance, is a portion of some four-legged animal, probably a cow, goat, or sheep. The head of this animal, and most likely another figure, are eroded beyond recognition. The scene depicted is some sort of sacrifice and has been designated by knowledgeable scholars as pre-Hittite.

The Hittites, if you recall, were a major nation at the time of Abraham. Abraham lived not too long after the Flood, so if this cave is pre-Hittite, then very likely it was carved by the descendants of Noah soon after the Flood.[6]

August 8, 1973

We climbed to just below the entrance—no problem. But the last 20 feet or so are vertical and no one seemed to want to climb, so the biggest chicken of all went first. It's probably not hard for an experienced rock climber, but I felt it was rather

The entrance to the pre-Hittite cave in 1973, before it was opened. The priest on the right is approximately six feet tall. (Photo by Ikenberry)

difficult. Once inside, I noticed another opening up above. I crawled through that one and saw Luke (Durnal) over on another pinnacle. Even though the way was treacherous, he could more easily arrive at the second opening that way than the way I had come.

By this time, Larry (Ikenberry) had climbed up to the main entrance, but could not make the last step into the entrance tunnel without help, so I grabbed his hand to help him in. Larry had the flashlight, and with its help we took many flash pictures.

The entrance level rooms are quite obviously hand carved, as is the entire cave. Several niches are carved back into the walls, no doubt used as storage bins and fixtures for holding torches.

The staircase going down into the next floor was shorter than I had imagined and the opening was bigger. Originally, a stone slab had covered the passageway; but it had been broken and the pieces of the slab were piled neatly at its head. Just off to the right of the stairway was the underground entrance to a water cistern about 30 feet deep, semicircular in shape and elaborately shored up by stone blocks. To the left of the stairway appeared to be an opening into another room; but it was entirely silted up.

The end of the tunnel running behind the pre-Hittite cave. Note the stone archway. This tunnel has never been excavated.

We slithered through the small opening, head-first, into the second level of the cave at the foot of the staircase. We found ourselves in a sort of foyer; before us opened two small rooms. A great deal of loose rock and silt covered everything, and we were only standing a few feet below the ceiling of the second level. One of the two rooms definitely appeared to have something buried in its center, perhaps even a coffin as suggested by its surroundings. In the other room, a vertical shaft went upward as far as we could see. It may have been a ventilation shaft previously, but was clogged up now. In this room I found a portion of a calcium ball, which was undoubtedly handmade.

All of the inner facings of the cave appear to have once been covered by a plaster-like substance, which has chipped away. Some remnants of color indicate that they may have been painted or inscribed with long-forgotten lore.

By this time, Luke had worked his way over to the upper entrance. It turned out to be quite well camouflaged. He had found an area that had been part of the original buttress, but had been gutted by fire and rebuilt. Doc (Davies) had stayed below and was passing up equipment by means of a rope.

We decided to leave by means of the upper entrance instead of the more dangerous vertical descent. Exiting, we noticed for the first time the immense care with which the tunnel which comprised the upper opening had been constructed. At least eight linear feet of it was mortared in with wedge-shaped blocks.

Just outside the upper entrance, I peeked into an adjacent hole. I had looked into it before but it seemed to go nowhere. However, I could see this time with the flashlight that it extended back about 30 feet. It ran almost parallel to the axis of the upper tunnel and behind the cave.

Quickly I jumped in, marveling at the huge tapered blocks of stone supporting the entrance. The tunnel sloped upward at about a 10% grade and the bulk of it was unsupported, with the exception of two large stone archways, one near the entrance and one at the far end, where passage was blocked by silt and loose rock. But the archway at that point gives the distinct impression that the tunnel does not end there. In the moist dirt at the tunnel's end it appeared that someone previously bored or prodded with a round stick. The hole went back about 18 inches and seemed to open up, but it was hard to tell. Rooting around in the debris, we discovered several bits of pottery. Again, Larry and I took pictures.[7]

Turkey has rightly been termed an archaeologist's paradise. In the past, European and American museums have stocked their displays with artifacts taken from Turkey. Even in spite of recent prohibitions on removing any artifact from Turkey, an elaborate smuggling ring continued to operate, forcing stricter measures. In the spring of 1973 stiff penalties were promised to anyone attempting to remove any object of even minor historical value.

The "Isak Pasha" now in ruins, but formerly a beautiful palace. It was part of Old Bayazit. (From *Penashkharhik Pararan*)

So, without proper excavation permits, it is entirely impossible to do any more with this cave than has already been done. It is hoped that soon a professional archaeological effort will be launched to open up these underground apartments and tunnels. If they truly date from the suspected ancient Pre-Hittite civilization, then it is just possible that information and artifacts are contained inside which would shed great light on the days of Noah soon after the Flood.

Permits Granted

Meanwhile, back in Ankara, all of the various teams had given up hope for the summer and returned home. Finally, only John Morris and Dr. Hewitt remained. On exactly the same day that the ICR application received its final no, Hewitt announced that his permits had come through, from an entirely different source. The date was August 16, normally the time to call a halt to the summer's work.

But this summer was different. The heat wave and drought had continued and the glacier had steadily receded. The old-timers around the mountain claimed that it had receded farther back than at any time in their memory. Unprecedented amounts of the upper reaches of the mountain lay exposed for the first time.

Hurriedly a makeshift team was assembled back in the States, made up of the various expedition members who were not hampered by other commitments. Two inexperienced but capable climbers under the direction of an instructor supplemented the older Ararat veterans: Cummings, Burdick, and Hewitt, all of whom eventually developed serious physical conditions; Burdick pneumonia, Cummings brain concussion and infection, and Hewitt mountain sickness.

The three high altitude climbers were able to put to rest the speculation that an unusual rock formation in the Cehennem Dere might be the "unidentified object" photographed some years earlier. The Australian member of the Trans-World team, Joeff McMahon, who had never before climbed a mountain of any sort, descended alone into a most inaccessible region to the formation itself, photographing and studying it. He measured the uniformly shaped basaltic rock as approximately 300 feet long by 60 feet wide and 20 feet high. A white chemical deposit marked its top. Even though it was a most unusual geological freak of nature, it was not the "unidentified object," nor was it the Ark; but it could easily have been mistaken for it from a distance.

After solving that mystery, they were able to study some of the vast areas usually hidden by ice and snow, but no discovery was made. Dr. Burdick systematically continued his valuable study of the awesome geology of Mt. Ararat, and Dr. Hewitt resumed his botanical studies.

Much important new information was gathered. Eryl Cummings remarked that despite all the personal frustrations it was probably the most successful expedition in which he had participated. Dr. Burdick's conclusion soon appeared in the *Bible-Science Newsletter*.

Our climbers spent nearly ten days searching out all the canyons in the area designated, without success. Were we looking in the wrong area? After comparing photos of Ararat taken on September 1, 1966, I came to the conclusion that the ice cap did not melt back far enough to uncover the Ark. Perhaps another year we might have better luck, especially if we get to work earlier in the summer. We are convinced the Ark is still on Mt. Ararat. There have been too many reports of sightings; and where there is so much smoke, there must be some fire.[8]

[1]*Area Handbook for the Republic of Turkey* (Washington, D.C.: U.S. Government, 1973).

[2] Father Eprikian, *Penashkharhik Pararan* (Venice: 1903), p. 153.

[3] Cited in *The Mythology of All Races* (Boston: Boston Archaeological Institute of North America, 1925) vol. 7, p. 3.

[4] Mardiros H. Ananikian, "Armenian Mythology" in *The Mythology of All Races* (Boston: Boston Archaeological Institute of North America, 1975), vol. 7, p. 228.

[5] C. L. Burdick, "Expedition to Mt. Ararat," *Bible-Science Newsletter* (October 15, 1969), p. 3.

[6] John D. Morris, *Adventure on Ararat* (San Diego: Creation-Life Publishers, 1973), pp. 50-51.

[7] John D. Morris, "Frustration on Ararat" (unpublished manuscript), pp. 49-50.

[8] C. L. Burdick, "Update on Ararat," *Bible-Science Newsletter* (February, 1974), p. 4.

27

Satellite Photos

To many interested people on the fringe of the continuing and frustrating search for Noah's Ark, there seems to be a simple solution, a way to gain all the necessary information without so many years of hard work. The idea is brought up and battered about at almost every lecture and discussion on the subject. "Why don't you just get the Federal Government to give you aerial photographs of Mt. Ararat? Surely you could see the Ark in them."

The concept is so simple. It is true that the American government and several other first-rate world powers are constantly scanning and photographing the globe, even the more remote areas, and the American people have grown more and more dependent upon the government to do things that traditionally the people have had the right to do. And the government has responded by expanding into a bureaucratic monolith.

And so, let's get the government to work for us. It sounds so simple, but wait.

Of course the first question of several that must be answered positively is: Do the capabilities exist to take such pictures? Are there orbiting or fixed wing devices capable of gathering such data? The answer is undeniably yes. The sky is full of all sorts of satellites circling the globe in prearranged patterns, designed to scan every square foot of surface periodically, radio-beaming their information back to earth. Other short-term satellites return their precious data back to eager eyes in the form of high-resolution film. Manned probes, such as SKYLAB, store data both with on-board film and earth-borne scanners.

Another type of data gathering was notoriously exposed in 1960 when the American pilot Gary Powers was shot down over Russia in his U-2 spy-plane on a photographic mission. In recent years the marvelous U-2 has been replaced by the sleek and ominous SR-71, capable of remaining in the air almost indefinitely with in-flight refuelings.

Even private industry gets into the act. Many large firms are presently orbiting satellites on various missions: communication, weather, cosmic, mineralogical, educational, to name a few. The capacity for getting pictures of Mt. Ararat does, without a doubt, exist!

The next question: Are the instruments on board these vessels capable of detecting an object on the earth's surface the size of Noah's Ark? Once again the answer is yes, although the range of sensitivity among them varies widely.

Most private satellites are not designed to gather detailed information. They are more concerned with general terrain features (helpful in locating oil-bearing strata or mineral-rich soil, or determining agricultural potential, etc.), water or wind patterns (for transportation purposes), weather fronts (for predicting the weather), stellar observations (for a better understanding of outer space)—the list could go on and on. These devices have specific functions which do not normally include photographing 450- by 75-foot objects icebound on a remote mountain in the Middle East.

The government-oriented space probes vary widely in both scope and purpose. As might be suspected, only the most secretive and potentially rewarding efforts put to use the highest caliber equipment. Consider the following quote from NASA scientist Tom Henderson, who, after consultation with ERTS photographic experts, transmitted the following in personal correspondence dated December 22, 1971:

Another problem is that by examining a photo one can deduce the specifications of the camera that took it. This has been a particular problem for us at NASA. As a result, we have even had to use "less than the best" cameras and film on multi-billion dollar space missions.

Much of NASA's work falls within the range of public domain, and taxpayers have relatively free access to their file banks. For reasons of national security, they cannot allow the best quality information to be available to everyone and so are forced to use second-class equipment and material.

The combined military and espionage network of this country does not operate under such conditions. They retain, and in the author's opinion must always retain, the privilege of classifying their material, allowing only those who have a specific, declared and official "need to know" to see certain items. These classifications range from unclassified, to secret, top secret, and so on. Information, whether it be photographic or any other type, is not necessarily given a classification according to its content, as might be expected. Again, Mr. Henderson:

Photo of the Ararat area taken from Skylab. Mt. Ararat is the little white dot in the lower righthand corner.

Releasing photos is difficult for several reasons. One is the system of classification. For example, although the photo we want may not contain classified information, it no doubt was taken on a photographic mission that was classified. If one starts to declassify photos here and there, in effect, the system of classification crumbles.

Pictures of Ararat

With few exceptions, then, the mission determines the classification. One only has to recall the site of Mt. Ararat, on the tri-border of Turkey, Russia, and Iran, within easy sight of a number of military installations and traditionally a hot-spot for international intrigue, to realize that most photographs taken of the area would have been taken on classified missions.

The Department of Defense does not readily disclose the exact specifications of its most sensitive camera equipment, and we as citizens should not expect them to. Reports do persist, however, that from extremely high altitudes the ability exists to read newspaper headlines, count bumps on a golf ball, and recognize individuals. Suffice it to say that certainly a vessel the size of Noah's Ark could indeed be studied in great detail through the use of Defense photographs.

The next question: Can pictures of Mt. Ararat be obtained by private individuals and organizations of sufficient resolution and character to aid in the search? Unfortunately, this question has not yet been answered, at least in the affirmative.

As mentioned previously, much of the work done by NASA is, by law, available to the public. A picture of Mt. Ararat, taken by the crew of SKYLAB, can be obtained at very little cost. It makes a nice conversation piece, but little more. It was taken out of the window of the craft by one of the crewmen with a hand-held Hasselblad camera from an altitude of about 100 miles.

More pictures, also readily available to the taxpayer, were taken by the Earth Resources Technology Satellite (ERTS). This satellite was launched on July 23, 1972, and placed in a "sun synchronous polar orbit around the earth. The satellite has the capacity for producing coverage of most of the earth on an 18-day repetitive cycle."[1]

Jumping to Conclusions

One group of pictures of particular interest to Ark searchers was taken on July 13 and 14, 1973, over Mt. Ararat. No official detailed study was made of them until January of 1974 when a NASA employee (himself interested in the Ark) noticed a rather uniform formation in the area of Mt. Ararat under consideration as a possible resting place for the Ark.

A lively discussion followed, and Dr. John Montgomery, whose interest in the Ark was well known, was notified. It was not long before the following news release hit the papers. Almost every newspaper in the country carried the article, as did almost every radio and television newscast.

Salt Lake (UPI) Feb. 21, 1974

A speck on a photograph made by a U.S. space satellite may be a picture of Noah's Ark, Senator Frank E. Moss, Democrat, Utah, said Thursday.

Moss told a meeting of the American Congress on Surveying and Mapping that the photos made by the Earth Resources Technology Satellite (ERTS) support evidence that an object 14,000 feet up the side of Turkey's Mt. Ararat is the Ark.

"ERTS photographs taken from 450 miles above the earth show a formation at the lower end of the satellite's resolution capability which appears to be foreign to other materials found on the mountain," said the Utah Democrat, who is chairman of the Senate Space Committee.

"It is about the size and shape to be the Ark," he said.

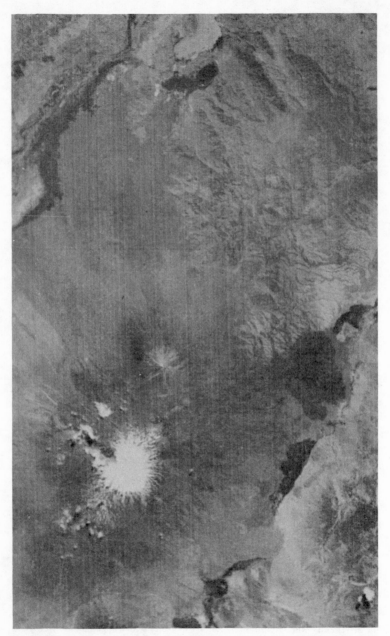

ERTS photography, reported as showing Noah's Ark. Note white ice cap, with the Ahora Gorge trending to the northeast from the summit; Lesser Ararat lies to the southeast.

Moss quoted from a "confidential memorandum" he received from Dr. John Montgomery, a professor at Trinity Divinity School who has been investigating the possibility that the remains of the Ark are on the mountain near the Iranian and Russian borders.

Dr. Montgomery believes the ERTS imagery further corroborates mounting evidence that the object on the mountain top is the Ark, the Senator said.

SKYLAB photos being processed now are expected to improve the ERTS pictures of the area.

Moss said the location of the Ark-like object is at about 14,000 feet on the northeast quadrant of the mountain in a canyon filled with ice, a location consistent with other sightings dating back 150 years.

But the Senator said ground search is "the only way accurately to establish what the formation is."

"A manned expedition is difficult," he added, "because the mountain is hard to climb and is now considered a military reservation."

"It is almost impossible to get permission to enter the area," Moss said, "but Dr. Montgomery is currently seeking permission to take an expedition to the site of the formation."

The Photos Explained

As might be expected excitement was generated, not only among the various groups attempting to launch expeditions to Mt. Ararat, but also among all those who so desperately wanted to see the Ark found. Within a matter of a few hours, however, cooler heads prevailed. Tom Henderson had been for several years closely connected with the work of the Institute for Creation Research, having participated along with Mike Turnage in excavation of the provocative and revealing fossil footprints in the Paluxy River basin near Glen Rose, Texas, showing beyond a doubt that man and dinosaur had lived together in the area as evidenced by literally thousands of their tracks in the same strata. The reader need not be told what havoc this find wreaks on the standard geologic timetable.* Henderson, in the course of his work at NASA, regularly studied the ERTS imagery. Because of his interest in the work of ICR he made it a point to check the photos of Ararat as they became available. The photos taken in July of 1973 were particularly cloud-free, and he had seen the formation referred to in the news release. He was without reservation in his opinion that it was not the Ark. His reasoning can best be summed up by quoting from various publications put out by the Department of the Interior on the specifications and capabilities of the

ERTS satellite and its pertinent type of image sensor, the Multi-Spectral Scanner (MSS).

The sensors on board the spacecraft transmit images to NASA receiving stations, and are converted from electronic signals to photographic negatives.

The MSS is a line-scanning device which uses an oscillating mirror to simultaneously scan the terrain passing beneath the spacecraft. The scanner produces four synchronous images, each at a different wave band.

The electronic signals are converted to 70 mm System Corrected Images. The image scale is approximately 1:3,369,000 and the swath width is approximately 100 nautical miles wide. Although the scanner data are acquired in a continuous swath, in the process of electronic signal to image conversion the images are divided into frames.[2]

The MSS sensor instantaneous field of view (IFOV) corresponds to 79 meters as measured on the ground. Resolution is limited to the IFOV dimension and refers to the ability of an observer to recognize adjacent fields of a certain width, (e.g., 80 meters). It is possible that the existence of boundaries between radiance fields as small as ½ IFOV can be sensed in certain scenes. However, this is not the same as recognizing the actual field dimension.

Once the data is digitized in the sensor, there will be no degradation to resolution until it reaches the D/A converter where it is reconverted to an analog video signal. From this point on, the various equipments in the photo processes all contribute some degradation to the resolution quality of the MSS data.

A human observer, hypothetically placed at the MSS output, could recognize adjacent fields of wheat and mildewed barley if they each exceeded 100 meters in width. If he were viewing a (photo) image, he could recognize the same fields if they exceeded 300 meters in width.[3]

Of course, several factors are involved. Mr. Edward Waltz, another NASA expert, comments in a recent article.

The ability of the Ark to be detected by the MSS is a function of several factors: 1) contrast of the Ark material against the background; 2) size of the Ark or exposed portions; 3) position of the Ark with respect to the direction of the satellite sensor scans. The Ark dimensions (approximately 135 x 25 meters from the top view) of Genesis 6:15 are at the very limits of the 50-90 meter ground resolution of ERTS. Under *optimal conditions* with the Ark *fully* exposed, it *could* appear as a *single* dark dot in the image.[4]

Obviously, the Ark has not been identified on the ERTS imagery, nor could it be specifically identified even if it were detected. There was some hope that the second ERTS satellite, which would have on board more sensitive gear, would provide better coverage. But even that was ruled out when the recording device on board the first ERTS broke down, and the second was hastily launched about one year early on January 22, 1975, to replace it, without the sensitive gear. ERTS (now re-named LANDSAT) does not plan another launch for several years.

Obtaining Better Photos

The fact that ERTS is incapable of sensing Noah's Ark in no way rules out the possibility of military photographs coming to the rescue. But the likelihood of identifying the existence of such photographs and obtaining them is open to question. Only through unofficial and "grapevine" sources can a private citizen learn of such top-quality data, since the government does not publish listings.

Over the course of time, however, the authors have learned of three distinct sets of military photographs taken of Mt. Ararat, two of which are reported to show the Ark, and the third, of even better quality than the others, having the potential. Great amounts of time are being devoted to effect their release.

Prior to the Watergate era, there existed no good way to approach the Department of Defense to see if such individual and non–security-risk photos, however classified, could be downgraded and obtained by the public. That is no longer the case. The current anti-establishment craze has provided a tool whereby progress along these lines is possible.

On February 19, 1975, the new Freedom of Information Act went into effect, with the stated purpose "to make available to the public the maximum amount of information concerning its (Dept. of Defense's) activities and operations."[5]

There are only three possible reasons for denial of a request: (1) that the record falls into a specific category of exemptions "and a significant and legitimate governmental purpose is served by withholding"; (2) "The record cannot be found because it has not been described with sufficient particularity to enable a responsible authority to locate it with a reasonable amount of effort"; (3) "The requester has unreasonably failed to comply with the procedural requirements imposed by the Act."[6]

Records include all books, papers, maps, photographs, or other documentary materials, regardless of physical form or characteristics, made or received by any agency of the United States under Federal Law.[7]

Any records that are vital to national security should not be released and the authors in no way wish to indicate that they should. They should receive the proper classification and be used solely for their intended purpose. It is our contention, however, that individual photographs

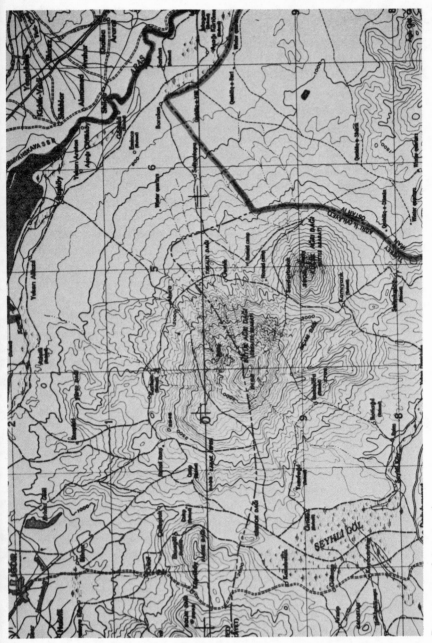

Recent map of Ararat region.

which contain no classified material, even though they were taken on a classified mission, could and should be downgraded upon request.

We must recognize another problem, that of our relationship with foreign powers, in this case Turkey. Again, Mr. Henderson:

Turkey has allowed the U.S.A. to photograph and map their country, but they don't want detailed geophysical information disseminated that might aid in the overthrow of their regime. As a result of this policy, for instance, only the 1:1,000,000 scale ONC maps of Turkey are available to the general public. The 1:500,000 scale T.P.C. maps have restricted distribution within the government. Larger scale maps are either classified or are othervise unavailable. (In my opinion, neither the 1:1,000,000 or the 1:500,000 scale topographic maps of Mt. Ararat would show enough contour detail to be very useful.)

In order to obtain Defense photographs of Mt. Ararat then, one must first gain approval of the U. S. government through the Freedom of Information Act and in addition obtain release from the Turkish Department of Interior and the military hierarchy whose power is centered in the Turkish General Staff, which is, to say the least, a mammoth task, but not an impossible one.

---

*Authors' Note: Readers wishing more information on this subject should contact ICR. Note is also made of an excellent documentary film on the find, released by Films for Christ, 1024 N. Elmwood, Peoria, Illinois 61606, entitled *Footprints in Stone*.

[1]ERTS Data Fact Sheet (1972), p. 1.
[2]ERTS Data Fact Sheet (1972), pp. 1-2.
[3]ERTS Specifications (1972, revised), pp. F-16 to F-19.
[4]Edward L. Waltz, "Space Age Ark-geology," *Bible and Spade* 3:4 (Autumn, 1974), p. 125. Emphasis ours.
[5]Department of Defense Directive No. 5400.7 (February 14, 1975), p. 2.
[6]Department of Defense Directive No. 5400.10 (February 11, 1975), pp. 4-5.
[7]Department of Defense Directive No. 5400.7, p.4.

28

Anti-Climax or Ante-Climax: 1974, 1975, 1976

When is it all going to end? Better yet, will it end? Will the long, drawn-out, but exciting search for the remains of Noah's Ark ever reach a conclusion? Or will the search continue, an endless procession of expeditions hoping year after year to procure permission from the Turkish government to explore Mt. Ararat?

The encouraging success in 1972, the glacial melt of 1973; worldwide interest due to the ERTS' photograph, as well as increased press coverage; the publication of several widely read books; and increased support from the general public indicated that the search was heading toward a climax, that a successful expedition was inevitable.

The Turkish Political Scene

Even the Turkish political scene appeared to be cooperating. Prime Minister Naim Talu had maintained his provisional role until after two events of national scope transpired in the fall of 1973. On October 14, Turkey held its regularly scheduled general elections, during which the holder of almost every elected office in Turkey was determined. The elections were held with only a minimal amount of disturbance, a surprise to everyone; but unfortunately no one party was able to gain a majority of seats in Parliament. Within two weeks, on October 29, Turkey celebrated the fiftieth anniversary of the formation of its Republic, again with only minor demonstrations.

As soon as the elections were over, Talu resigned, leaving Turkey without an effective government and forcing President Koutürk to choose a successor. Once again a coalition government was in order, since no party had enough support in Parliament to obtain a vote of confidence. The job of organizing such a coalition was undertaken by Bulent Ecevit, the leader of the Republican Peoples Party, which controlled over 45 percent of the seats and maintained a slightly left-of-center stance. Finally, early in 1974, an agreement was reached with a small extreme right-wing (radical Moslem) party called the National Salvation Party, whose few delegates provided a majority.

This strange amalgamation was marred from the start by fierce opposition without and dissension within. But as Ecevit began to take control, his position strengthened, and his popularity grew.

Ecevit and members of his cabinet (with the exception of the NSP members) have always maintained both personal and political ties with the West, and a somewhat favorable initial response was received by the various groups interested in exploring Mt. Ararat. In fact, a springtime trip to Ankara by John Morris resulted in approval of ICR plans for an expedition in July and August. Since the approval came immediately after his appearance in an interview on the NBC Today Show and the reported ERTS claims, the nation was primed for a discovery!

But alas, it was not to be. Ark enthusiasts were to be disappointed once again. Three situations of international importance forced the Turks to reconsider.

First, a thirteen-year-long civil war between the Kurdish nomads and the governments of Syria and Iraq increased in intensity early in 1974. The Kurds of Eastern Turkey (by far the largest single group of Kurds in the Middle East) did not participate in the war for an independent Kurdish state, but they did support it. Their growing unrest caused Turkish officials to wonder if a confrontation was on its way. Indeed, the fighting did spill over the southeastern border into Turkey for a time.

Mt. Ararat and the surrounding region is one of the areas almost completely populated by Kurds. Turkish military officials mobilized and reinforced their nearby troops just in case of trouble, and the entire area was placed under martial law and sealed off to all non-essential travelers.[1]

Second, in violation of a loose agreement between the U.S. and Turkey, Ecevit announced to Parliament that on July 2, 1974, the peasants of eastern Turkey could resume the growth of opium poppies, which had long been their main crop. In 1972, the U.S. had instituted a three-year program of economic aid to Turkey, to offset the loss of income to the growers and to replace their habits with a more acceptable one.

Inflation in Turkey was running wild and unemployment was high. By the thousands, the rural Turks were flocking to the cities to find work. In

Turkey's 1973 decision to resume the tradition of growing opium poppies resulted in an international uproar and the temporary severing of diplomatic relations with the U.S.

order to shore up this sagging economy, Ecevit decided to allow his people to grow opium poppies once again.

The decision obviously horrified American congressmen who cited figures showing that heroin addiction had dropped to one-third its 1972 figure. But the Turks have absolutely no drug problem of their own and regard the poppy situation as one of social and economic import only.[2]

Of course, economic aid to Turkey was immediately dropped. Even though Turkey implemented firm controls to see that the opium was to be used for legitimate uses only, America recalled its ambassador to Turkey, in effect severing diplomatic relations with its long-time NATO ally.

In 1974 when Turkey was forced to go to war by the overthrow of the government of Cyprus, fortifications around Mt. Ararat stiffened. Note Mt. Ararat in background.

Once again, such strained relations did not aid the efforts of American groups attempting to search for Noah's Ark.

The clincher came right on the heels of this opium problem. On July 15, 1974, the provisional government of Cyprus was overthrown by Cypriot insurrectionists sponsored by the illegal Greek military dictatorship. President Makarios was ejected and fled to Britain, supposedly the guarantor of the Cypriot State, who had pledged to maintain the sovereignty of the government and the rights of both Greeks and Turkish communities.

Greece and Turkey have been bitter enemies throughout the twentieth century and, since Cyprus is far from the Greek mainland and only a few miles off the southern coast of Turkey, the new self-proclaimed Cypriot military regime was unacceptable to Turkey. After waiting until July 20, long enough to see that Britain was not going to step in and correct the situation, Turkey invaded.

The Turkish community, comprising about one-fourth of the Cypriot population, had long been subjected to persecutions from the Greeks.

Such harassment had been a source of agitation to the mainland Turks who took this opportunity to vent their anger on the Greek Cypriots. Air raids and ground armor made short work of the Greek forces. When a hasty cease-fire was called on July 21, Turkey controlled significant parts of the island.

One of the positive peripheral effects of Turkey's action was that on July 23 the military dictatorship in Athens, which had suppressed democracy in Greece for seven years, resigned, and the government was returned to the civilians. On the same day, the Greek-supported military regime on Cyprus also withdrew.[3]

Within a matter of days, President Nixon was compelled to resign his own position, and the instability of international politics was acutely felt at the negotiation table between Greece, Britain, Cyprus, and Turkey. Bargaining broke down time and again and the fighting broke out repeatedly throughout mid-September. In the end, Turkey had captured approximately 40 percent of the island, and hundreds of thousands of refugees on both sides had been left homeless. In the fighting, Rodger P. Davis, U.S. Ambassador to Cyprus, was slain by Greeks.

It is not hard to figure out that the Cyprus conflict had an effect on the consideration of applications for permits by the various Ark groups. As a matter of fact, all such permits were either rescinded or refused. No outsider was given permission to enter the sensitive military reservation of Mt. Ararat.

Three Summer Expeditions

Unfortunately, three American groups chose to climb Ararat without official sanction. All were subject to extreme danger and none accomplished anything that furthered the search.

One of these groups is already familiar to the reader, that of the unique cult from Palestine, Texas, called the Holy Ground Mission Changing Center. They returned from Turkey in September, announcing to the world that they had not only been on Mt. Ararat, but had actually seen the Ark from a distance of 2,000 feet. They sported a picture which they claimed showed "the planking on the side."

Their story was not accepted by everyone. Those who are knowledgeable know that the Mission does not have a very good track record, that many of the statements made are open to serious doubt. They have consistently used the material of others, claiming it was their own, and drawn false conclusions from it. For example, the intriguing picture of the "unidentified object" taken by ARF expedition in 1966 has now appeared in many newspapers and personal lectures sponsored by the Mission and used as proof that they have found the Ark.

Their most recent picture is billed as a telephoto of the Ark taken from 2,000 feet. The photograph is far out of focus and shows a mountainous region and an unusual rock formation. However, very sharp and distinct lines appear on the picture running parallel along the formation. Any photographer knows that in a telephoto taken from 2,000 feet, if anything is in focus, everything is in focus. But in this picture, the only thing that does appear sharply is the only proof offered by the Mission to substantiate their claim of seeing "the planking on the side" of the Ark. The CIA has analyzed the picture and labeled it as a very amateurish example of a retouched photograph.

In short, the authors place absolutely no credence in their claim that the Ark has been found. There is even some question to their claim to have been on the mountain at all. It is reported that soon after arriving in Dogubeyazit, they were arrested and given three days to leave the country. Perhaps they returned secretly later.

The second group contained some new names and one old one. A Los Angeles based film company known as the National Association for Media Evangelism (NAME) recognized the value of Noah's Ark as an evangelistic tool. Desiring to make a movie of the search, they contracted with John Montgomery, who was to be responsible for the acquisition of permits and logistics for the expedition. The group ascended the mountain at night "because of political difficulties." They were only able to spend portions of two days at the "Navarra site" filming the glacier from which wood has reportedly been taken.[4]

The movie, which, as of this writing, has not yet been released, will be mainly used for television, sponsored by churches in each local area. The producer and photographers are experienced professionals, and the movie is expected to be top quality work.

Another Hollywood producer caught Ark fever in 1974 and journeyed to Ararat to make a movie, this time for theater release. Bart LaRue, of Jannus Hollywood, recognized the political problems before starting out and literally bribed his way up the mountain. He also climbed at night with the aid of Kurdish smugglers to avoid detection.

He spent only a short time at the Navarra site, but his movie, released nationwide in the spring of 1976, detailed the numerous problems involved in the search as well as much of the research and background.

Before his trip to Turkey, LaRue contracted with SEARCH, Inc., still "persona non grata" in Turkey, for all of their archival material. A great deal of film taken by the ARF expeditions in the 1960s and the SEARCH expedition in 1969 was used in the feature length film. A lengthy interview with Navarra and studies of some of the ancient traditions of the area included.

Even though the film is completely secular in origin and content, it does contain much useful information and is recommended for those interested in the subject.

Each of these groups flirted with possible arrest and even death as the Cyprus conflict unfolded. Most Turks felt that America has sided with the Greeks, and anti-American sentiment ran high. Indeed, Dr. Jim Davis, the ICR representative in Ankara attempting to resecure permission for the nine-man ICR team, recognizing that there was no chance for success and a very real chance of harm recommended that ICR await more favorable conditions.

Anti-Americanism Festers

But conditions did not improve with time. Quite the contrary, in fact. In October, 1974, Congress voted to cut off all military aid to Turkey. President Ford vetoed the bill, and the matter was delayed until December.

Meanwhile a serious split had occurred within Prime Minister Ecevit's coalition government. The right-wing faction refused to support Cyprus peace negotiations. But, since Ecevit had greatly increased in popularity due to his strong stand and decisive action during the Cyprus conflict, he felt confident that he could gain complete control of Parliament if a new general election were held. So he resigned his position and called for new elections.

The opposition parties effectively blocked efforts to hold elections, and as the matter dragged out, Ecevit's popularity dwindled. Finally, on April 12, 1975, Suleyman Demirel, the Prime Minister from 1965 to 1971, was returned to power as head of a curious four-party conservative coalition. His narrow victory touched off a brawl on the floor of the National Assembly. Ecevit, the single most influential man in Turkish politics, remained on the outside.

Another old problem cropped up again. The Kurdish civil war in Iraq and Syria finally came to a close when Iran signed a pact with Iraq agreeing to stop supplying arms to the rebelling Kurds. On April 1, 1975, the war was over and hundreds of thousands of Kurds fled for their lives in front of the advancing armies. They were offered partial sanctuary in Iran; but their leaders pleaded with Turkey to allow them to settle in the eastern provinces, already predominantly Kurdish. Turkey refused, wary of a civil war withn its own boundaries.[5]

Many Kurdish refugees did cross over into Turkey, however. The gravity of the situation was displayed when Turkey mobilized its armaments there.

The Ararat area was most unsafe. Ararat had always been a haven for Kurdish renegades, and the addition of so many homeless, desperate, and armed refugees made the situation extremely volatile.

At about the same time, scattered Armenians requested the United Nations to institute a "Day of Remembrance" for the great numbers who lost their lives in the bloody aftermath of World War I in eastern Turkey. They desired to create worldwide anti-Turkish propaganda. The Turks are not proud of the actions in question, but they realize that no war is ever pretty and conquered nations will never be satisfied with the results. Furthermore, absolutely no good can come of rehashing the occurrences of two generations ago.

Once again, calling attention to the Ararat area would favor both the Armenian and Kurdish causes, something which the Turks are reluctant to do.

If the internal situation and negative propaganda were not enough, Turkish-American relations were on a downswing. On Feburary 5 a December Congressional vote went into effect, cutting off all military aid to Turkey as a punishment for having used American supplied NATO weaponry during the Cyprus invasion and imposing an arms embargo. Turkish officials expected and in some cases welcomed the stoppage of American aid but were not prepared for the rest of the decision. In commenting on the shutdown, a State Department spokesman woefully admitted to the Associated Press in Washington on February 5, 1975 that

U. S. government agencies have been informed to cut off all sales of defense items and services to Turkey, as well as all credits to finance such transactions.

No licenses will be issued by the government for the transportation of arms, ammunition, and implements of war, including technical assistance, and any equipment now en route to Turkey will be stopped and diverted elsewhere.

All in all, Turkey had previously bought and paid for $185 million worth of equipment that was not to be shipped. Spare and replacement parts could not be purchased. Furthermore, any equipment, such as airplane engines, that had been shipped to the States for repair was confiscated. It was obvious that in the face of such unwarranted action Turkey was not going to back down and issued an ultimatum for the lifting of the embargo or withdrawal of American troops from Turkey.

Congress toyed with the idea of lifting the embargo. President Ford lobbied long and hard for reinstating normal relations with the most powerful country in all of eastern Europe and our long-time NATO ally, recognizing that Turkey comprised the front line of resistance of the free world in case of a Communist attack.

Unfortunately, it seems that ethnic politics influenced the Congressional decision. Greek and Armenian Americans coerced the House to reject efforts to lift the embargo. All indicators show that an emotional and organized lobby used this method to strike back at the Turks. One wonders just what power these wealthy minorities have over this country's legislative process.

The lobby worked. On July 25, the House refused to lift the ban, defying all logic. And, sure enough, on the very next day Turkish troops began taking over American-manned NATO bases in Turkey. Included on these bases were some very sophisticated weaponry, intelligence equipment, and even nuclear warheads. The Greek lobbyists did a double take when they realized that they were responsible for turning their archenemy into a nuclear super power overnight.

It should be noted that while the breach between the U.S. and Turkey was widening, Greece and Turkey were making progress toward a peace settlement on Cyprus on their own, while Greece was likewise kicking the American Naval bases out of the country. American diplomacy had, against all odds, succeeded in alienating both sides.

Ecevit, the out-of-power politician, was using these circumstances to his own benefit by indirectly encouraging anti-American riots throughout the country. Demeril was forced to maintain a hard stance also to appease the people.

In October, 1975, Congress made provisions to lift the arms embargo, finally realizing that Turkey was not playing games. But even if the U.S. were to bend over backwards to try to reinstate friendly terms with Turkey, irreparable damage has been done. The Turks feel that they could never fully trust America again. In their eyes they are being punished for merely reacting to a Greek violation of the treaty on Cypress. And while their military strength was being sapped by America, the Greeks were being given large amounts of armaments. Turkey has vowed never again to be in such a position of total reliance upon America.

Will It End?

Where will it end? Who knows? We do know that such turmoil has effectively clamped a lid on any search for the Ark. In fact, in May, 1975, when John Morris journeyed to Turkey to encourage sanction of the proposed ICR expedition, he met with a firm anti-American policy. The officially unsanctioned expeditions of the previous year did not help, and several time authorities questioned him about any connection with them.

Each expedition met the same fate. Once again, the Holy Ground Mission was asked to leave the country but vowed to return to the mountain anyway. A filming crew which had accompanied them to document their "finds" abandoned them once they realized the hopelessness of the situation. The Trans-World group held out hope until the very end of the summer, but the permits never came through.

Meanwhile, Bart LaRue released his feature length film *The Ark of Noah*, in selected areas. The basic theme of the film is anti-Turkish. He

Mt. Ararat, in a military zone, is heavily fortified and guarded. Access to the mountain is restricted.

challenges Turkey to re-evaluate its position on the search for the Ark, to recognize the worldwide importance of the relocation, and to allow the explorations to continue, with a full-fledged scientific expedition manned by qualified personnel and stocked with proper equipment.

On a positive note, Sun Classic Pictures, Inc., a major film company, released a family oriented film entitled *In Search of Noah's Ark*[6], in the spring of 1976. This film, which for the first time will bring the news of the search and research to everyone, dramatizes many of the sightings, interviews many of those involved, and presents the whole issue from a proper perspective. It remains to be seen what effect the film will have on the potential for further exploration, but it will no doubt heighten interest nationwide.

Humanly speaking, it seems that the search for the Ark has come to a standstill. This chapter, while dealing with the international political situation, graphically depicts the obstacles confronting future exploration efforts.

The one ray of hope, under present conditions, is for the Turks themselves to take an active interest. Needless to say, their tourism industry has taken a nose dive. Such a find would not only be a grand attraction, but the discovery of the Ark would shift world opinion, and Turkey could regain some of its lost popularity.

Such interest among the Turks is not out of the realm of possibility. In May, John Morris spent many hours in consultation with influential Turks, who began to see the importance of the Ark's relocation and documentation. All of the ICR research material was bared and discussed, and the most likely locations were displayed.

Even in the face of such overwhelming odds, it is refreshing to note that we do not need to rely solely on our human resources. If God is in the project, and we are confident that He is, we can expect Him to bless. As will be discussed in a later chapter, we have reason to expect Him to intervene soon.

---

[1]See "Kurds in Combat," *TIME* (April, 1974), p. 41.

[2]See L. Edgar Prina, "Turkey Lifts Opium Poppy Ban," *Copley News Service* (July 21, 1974), and "Opium's Lethal Return," *TIME* (July, 1974).

[3]See *Crisis on Cyprus 1974* (Washington: U.S. Government, Oct. 14, 1974).

[4]John Montgomery, *The Quest for Noah's Ark*, revised (Minneapolis: Bethany Fellowship, 1974), pp. 318-20.

[5]See "Barzani Declares Kurds Will Never Resume War in Iraq," Associated Press, Tehran, Iran, May 4, 1975.

[6]Dave Balsiger and Charles E. Selliger, Jr., *In Search of Noah's Ark* (Los Angeles, Sun Classic Books, 1976).

29

Biblical Narrative

And it came to pass, when men began to multiply on the face of the earth, and daughters were born unto them, that the sons of God saw the daughters of men that they were fair; and they took them wives of all which they chose. And the Lord said, My spirit shall not always strive with man, for that he also is flesh: yet his days shall be an hundred and twenty years. There were giants in the earth in those days; and also after that, when the sons of God came in unto the daughters of men, and they bare children to them, the same became mighty men which were of old, men of renown.

And God saw that the wickedness of man was great in the earth, and that every imagination of the thoughts of his heart was only evil continually. And it repented the Lord that He had made man on the earth, and it grieved Him at His heart. And the Lord said, I will destroy man whom I have created from the face of the earth; both man, and beast, and the creeping thing, and the fowls of the air; for it repenteth me that I have made them. But Noah found grace in the eyes of the Lord.

These are the generations of Noah: Noah was a just man and perfect in his generations, and Noah walked with God. And Noah begat three sons, Shem, Ham, and Japheth. The earth also was corrupt before God, and the earth was filled with violence. And God looked upon the earth, and, behold, it was corrupt; for all flesh had corrupted his way upon the earth. And God said unto Noah, The end of all flesh is come before me; for the earth is filled with violence through them; and, behold, I will destroy them with the earth.

Make thee an ark of gopher wood; rooms shalt thou make in the ark, and shalt pitch it within and without with pitch. And this is the fashion which thou shalt make it of: the length of the ark shall be three hundred cubits, the breadth of it fifty cubits, and the height of it thirty cubits. A window shalt thou make to the ark, and in a cubit shalt thou finish it above; and the door of the ark shalt thou set in the side thereof; with lower, second, and third stories shalt thou make it. And, behold, I, even I, do bring a flood of waters upon the earth, to destroy all flesh, wherein is the breath of life, from under heaven; and every thing that is in the earth shall die. But with thee will I establish my covenant; and thou shalt come into the ark, thou, and thy sons, and thy wife, and thy sons' wives with thee. And of every living

TAB. XXXV.

GENESIS Cap. VI. v. 14.
Arca ex Gopher.

I. Buch Mosis Cap. VI. v. 14.
Die Arch gebauet aus dem Holtz Gopher.

thing of all flesh, two of every sort shalt thou bring into the ark, to keep them alive with thee; they shall be male and female. Of fowls after their kind, and of cattle after their kind, of every creeping thing of the earth after his kind, two of every sort shall come unto thee, to keep them alive. And take thou unto thee of all food that is eaten, and thou shalt gather it to thee; and it shall be for food for thee, and for them. Thus did Noah; according to all that God commanded him, so did he.

And the Lord said unto Noah, Come thou and all thy house into the ark; for thee have I seen righteous before me in this generation. Of every clean beast thou shalt take to thee by sevens, the male and his female: and of beasts that are not clean by two; the male and his female. Of fowls also of the air by sevens, the male and the female; to keep seed alive upon the face of all the earth. For yet seven days, and I will cause it to rain upon the earth forty days and forty nights; and every living substance that I have made will I destroy from off the face of the earth. And Noah did according unto all that the Lord commanded him. And Noah was six hundred years old when the flood of waters was upon the earth.

And Noah went in, and his sons, and his wife, and his sons' wives with him, into the ark, because of the waters of the flood. Of clean beasts, and of beasts that are not clean, and of fowls, and of every thing that creepeth upon the earth, there went in two and two unto Noah into the ark, the male and the female, as God had commanded Noah. And it came to pass after seven days, that the waters of the flood were upon the earth.

In the six hundredth year of Noah's life, in the second month, the seventeenth day of the month, the same day were all the fountains of the great deep broken up, and the windows of heaven were opened. And the rain was upon the earth forty days and forty nights. In the selfsame day entered Noah, and Shem, and Ham, and Japheth, the sons of Noah, and Noah's wife, and the three wives of his sons with them, into the ark; they, and every beast after his kind, and all the cattle after their kind, and every creeping thing that creepeth upon the earth after his kind, and every fowl after his kind, every bird of every sort.

And they went in unto Noah into the ark, two and two of all flesh, wherein is the breath of life. And they that went in, went in male and female of all flesh, as God had commanded him and the Lord shut him in. And the flood was forty days upon the earth; and the waters increased, and bare up the ark, and it was lift up above the earth. And the waters prevailed, and were increased greatly upon the earth; and the ark went upon the face of the waters. And the waters prevailed exceedingly upon the earth; and all the high hills, that were under the whole heaven, were covered. Fifteen cubits upward did the waters prevail; and the mountains were covered. And all flesh died that moved upon the earth, both of fowl, and of cattle, and of beast, and of every creeping thing that creepeth upon the earth, and every man: all in whose nostrils was the breath of life, of all that was in the dry land, died. And every living substance was destroyed which was upon the face of the ground, both man, and cattle, and the creeping things, and the fowl of the heaven; and they were destroyed from the earth: and Noah only remained alive,

TAB. XLII.

GENESIS Cap. VII. v. 7. 8. 9.

Animantium in Arcam introitus.

1 Buch Mosis Cap. VII. v. 7. 8. 9.

Eingang der Thiere in die Arch.

and they that were with him in the ark. And the waters prevailed upon the earth an hundred and fifty days.

And God remembered Noah, and every living thing, and all the cattle that was with him in the ark: and God made a wind to pass over the earth, and the waters assuaged; the fountains also of the deep and the windows of heaven were stopped, and the rain from heaven was restrained; and the waters returned from off the earth continually: and after the end of the hundred and fifty days the waters were abated.

And the ark rested in the seventh month, on the seventeenth day of the month, upon the mountains of Ararat. And the waters decreased continually until the tenth month: in the tenth month, on the first day of the month, were the tops of the mountains seen.

And it came to pass at the end of forty days, that Noah opened the window of the ark which he had made: and he sent forth a raven, which went forth to and fro, until the waters were dried up from off the earth. Also he sent forth a dove from him, to see if the waters were abated from off the face of the ground; but the dove found no rest for the sole of her foot, and she returned unto him into the ark, for the waters were on the face of the whole earth: then he put forth his hand, and took her, and pulled her in unto him into the ark. And he stayed yet another seven days; and again he sent forth the dove out of the ark; and the dove came in to him in the evening; and, lo, in her mouth was an olive leaf pluckt off: so Noah knew that the waters were abated from off the earth. And he stayed yet other seven days; and sent forth the dove; which returned not again unto him any more.

And it came to pass that in the six hundredth and first year, in the first month, the first day of the month, the waters were dried up from off the earth: and Noah removed the covering of the ark, and looked, and, behold, the face of the ground was dry. And in the second month, on the seven and twentieth day of the month, was the earth dried.

And God spake unto Noah, saying, Go forth of the ark, thou, and thy wife, and thy sons, and thy son's wives with thee. Bring forth with thee every living thing that is with thee, of all flesh, both of fowl, and of cattle, and of every creeping thing that creepeth upon the earth; that they may breed abundantly in the earth, and be fruitful, and multiply upon the earth. And Noah went forth, and his sons, and his wife, and his sons' wives with him: every beast, every creeping thing, and every fowl, and whatsoever creepeth upon the earth, after their kinds, went forth out of the ark.

And Noah builded an altar unto the Lord; and took of every clean beast, and of every clean fowl, and offered burnt offerings on the altar. And the Lord smelled a sweet savour; and the Lord said in His heart, I will not again curse the ground any more for man's sake; for the imagination of man's heart is evil from his youth; neither will I again smite any more every thing living, as I have done. While the

TAB. LXIII.

GENESIS Cap. VIII. v. 10. 11.

Folium Olivarum.

I Buch Mosis Cap. VIII. v. 10. 11.

Das mitgebrachte Oelblatt.

earth remaineth, seed time and harvest, and cold and heat, and summer and winter, and day and night shall not cease.

And God blessed Noah and his sons, and said unto them, Be fruitful, and multiply, and replenish the earth. And the fear of you and the dread of you shall be upon every beast of the earth, and upon every fowl of the air, upon all that moveth upon the earth, and upon all the fishes of the sea; into your hand are they delivered. Every moving thing that liveth shall be meat for you; even as the green herb have I given you all things. But flesh with the life thereof, which is the blood thereof, shall ye not eat. And surely your blood of your lives will I require; at the hand of every beast will I require it, and at the hand of man; at the hand of every man's brother will I require the life of man. Whoso sheddeth man's blood, by man shall his blood be shed: for in the image of God made He man. And you, be ye fruitful, and multiply; bring forth abundantly in the earth, and multiply therein.

And God spake unto Noah, and to his sons with him, saying, and I, behold, I establish my covenant with you, and with your seed after you; and with every living creature that is with you, of the fowl, of the cattle, and of every beast of the earth with you; from all that go out of the ark, to every beast of the earth. And I will establish my covenant with you; neither shall all flesh be cut off any more by the waters of a flood; neither shall there any more be a flood to destroy the earth. And God said, this is the token of the covenant which I make between me and you and every living creature that is with you, for perpetual generations: I do set my bow in the cloud, and it shall be for a token of a covenant between me and the earth. And it shall come to pass, when I bring a cloud over the earth, that the bow shall be seen in the cloud: And I will remember My covenant, which is between Me and you and every living creature of all flesh; and the waters shall no more become a flood to destroy all flesh. And the bow shall be in the cloud; and I will look upon it, that I may remember the everlasting covenant between God and every living creature of all flesh that is upon the earth. And God said unto Noah, this is the token of the covenant, which I have established between Me and all flesh that is upon the earth.

And the sons of Noah, that went forth of the ark, were Shem, and Ham, and Japheth: and Ham is the father of Canaan. These are the three sons of Noah: and of them was the whole earth overspread.

And the whole earth was of one language, and of one speech. And it came to pass, as they journeyed from the east, that they found a plain in the land of Shinar; and they dwelt there. And they said one to another, go to, let us make brick, and burn them throughly. And they had brick for stone, and slime had they for mortar. And they said, go to, let us build us a city and a tower, whose top may reach unto heaven; and let us make us a name, lest we be scattered abroad upon the face of the whole earth. And the Lord came down to see the city and the tower, which the children of men builded. And the Lord said, behold the people is one, and they have all one language; and this they begin to do: and now nothing will be restrained from them, which they have imagined to do. Go to, let us go down, and

TAB. LXV.

Signum Iridis.

Der Regen-bogen ein Gnaden Zeichen.

GENESIS Cap. XI. v. 4.
Scenographia Turris.

1. Buch Mosis Cap. XI. v. 4.
Der Perspectivische Riß des Thurns.

there confound their language, that they may not understand one another's speech. So the Lord scattered them abroad from thence upon the face of all the earth: and they left off to build the city. Therefore is the name of it called Babel; because the Lord did there confound the language of all the earth: and from thence did the Lord scatter them abroad upon the face of all the earth.

Genesis 6:1—9:19; 11:1-9.

NOTE: The series of engravings appearing in this chapter appear anonymously in an old Bible dated 1707 in the possession of Dr. Arnold Ehlert. For details, see *The Bible Collector*, No. 30 (April-June 1972).

30

Universal Flood Traditions

Hey you women! Down by the river! You better shut up! Stop making so much noise! You're gonna make the lizards mad! There's gonna be another flood if you don't watch out!

Such a sexist outburst is somewhat common in the dense rain forest of Western District, Papua New Guinea. The siesta-loving Samo-Kubo tribesmen are quite certain that, if you make the lizards mad, they will cause another flood in which everyone will perish.

It seems, that many many years ago, back in the dawn of time, someone made the lizards mad. They first made a lot of noise, then teased them until they couldn't stand it any longer, finally incurring the wrath of the Lizard Man. It began to rain. The rain poured down for days. The water began to rise, and still the rain came. Finally, all the people climbed up the highest mountain they could find. But still the waters crept up.

People everywhere were drowning. It looked like the whole world was coming to an end. Finally, two brothers built a raft. It was only a small raft. They climbed aboard. Soon, all the others tried to climb on, but the raft only held two. They sailed off, and left the others behind.

The brother concept among the Samo-Kubo is strong. The most meaningful relationship a man can have is with his brother. Even in this piece of folklore it stands out. It does not seem to occur to the tribe that the repopulation of the earth by two brothers is biologically impossible.

The significant thing, however, is that a hitherto unknown tribe, deep in an almost impenetrable jungle with almost no contact with the outside world, has in its traditions a story remarkably similar in many ways to the story of Noah's Flood that we find in the Bible. True, many local embellishments have been added, as would be expected, but the essence of the story remains.

Flood traditions such as this one have been found to exist all over the world, on every continent, in nearly every culture. Surprisingly, just as in the Samo-Kubo legend, they have retained their integrity to the extent that they are recognizable as forming a piece of evidence, the total compilation of which overwhelmingly supports a worldwide flood. The great majority of all these flood traditions speaks of the same events and circumstances that are so clearly related in the Bible. They speak of a worldwide flood brought on by the wickedness of man in which members of a favored family were forewarned and escaped in a boat which, in many cases, carried animals and eventually grounded on a high mountain.

The heretofore unpublished Samo-Kubo story was related just a few years ago to Dr. Dan Shaw, cultural anthropologist, linguist, and Wycliffe Bible translator. The tribe is so remote, chance of outside contact negligible, and the story so interwoven with the very cultural essence of the tribe that there seems to be absolutely no chance of contamination from outside sources.

Consider its similarities to the biblical story. Due to the wickedness of man (noise, etc.), the gods (the Lizard Man) caused a worldwide flood, in which everyone perished except for members of a favored family, in this case, two brothers on a wooden vessel. Once again, animals played an important part, as did a mountain, although their roles were somewhat different than in the biblical account. From these survivors, then, the present-day world population has descended.

More Flood Traditions

A great many scholarly works have been published, compiling and discussing these various traditions, over 200 of them! They will not be related here, although they are listed and analyzed in some detail. In each story, an endeavor was made by the authors to compare similarities and differences and to establish relationships and patterns. For instance, it can be easily shown that these traditions springing from ancient cultures in the Mesopotamian area bear close resemblance to the Hebrew account in detail but not necessarily in clarity of thought. The Babylonian, Sumerian, and Chaldean accounts weave highly mystical animalistic and polytheistic tales, which under no circumstances can be understood in their literal sense, but do remarkably parallel the Genesis account in detail. It almost goes without saying that the beautiful story handed down, likely in written form, from Noah through the patriarchal line, finally to be incorporated into the book of Genesis by Moses, stands in a class by itself when compared with other versions for meaningful transmission of information. If the universal law of cause and effect has any meaning at all—that is, that the effect cannot be greater than its cause—then there can be no doubt that the less accomplished writings and tales of secular historians are merely corruptions of the original and meaningful Genesis history.

Furthermore, as a general rule, it is noted that the farther from the Hebrew influence a culture has migrated, the more likely their tradition or memory of the Flood will vary from the original.

One thing is sure. Peoples all over the globe "remember" the Flood. Not because they experienced it, but because every man alive is indeed a direct descendant of Noah himself! If the Flood is actually a historical event, and if it was a global catastrophe, as almost all the traditions claim it to be, then no one could have survived without the Providential protection of the Ark. All men consequently descended from the survivors on board Noah's Ark. As they migrated in family groups from the Ararat area and later from Babel, they carried with them not only the story of destruction of the world by water, due to the wickedness of man, but of God's grace and method of salvation for the righteous—that of a huge boat which landed on a mountain top. In their travels, the story changed and was adapted to their adopted culture, but the essence remained the same.

The following list of cultures containing flood traditions, grouped by general global areas, can be considered fairly complete, except in the Middle East itself, where many cuneiform fragments of tales of a flood have recently been unearthed. These are most likely variations of the major ones that are listed here.

Table I. A list of Flood Traditions, grouped by global distribution in continents or area.

Middle East and Africa

Africa (Central)	Jumala Tribe
Babylon	Lower Congo
Bapedi Tribe (S. Africa)	Masai Tribe
Chaldea	Otshi Tribe (Kabinda)
Egypt (Pharaoic)	Persia (Ahriman)
Egypt (Priestly)	Persia (Bundehesch)
Hottentots	Persia (Testrya)

Middle East and Africa (Cont'd.)

Persia (Yima)
Persia (Zala-Cupha)
Syria

Pacific Islands

Alamblack Tribe (New Guinea)
Alfoors of Ceram
Ami
Andaman Islands
Australia
Bunva
Dutch New Guinea
 (Mombrano River)
East Indian Island
Engano
Falwol Tribe (New Guinea)
Fiji
Fiji (Rokora)
Flores Island
Formosa Tribesmen
Hawaii (Mauna-Ka) Tribesmen
Hawaii (Nu-U)
Kabidi Tribe (New Guinea)
Kurnai Tribe (Australia)
Leeward Islands

Maoris (New Zealand)
Melanesia
Micronesia
Nais
New Britain
Otheite Island
Ot-Danoms
Polynesia
Queensland
Rotti Tribe
Samoa
Samo-Kubo Tribe (New Guinea)
Sea Dyaks (Borneo)
Sea Dyaks (Trout)
Sea Kyaks (Sarawak)
Sumatra
Tahiti
Toradjas
Valman Tribe (New Guinea)

Far East

Anals (Assam)
Bahnara (China)
Bengal Kolhs
Benua-Jakun (Malasia)
Bhagavata—Purana
China (Fo-hi)
China (Joa)
China (Tao-tse)
Cingpaws (Upper Burma)
India (Rama)
Kamars (C. India)

Kamchadales (India)
Karens (Burma)
Lolos (S. China)
Mahabharata
Matsya—Purana
Menangkabans (Sumatra)
Satapatha Brahmana
Singphos (Burma)
Sudan
Tartary Mongols

Europe & Asia

Celts
Druids
Finland
Iceland
Kelts
Lapland
Lithuania

Norway
Rumania
Russia
Siberia
Transylvania
Wales

Hellenic

Apamea (Cibotos)
Apollodorus
Aristotle
Athenian
Cos (Merops)
Crete
Diodorus
Hellenucus
Lucian
Megaros
Ogyges (Boeotia)

Ovid
Perirrhoos
Pindar
Plato
Plutarch
Rhodes
Samothrace
Sithnide Nymphs
Stephanus
Thessalonica

North America

Acagchemens
Aleutian Island Indians
Algonquins (Manabozho)
Appalachian Indians
Araphos
Arctic Eskimos
Athapascans
Blackfoot Indians
Caddoques
Central Eskimos
Cherokees
Chippewas
Crees
Delaware Algonquins
Dogribs
Eleuts
Eskimos (Alaska)
Eskimos (Norton Sound)

Esquimax
Flatheads
Greenland
Great Lakes Indians
Haidas
Hareskins
Huron Indians
Innuit Eskimos
Iroquois
Kathlamets
Knistineaux
Kolosh
Koloshes
Lake Tahoe Indians
Lenni Lenape Indians
Luisenos
Mandans
Mantagnais Algonquins

North America (Cont'd.)

Menominees
Montagnais
Natchez Indians
New California Indians
Nez Perces
Ojibway
Pacullies
Papagos
Pimas
Potawatomi Indians
Rio Erevato Indians

Salteaux Algonquins
Sarcees
Smith River Indians
Spokanas
Thlinkuts
Thlinkuts (Yehl)
Thompsan Indians
Tinneh Indians
Twangs
Virginia Indians
Yakimas

Central America

Achagnas
Antilles
Aztecs
Aztecs (Coxcoxtli)
Canaris
Cholulans
Cholulas
Coras (Highland)
Coras (Lowland)
Cuban Indians
Huichals

Mayas
Mexico (Coxcox)
Mexico (Mexitli)
Michoacans
Muratos
Nicaragua Indians
Panama Indians
Rio-Crevato Indians
St. Domingo Indians
Tlascalans
Toltecs

South America

Abederys
Ackawois
Araucanians
Arawaks
Brazilian Mountain
   Indians
Brazilian Sea Coast
   Indians
Caingangs
Carayas
Chiriguanos
Colombian Indians
Incas

Kataushys
Macusis
Maypures
Orinoco Indians
Pamarys
Peru (Bomara)
Peru (Guancas)
Peruvian Indians
Peru (Manco Capak)
Rio de Janeiro Indians
Tamanacs
Terra-Firma Indians
Tierra del Fuego Indians

In each of the traditions, an effort was made to answer a set of nineteen questions. Of course, in some instances, sufficient data were not available to answer each. However, the percentages of positive answers out of the total answers to each question are tabulated and discussed. In questions 1-8, the choice had to be made between questions 1 and 2, 3 and 4, 5 and 6, and 7 and 8.[1]

1. Is there a favored family?   88%
2. Is there a remnant?   12%
3. Is survival due to a boat?   70%
4. Is survival due to other means?   30%
5. Is catastrophe only a flood?   95%
6. Is flood connected with other events?   5%
7. Is flood due to wickedness of man?   66%
8. Is flood due to natural causes?   34%
9. Were animals also saved?   67%
10. Did animals play any part?   73%
11. Was flood universal?   95%
12. Did the survivors eventually end up on a mountain?   57%
13. Were birds sent out?   35%
14. Was the rainbow mentioned?   7%
15. Did survivors sacrifice, etc., afterwards?   13%
16. Were the favored ones or remnant forewarned?   66%
17. Was the geography local? (Local mountain?)   82%
18. Were specifically eight persons saved?   9%
19. Were there incidental circumstances?   37%

The remarkable similarity of all these traditions is evident. And even their differences appear in a predictable pattern, predictable, that is, if you assume that all are descendants of Noah and migrated from the Ararat area after the Flood. As might be suspected local geography is usually specified when any is mentioned. The tribes "relocated" their landing place to the nearest high mountain in most cases, making the personal impact of the story greater. The farther from the Mesopotamian area a tribe had migrated, the more incidental circumstances crept into the story, and the story in many cases took the viewpoint of an outside observer as opposed to Noah's seemingly confined observations. In fact, the reference in the Bible to "the mountains of Ararat" is in itself important. The Israelites had no personal knowledge of the land to the north of Palestine before Moses' death. The reference to a specific mountain far from their land is quite unique. Some of the legends mention a faraway mountain, but never a specific one. Anthropologists feel that this testifies to the accuracy of the biblical account.

Animals consistently played a part. In many tales, birds or other animals were used directly to gauge or alter the recession of the flood waters during the latter stages. Frequently, animals were included in the Ark or were used to forewarn the survivors. In almost every case when a favored family of righteous ones was saved, they were forewarned. This would not necessarily be so if the traditions were unrelated, but the fact that there is a correlation parallels the biblical account.

In a few of the stories the striking and precise a counts of the appearance of the rainbow as a token after the flood, the sacrifice of thankfulness, and the specific mention of the salvation of an eight-member family all appear. These details cannot be coincidental. They must stem from a common source. One would expect many traditions to incorporate the landing place of a mountain into their story, because in time of a severe flood, local or otherwise, a mountaintop or a boat provides the most likely solution. But these other minute details are not what would be expected if the stories came from unrelated sources or events.

Critics of the global Flood theory have always been quick to claim that many of these Flood traditions actually come from contact with missionaries, reaching into out-of-the-way places spreading the Christian faith. And, to be sure, one case of this has been documented in an Indian tribe of North America. But the use of that excuse generally must be rejected by a logical mind on several accounts. First, most of the traditions were gathered by those whose interests were purely anthropological, those whose motives did not include vindicating the Christian Bible, and any suspicion would be noted. In fact, many of the ancient written accounts were penned by pagans who were very much in opposition to everything the Hebrews held dear.

Second, missionaries who dedicate their lives to spreading Christianity usually spend their time imparting the spiritual truths of the Gospel, not of Jewish history. If they felt a desire to relate the miraculous events of the past, we should find similar traditions of the miracles concerning Jonah and the whale, the crossing of the Red Sea, the plagues of Egypt, destruction of Sodom and Gomorrah and others, equally worthy of incorporation into the body of folklore of a culture. But we find no such thing. We do find many, many traditions of the creation of the world, the fall of man into sin, and the Tower of Babel and confusion of tongues, but this is understandable. It was after these events that the nations began to disperse.

Third, if missionaries are responsible for the similarities in the stories, what or who is responsible for the differences? Most of the stories tell of the gods' disfavor with man. But the means of expressing such disfavor vary so widely that it cannot have come from a recent source wishing to convey meaningful truth. For instance, incurring the wrath of the almighty Lizard Man by irritating the river lizards corresponds to the Genesis account in concept, but such details could not have been passed along in recent times by anyone knowledgeable of the biblical story.

The conclusion must stand. The universal Flood traditions can only have come from a common source, embellished with local color and culture, but retaining enough pertinent data to convey both historical and moral concepts.

Dispersion after the Flood

The fact that traditions of the pre-Flood world and the Tower of Babel also survive is in itself significant. We will not take this opportunity to analyze them. But, again, details appear which seem to stem from a common origin. The original perfect state, long age spans, eating of forbidden fruit, conflict with the serpent, a resulting evil society, and God's eventual judgment are all elements of these traditions. After the Flood, we see another wicked society springing up, construction of a tower, confusion of languages, turmoil, and migration.

It should be noted at this point that Mt. Ararat occupies a very unique position on the face of the earth. By consulting the map of the world it becomes evident that migration from the Ararat area to any land on earth is uninhibited and can be accomplished with a minimum of difficulty. The usual natural barriers, mountain ranges, deserts, or oceans are absent. Migration in any direction could occur easily.

Furthermore, a recent computer study by Andrew Woods, representing the Institute for Creation Research, has shown that the center of the earth's geographical land mass (i.e., that the unit area on the earth's surface from which the average distance to every other unit area is the least) is at Ankara, Turkey, the capital of the country, only 600 miles from Mt. Ararat.[2]

Mt. Ararat is uniquely suited as a starting place from which to replenish the earth.

Another interesting feature of Mt. Ararat is that the snow on its peak melts and runs down into a system of shallow rivers and underground streams which eventually form the headwaters of the Euphrates River. A well-known anthropological tendency has been noted. Migrations of nations generally follow the flow of a river, all other factors being equal. One would expect the major portion of the descendants of Noah to migrate down the Euphrates River. And that is exactly the case. Approximately 700 miles south of Ararat, in the once rich Tigris-Euphrates Valley, otherwise known as the Fertile Crescent, lie the remains of the ancient city of Babel. Archaeologists are uncertain, but most agree that the remains of the infamous Tower of Babel can still be seen in that desolate region.

Evidently, not everyone was present in Babel to participate in the awful rebellion and insolence that resulted in the building of the tower. In all likelihood, Noah, who lived 350 years after the Flood, was not there. Neither was Shem, to whom Noah imparted his spiritual integrity and from whom eventually would come Abraham and the chosen nation of Israel. Probably some of the descendants of Japheth had already begun to wander north into Asia and Europe.

Most of the populations of the world banded together in rebellion against God and built the tower in direct disobedience to God. God had given Noah and his family the command in Genesis 9:1 to "Be fruitful, and multiply, and replenish the earth." But only a few generations later, under the direction of the wicked Nimrod, most of the earth's inhabitants decided:

Let us build us a city and a tower, whose top may reach up into heaven; and let us make us a name, lest we be scattered abroad upon the face of the earth (Gen. 11:4).

Recognizing that man would never of his own accord migrate to the far corners of the globe, God came to earth and confounded the languages of the families and tribes, thus forcing them to abandon this project and wander off to be only with those with whom they could communicate (Gen. 11:5-9). The masterful and precise "Table of Nations" in Genesis 10 traces their migrations.

Once again, migrations from the area around Babel could have occurred with little difficulty, particularly to the Far East, the Middle East, and Africa. Could it be a coincidence that Noah's Ark landed so near the center of the earth's geographical land mass and in the ideal spot from which migration could occur with the greatest ease?

Additional References

Andree, Richard. *Die Flutsagen Ethnographisch Hetrachtet*. Germany: Viehweg und Sohn, 1891.

Baring-Gould, S. *Legends of the Patriarchs and Prophets*. New York: Hurst and Co., n.d.

Barton, George. *Archeology and the Bible*. Philadelphia: American Sunday School Union, 1916.

Bruce, Les P. "Alamblak Flood Tradition." In *Acts and Facts*. Vol. 4, No. 3. San Diego: Institute for Creation Research, April, 1975.

Catcott, A. *A Treatise on the Deluge*. London: M. Withers, 1761.

Custance, Arthur C. "Flood Traditions of the World." In *Symposium on Creation IV*. Ed. Donald W. Patten. Grand Rapids: Baker, 1972, pp. 9-44.

Dwight, H.G.O. "Armenian Traditions About Mt. Ararat." In *Journal of American Oriental Society* (1856), pp. 189-191.

Faber, George S. *Origin of Pagan Idolatry*. Vol. 2, Book 3, London: A. J. Valpy, 1816.

Frazer, Sir James G. *Folklore in the Old Testament*. London: Macmillan & Co., 1919.

Gaster, Theodor H. *Myth, Legend and Custom in the Old Testament*. New York: Harper and Row, 1969.

Heidel, Alexander. *The Gilgamesh Epic and Old Testament Parallels*. Chicago: University of Chicago Press, 1949.

Jastrow, Morris. *Hebrew and Babylonian Traditions*. New York: Charles Scribner's Sons, 1914.

Lenormant, Francois. *The Beginnings of History*. Translated by Francis Brown. New York: Scribner, 1891.

Lewis, Jack P. *A Study of the Interpretation of Noah and the Flood in Jewish and Christian Literature*. Leiden: E. J. Brill, 1968.

Morris, Henry M. *The Genesis Record*. San Diego: Creation-Life Publishers, 1976.

Nelson, Byron C. *The Deluge Story in Stone*. Augsburg, Minn: Augsburg Publishing House, 1931.

Pratt, Jane Abbott. *Consciousness and Sacrifice*. New York: Analytical Psychology Club of New York, 1956.

Pritchard, James B. *Ancient Near Eastern Texts Relating to the Old Testament*. Princeton: Princeton University Press, 1950.

Rehwinkel, Alfred M. *The Flood*. St. Louis: Concordia, 1951.

Rogers, Robert W. *Cuneiform Parallels to the Old Testament*. New York: Eaton and Mains, 1912.

"Story of the Flood." *Huntington Beach News*. August 10, 1906.

Titcomb, J. H. *Ethnic Testimonies to the Pentateuch*. London: Transactions of the Victoria Institute, 1872.

Zockler, Otto. "Oriental Traditions of the Deluge." *The Sunday School Times,* Vol. 29, No. 2. January 8, 1887, pp. 19, 20.

[1] A similar analysis was conducted in a more limited fashion by James E. Strickling in "A Statistical Analysis of Flood Legends" in *C.R.S. Journal* (December 1972).

[2] Andrew Woods, *The Center of the Earth* (San Diego: Institute for Creation Research, 1972).

TAB. XXXIV.

GENESIS Cap. VI. v. 14.
Arca ex Gopher.

I. Buch Moses Cap. VI. v. 14.
Arch Noa gebauet aus dem Holtz Gopher.

31

An Engineer Looks
At Noah's Ark

What did the Ark look like? How could Noah have carried two of every kind of animal on board the Ark? How did he collect them? How did he and his family care for and feed them?

Where did all the water necessary for such a flood come from? If it once covered the world, where did it go? Was the world drastically changed by the Flood?

By this time the reader is probably bursting with questions much like the ones listed above. They are common questions, ones that are frequently asked by layman and scholar alike.

The story of the great Flood is indeed a unique one. Its universal scope and impact are completely foreign to our present-day experience. The superlatives used in the narrative, the all-inclusive terms, make the story hard to believe. Many of the details are qualitatively almost beyond our comprehension, and, consequently, many skeptics have ridiculed this story more than almost any other in the Bible. The present-day scoffers, so precisely predicted by the Apostle in 2 Peter 3, take great delight in pointing out these seeming impossibilities, problem areas for believers in the Word of God and specifically in the Flood story.

As is generally the case, however, these advocates of the so-called "higher criticism" seldom take the time to investigate the problems with the serious scholarship they deserve. The usual ploy is simply to call attention to a seeming problem, call its supporters a few names, brand the whole affair as impossible and preposterous, and conclude with glee that the Bible is in error.

The purpose of this chapter is to study some of the aspects of Noah's Flood which have caused some to doubt the accuracy of the Genesis account. It is our contention that although qualitatively each problem area may be foreign to our experience (as indeed God promised that it would be), quantitatively each can be shown to be feasible.

We will not try to prove the Bible. We accept it as God's Word and believe it in its most straightforward and literal interpretation. But we feel that, if the Bible is really true, it ought to stand the test of scrutiny. Our confidence in the Bible is such that we are convinced that once true facts are discovered they will always agree with revealed Truth. In that light, an attempt will be made to answer some of the questions and accusations.

Size of the Ark

And this is the fashion which thou shalt make it of:
The length of the Ark shall be three hundred cubits,
the breadth of it fifty cubits, and
the height of it thirty cubits.
A window shalt thou make to the Ark, and in a cubit
shalt thou finish it above; and
the door of the Ark shalt thou set in the side thereof;
with lower, second and third stories shalt thou make it.
(Gen. 6:15,16)

There is quite a bit of disagreement between modern-day scholars on the exact value of a cubit. Most estimates range from 17.5 inches to 24 inches, with the most likely value being about 18 inches. For the purposes of this discussion, in order to be both as conservative and factual as possible, let us assume the latter value.

The dimensions of the Ark then are seen to be 450 feet in length, 75 feet in width, and 45 feet in height. A simple calculation shows that the volumetric capacity of the Ark was $450 \times 75 \times 45 = 1,518,750$ cubic feet. This vessel was of monstrous proportions, and only in the late 1880s was a vessel built with a length greater than that of Noah's Ark.

The purpose of the Ark is clear. The Flood was universal, and its purpose was to "destroy man whom I have created from the face of the earth; both man, and beast, and the creeping things, and the fowls of the air" (Gen. 6:7). The Ark then was to provide a method of salvation, a means of survival for Noah and his family and representative animals of God's creation.

But the pertinent question is, "Was the ark large enough to house two of every kind of unclean animal and seven of every kind of clean animal?"

It sounds impossible, and many have rejected it without any serious thought. Let us, however, analyze the subject and see.

The first thing we must determine is the modern equivalent of the Genesis "kind." The first mention of "kind" appears in the Creation

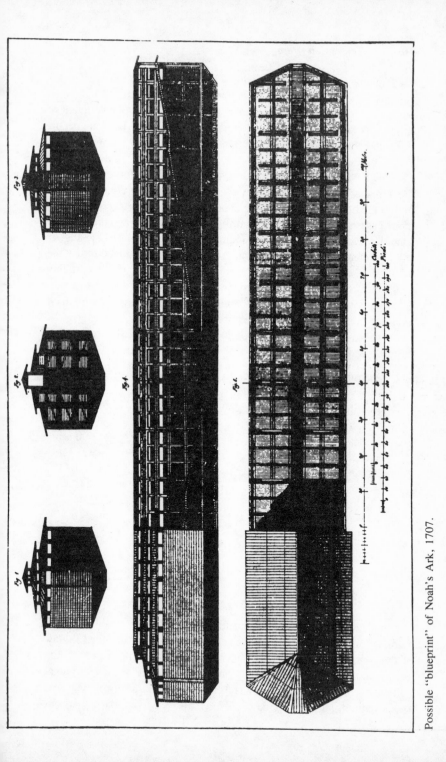

Possible "blueprint" of Noah's Ark, 1707.

story in Genesis 1, where ten times it is stated that God created the animals "after its kind." We don't know exactly what this "kind" was, but no doubt it represented the boundaries of variation of each plant or animal. Certainly adaptation and variation have occurred and are occurring today, but there always seem to be limits beyond which no variation is possible.

Some have felt, and with good reason, that "kind" approximates our modern classification of "family," and if so, the maximum number represented on the Ark would be about 700.[1] But since taxonomy is in many cases quite subjective, it is difficult to be certain, and that number should be considered a bare minimum. For our purposes, and to answer any argument raised by the skeptic, we feel it more realistic to use the number of "species" instead of "families." This figure would certainly be the maximum number on board the Ark estimated by any knowledgeable taxonomist, and if the Ark could accommodate the maximum, it could certainly handle a lesser number.

Ernst Mayr, probably the leading American systematic taxonomist, has provided the following table listing the number of animal species.[2]

Mammals	3,700
Birds	8,600
Reptiles	6,300
Amphibians	2,500
Fishes	20,600
Tunicates, etc.	1,325
Echinoderms	6,000
Arthropods	838,000
Mollusks	107,250
Worms, etc.	39,450
Coelenterates, etc.	5,380
Sponges	4,800
Protozoans	28,400
TOTAL ANIMALS	1,072,300

Not all of these animals needed to be on board the Ark. Only land animals that could not have survived otherwise had to be included. Many of the categories can be ruled out entirely. Fishes, tunicates, echinoderms, mollusks, coelenterates, sponges, protozoans, most arthropods and most worms could have survived outside the Ark. Many of the insect species among the arthropoda could have also survived, particularly in their larval stages, but those which needed to be on board would not have taken up much volume at all. The amphibians and many of the reptiles and marine mammals could also have survived without the aid of the Ark.

Simple subtraction, then, leads us to the conclusion that the Ark needed to house no more than 35,000 individual vertebrate animals. But let us be generous and add on a reasonable number to include extinct animals and then add on some more to satisfy even the most skeptical. For the purpose of our discussion, let us assume 50,000 land animals were on the Ark.

Very few land animals are large. Most are quite small in fact. Keep in mind that, in order to insure prime reproductive tendencies after the Flood, the specimens chosen for preservation on the Ark would, in all likelihood, have been young, healthy ones, not necessarily the strongest and largest of each species. For all practical purposes, we can be sure that the average size of all the animals was smaller than the size of a sheep.

Converting the volumetric capacity of Noah's Ark to an equivalent number of stock cars yields very significant conclusions. A standard railroad stock car consists of 2,670 cubic feet effective capacity. Simply by dividing the volume of the Ark by the volume of a stock car (1,518,750/2,670) we find that the ark's capacity was equal to that of 569 standard railroad stock cars.

Since 240 animals the size of a sheep could be housed in a standard two-deck stock car, by dividing the total number of animals on the Ark by 240 we find that all of the animals that needed to be on board the Ark could have been cared for in a space equal to that of only 208 standard stock cars, approximately 36% of the capacity of the Ark!

In other words, assuming a minimum size for the Ark and a maximum number of animals, we find that the Ark was not too small for the task, as many have claimed.

Such simple calculations are certainly not beyond the abilities of the scoffers. What does seem to be beyond them is the willingness to try to see if the biblical story is feasible.

Construction of the Ark

Some have ridiculed the idea that Noah and his three sons could have built such a huge vessel. Even if they did have 120 years to construct the Ark, the task seems too great. Construction techniques could not have been so far advanced, and four men simply could not have handled such huge timbers in order to build the three story barge.

The answer to this charge is so simple that it is hard to believe that intelligent people see a problem here. Obviously, Noah was an educated person, having at least been trained by the patriarch in the godly line of Seth. In all likelihood he was wealthy, or else he could not have abandoned his livelihood for 120 years to build the Ark. Furthermore, he must have had the help of at least two of the patriarchs, his father Lamech and his grandfather Methuselah, who died within a year of the Flood. Also, there is no reason not to assume that great numbers of workers had been hired to carry out the massive task of construction.

But, again, let us take the worst possible case. Suppose Noah could not, would not, or simply did not hire anyone to help with the construction of the Ark. Suppose that Methuselah and Lamech were unable to help. The only people who did any work at all were Noah and his three sons. The question becomes, "Could these four men have constructed the Ark all by themselves?"

Again, the scoffers are disappointed by a few simple calculations. We know that the volume of the Ark was approximately 450 feet by 75 feet by 45 feet, or 1.52×10^6 cubic feet. A very liberal guess would indicate that no more than 25% of the total volume was composed of wood structure. In other words, the maximum amount of wood needed for the construction of Noah's Ark was $(.25)(1.52 \times 10^6)$ or 0.38×10^6 cubic feet of wood.

We can only guess how much wood these four men were able to put in place in one day. Of course, they needed to cut the trees, work the timber, transport them to the construction site, and do the carpentry. In all likelihood, the construction took place in an area where lumber was available, which leads us to conclude that at the very least they could have installed fifteen cubic feet of wood per day between them.

Therefore, simply by converting the amount per day into the amount per year yields:

$$\frac{15 \text{ cubic feet}}{\text{day}} \times \frac{6 \text{ days}}{\text{week}} \times \frac{52 \text{ weeks}}{\text{year}} = \frac{4{,}680 \text{ cubic feet}}{\text{year}}$$

It is now easy to find how many years it took Noah to build the Ark, using these very conservative assumptions.

$$\frac{0.38 \times 10^6 \text{ cubic feet}}{4{,}680 \text{ cubic feet/year}} = 81 \text{ years}$$

Eighty-one years! That is the maximum length of time necessary for the building of the Ark. Noah, if you recall, was given the warning that the Flood was coming 120 years before the event took place. There was then plenty of time to warn others of the coming disaster, for vacations, and for providing for his family.

Noah's intelligence should not be open to question. Even a person of mediocre intelligence would be able to amass a great deal of useful information over the space of hundreds of years, and Noah was reported to be four hundred and eighty years old when work on the Ark began. But keep in mind that, only nine generations before, God had created Adam in a perfect state, to live forever and to have a close, personal, physical relationship with his intelligent Creator.

Medical science today has shown that man's brain is by far the most orderly collection of matter in the universe. But scientists have also found that most of it lies dormant. Experts estimate that we presently use only from 4% to 10% of our total brain. The rest is used, if at all, as a memory bank, storing unrecallable data.

It might be reasonable to speculate that Adam possessed the ability to use the entire capacity of his brain. At the time of his fall into sin, he began to lose it, having to spend most of his energies and time providing support for his family and no longer enjoying frequent communication with God. Certainly after the Flood, as life spans shortened and the physical earth changed, man's intelligence deteriorated rapidly, but not before a few marvelous civilizations sprang up with the ability to construct the Tower of Babel, the pyramids, etc.—intelligence which was soon lost.

Further speculation concludes that we may once again have full use of our brain during the eternal ages, but suffice it to say that there is no reason to assume that Noah was not a brilliant man, even by today's standards.

The Design of the Ark

The vessel itself was marvelously well designed for its intended use. No doubt it was supernaturally designed. Keep in mind that, once it was in use, it had no place to go, for the world was completely covered with water. The only requirements placed on the Ark were that it be able to withstand the vast hydrodynamic forces in operation at the time and that it be as stable and sturdy as possible.

The "gopher" wood reportedly used must have been extremely strong and durable. We do not know what type of wood it was. In fact, the translators of the Bible did not know either and simply transliterated the

Hebrew word "gopher." We may never know until samples are taken and analyzed.

God admonished Noah to pitch the boat "within and without with pitch" (Gen. 6:14). But the word "pitch" simply means "covering," leaving us with no clue as to the actual material used. The reader will remember that many of the reported sightings listed in this book relate that the wood of the Ark was covered with a hard shellac-like substance, probably a resin base. Other reports indicate that not only was the surface covered on all sides with the resin, but that the wood also seemed to be thoroughly impregnated with it.

Since the Ark was only to be used for one year, it seems unnecessary to take such elaborate precautions to waterproof and protect the wood. The wood would not even begin to deteriorate in such a short length of time. Perhaps a reason for the application of such a preservative can be found in the modern day search for the remains of the Ark. Perhaps God in His foresight made sure that the Ark would be able to survive 5,000 years or so in the ice cap of Ararat.

It is interesting to note that many modern day vessels are built on design specifications similar to those of the Ark. Modern day mathematical studies have shown that the Ark must have been a remarkably stable ship. Experienced designers will recognize that the ratio of length to width of six to one is considered to be the optimum design for stability and is used in construction of many different types of ships, from warships to racing sailboats.

The length of the Ark, 450 feet or so, would tend to provide insurance that the Ark would not be subjected to any wave of equal magnitude acting throughout its entire length. The Ark's chances of capsizing were therefore lessened.

The cross-section of 75 feet by 45 feet is also significant. The center of gravity for such a section can be calculated, as well as the buoyant forces of the water for any given degree of tilt, and conclusions drawn. It can be shown that for any degree of tilt up to 90 degrees, the Ark would tend to right itself! Noah's Ark was indeed optimally designed to perform under adverse conditions.[3]

Collection of the Animals

Once the Ark was completed and ready for action, Noah was faced with another impossible task, that of collecting two of every kind of unclean animal and seven of every kind of clean animal and convincing them to board his boat. The fact that it would have been a monumental task has caused some to ridicule the story.

The Bible does not go into great detail on this subject, and so we cannot be too dogmatic. There is, however, one very plausible and possible explanation which negates any justification for those who profess disbelief.

It has been noted by experts that many members of the animal kingdom possess the ability to sense imminent danger. Animals have been noticed leaving areas which soon were hit by a volcanic eruption, earthquake, or other natural catastrophe. This instinct seems to be possessed by nearly all types of vertebrates and many invertebrates as well.

Another tendency almost universally found among animals is the ability to migrate. Remarkable migratory patterns are well established in many animals. The animals use this ability to escape unbearable environmental conditions.

There is certainly nothing impractical in the assumption that these mechanisms came into play shortly before the Flood. Since seasons were less pronounced before the Flood, and individuals of each kind of animal were probably rather evenly distributed geographically, these instincts were not likely used until that time. Whether or not God specifically endowed selected pairs of animals with the migratory mechanism at this time, we can only guess. But it is very likely that He did. Those animals which He felt would be most capable of withstanding the rigors of an entire year on board the Ark and be most able to reproduce and replenish the earth afterward were given the ability to sense the oncoming danger and migrate to the place of safety.

Care of the Animals

Objections have also been raised over the care and feeding of such a large group of animals. The entire Flood account is thrown out by some because such a task is impossible. But once again, even though we cannot be dogmatic, we can suggest a plausible explanation.

Animals have been observed to undergo personality changes when confronted with overwhelming danger. During a forest fire, for example, predators and prey alike are often found fleeing together to places of safety and remaining in close proximity for long periods of time, unaware of their former relationship, oblivious to all but the overwhelming hazard of the fire. In the days before the Flood, aware of the imminent natural catastrophe and motivated only by the desire for survival, the animals may have been quite willing to mingle together in harmony. This willingness would have extended into the time of the Flood as conditions worsened.

It has been noted that an animal, when faced with adverse conditions, has three choices: it can die, adapt, or migrate. In the case in point, the animals had already migrated. Certainly death was not an option, so they had to adapt to the situation.

Zoologists have observed another almost universal tendency among animals. It is the ability to hibernate, the psychological state in which an animal can suspend or greatly retard his natural functions. This state enables the animal to survive long periods of complete inactivity during times of extreme stress or hardship.

Again, the Bible is not specific on this subject, but it seems likely that God would not have asked Noah to perform such an overwhelming task as caring for a floating zoo full of unruly animals. It is more within His character to place the animals in a state of hibernation or relative dormancy, greatly reducing the workload of Noah and his family. It should be noted that in such a situation the animals would eat, drink, and excrete less, and require much less room. The theory provides a workable solution.

All of the land animals that live today, as descendants of those on board the Ark, have evidently inherited the characteristics of premonition, migration, and hibernation given their ancestors by God at the time of the Flood.

Water Necessary for Flood

Probably the most commonly voiced skepticism has to do with the amount of water needed for a worldwide flood. Where did the water come from, and where did it go? The very idea of water covering the globe is so preposterous that few stop to study the problem, but those who do find once again that the problem disappears.

It may initially surprise the reader that plenty of water for such a flood exists on the earth's surface today. It has been calculated in recent years, due to vastly increased knowledge concerning the earth's surface, that if all of the globe were smoothed out into a perfect sphere (no mountains, no ocean basins), that the waters would cover the land to a depth of one and one-half miles. As it is, water covers approximately two-thirds of the surface of the earth, and the average elevation of the land is approximately at 7,800 feet below sea-level. Make no mistake, there is plenty of water.

The account in Genesis speaks of the "waters above the firmament," indicating that vast amounts of invisible water vapor were stored in the atmosphere. At the time of the Flood, torrential rains fell for forty days as the canopy of water vapor condensed and collapsed.

Another source of water is mentioned in Genesis 7:11 when "the fountains of the great deep" broke up, spewing untold amounts of primary water onto the surface of the earth. Volcanism also occurred on an unprecedented scale, another source of primary water. The cumulative effect of all of this activity was that even the highest mountains were covered with water.

On the 150th day, the waters began to abate. Realistic assumptions show that the waters receded at an average rate of fifteen to twenty feet per day. But where did the waters go?

Obviously the waters are now in the ocean basins. We can conclude then, that during the later stages of the Flood, the ocean basins were forming, widening and growing deeper as the ocean floors dropped. The waters rushed into these newly formed basins, and the land reappeared.

The new continents were greatly different from the old ones. A year of violent geologic upheavals, volcanism, earthquakes, tidal waves, erosion, and deposition had left its mark. As the water washed off, it gouged out river systems, valleys, and canyons, leaving scars everywhere.

Finally, 371 days after entering the Ark, Noah and his family and the animals disembarked to begin their new life on the vastly changed earth.

The first thing Noah did was to build an altar and give thanks to God for His merciful protection during the year of the Flood. God made a promise to Noah, vowing never again to destroy the earth and mankind with such a Flood. As a token of the promise, God pointed out the rainbow arching over the plain below Mt. Ararat.

The rainbow was a completely new experience to Noah. It had not been seen before. Such a refraction and separation of the visible light spectrum is due to the sun's rays striking water droplets in the sky. Before the Flood, the sky had been filled with water vapor, an invisible gas which cannot so separate the light. But after the Flood, as today, clouds of minute water droplets are capable of producing the beautiful rainbow. No doubt, the patriarch Noah welcomed the sight of the rainbow whenever he saw it from then on.

Noah and his family probably considered dismantling the Ark to re-use the wood. But such large timbers at such a high elevation were impossible to move. Furthermore, the weather on top of the mountain was not at all inviting. Eventually, it began to snow, no doubt covering the Ark. Soon glaciers formed, making travel and survival difficult.

It wasn't long before the Ark was inaccessible most of the time, and those who occasionally visited it could only take small pieces for a souvenir. As the years passed, and the nations migrated, they carried with them the legend of the Ark. Of the people who stayed in the area, only a rare few visited or accidentally spotted it.

And, so, there it sits in glorious solitude, on the upper slopes of Mt. Ararat, locked in its icy grave, waiting—waiting for the next chapter in this long history of the search for and the eventual relocation of Noah's Ark.

[1]See Arthur J. Jones, "How Many Animals in the Ark?" *Creation Research Society Journal,* 10:2 (Sept., 1973), pp. 102-107.
[2]Ernst Mayr, *Principles of Systematic Zoology* (New York: McGraw-Hill, 1969), pp. 11, 12.
[3]Henry M. Morris, "The Ark of Noah," *Creation Research Society Journal,* 8:2 (Sept., 1971), pp. 142-144.

32

A Reasonable Conclusion

Two conclusions dominate regarding the possible discovery of Noah's Ark: "Preposterous," and "Imminent." There are others, of course, but they range somewhere between the two. We think the holder of either view is more influenced by his preconceived ideas regarding the historicity of Noah and the Flood in his day than by the evidence for the existence of the remains of the Ark in ours.

When the director of one of the nation's leading university museums, a respected archaeologist, was asked what he thought the chances were of discovering the Ark, he replied, "Anything is possible in this world, but if there is anything that is impossible in archaeology, this is it." When Dr. Clifford A. Wilson, former director of the Australian Institute of Archaeology was asked the same question, his response was, "It is quite possible." Both of these men are competently trained and highly respected archaeologists. Dr. Wilson, however, has a profound conviction that the Bible is the Word of God. Consequently, he already believes that Noah and his Ark did indeed exist some 5,000 years ago. When he hears the stories recounted in this book, he will naturally consider the possibility of its discovery feasible. But those who question the validity of the Bible's story in the first place are too skeptical to be persuaded by "stories." The only thing that will convince them is the actual discovery and examination of the Ark itself.

Admittedly, we don't have that kind of evidence yet, but we think there is enough similarity in these stories of people who claim to have seen it to conclude that it may yet be found in our lifetime. We must also admit, however, that like Dr. Wilson, we believe Noah and his Ark did in fact once exist, so it is easier for us to believe than for those who question the Bible record.

Fact: Noah's Ark Was Real

Until the Ark has been discovered you will not personally have the opportunity to examine that ancient structure. But, until that time, you would do well to settle in your mind that Noah and the Ark are fact—not fable—or you will not be able to accept the evidence in this book. We have already given sufficient proof for so believing in chapter 30 when we showed that the universal flood stories demand a common truth source and in chapter 31 where we show that the story of the Ark is mathematically and hydrodynamically feasible.

The most formidable reason for so believing, however, is that Jesus Christ lifted the story of Noah and the Flood out of the realm of fiction and forever established it as a fact by referring to it as a true fact of history (Matt. 24:37-39; Luke 17:26-27). There isn't space in this book to launch into the many evidences for the divinity of our Lord, but we have made

Artist's conception of Noah's Ark on Mt. Ararat, attempting to show how the Ark could be protruding from a glacier, in a small lake, and on the edge of a cliff at the same time, thus harmonizing various eyewitness accounts. (Drawn by Joe Morris)

such a study and are convinced that He is what He said He was—"The Son of God."[1] Therefore, we can accept His statement as to the reliability of His words, "Heaven and earth shall pass away, but my words shall not pass away" (Matt. 24:35), as ample evidence for the fact of Noah's existence, as well as his Ark and the Flood.

The Ark and "The Last Days"

There is nothing in the Bible that demands that the Ark be discovered, either in our day or any other time. But it is fascinating to us that Christ Himself referred to Noah and his days when prophesying about the last days. It is so fascinating in fact, that we can't help but wonder if He might just have had that in mind.

Admittedly, tying the potential discovery of Noah's Ark to prophecy is uncertain, and we certainly do not wish to imply that the prophetic teachings demand such a revelation. But God has repeatedly established the pattern of clearly revealing His will to men, giving them ample evidence for accepting His word, particularly just prior to times of great judgment. What better authentication of Himself, His Word, and His Son, Jesus Christ, than the irrefutable evidence of sufficient portions of Noah's Ark to prove it exists just as the Bible teaches. You can imagine what the discovery of a ship the size of a modern aircraft carrier at the 14,500 foot altitude on Mt. Ararat would do to those committed to the idea of evolution. Such a disclosure would establish the fact of a worldwide flood, as taught in Scripture, thus stripping the evolutionist of his so-called "evidence" in the fossils found in the geologic column. It is our opinion that no other one event, except the return of Christ, would be so devastating to the atheistic philosophies based on evolution that currently dominate every major discipline in the Western World. Such a revelation would certainly not be out of character for the God of the Bible.

There is no question that Christ taught that conditions in "the last days" would be similar to conditions prior to the Flood (Matt. 24:37-39).

Since He said the last days would be "like" the days of Noah, we ought to examine the conditions prior to the Flood to see if there is any similarity to conditions in our day. Even a casual examination shows there were four major characteristics of Noah's day listed in the Scripture.

1) They were days of sexual abuse. Genesis 6 explains they had violated the marital statutes of God, and the holy relationship of husband

and wife was perverted. This led to a breakdown of the home and began polluting the race.

2) They were days when "the imaginations of men were evil continually." Whether they had hard-core pornography, prostitution, x-rated movies, and "massage parlors" is not stated, but they were obsessed with the same desires—"evil imaginations continually."

3)   The people were "lovers of violence." The selfishness of man, when unchecked, produces a violence toward his fellow man that makes society unsafe. It has been hundreds of years since such conditions as these violent days of Noah stalked this earth, but with 517 recorded killings in New York City alone last year, who can deny that Noah's days are being revisited?

4)   Disobedience to and unbelief in God. Noah's contemporaries not only defied God by personally violating His laws, they refused to believe His prophet, Noah, that judgment was about to come. In fact, the heart of man was so cold toward God in that day that none believed Noah's preaching except his own immediate family—until it was too late, and God shut the door and the floods came.

The ebb and flow of society change from generation to generation. Consequently, there have been social highs and lows throughout history. This may be just one of those social declines that can be expected periodically. But the thing that we find intriguing is that the period that has produced the most significant sightings of Noah's Ark (1840 to present) is the same period when social and moral conditions have plunged to a tragic low. Could that be coincidental? Or could the fact that today's climate resembles that of Noah's day indicate that we are in the last days?

If indeed we are in the last days we can expect one final call from God because the worst period of divine judgment since Noah's day is about to shake this earth. That period is known as "The Great Tribulation." Jesus said there has never been a day like it and never would be again (Matt. 24:21). It may be that the fulfillment of prophecy (as outlined in the author's book, *The Beginning of the End*[2]) is all the warning that God will give this generation—or He may give something else. But we feel it is well within His character and consistent with His past revelatory practice to shake this skeptical world in which we live by revealing the remains of Noah's Ark.

Before or After Rapture?

Students of prophecy are familiar with the Bible teaching that before the world is plunged into this awful time of tribulation all true Christians will be taken out of the world (1 Cor. 15:52-58; 1 Thess. 4:13-18). This is called the Second Coming of Christ for the church, or "the Rapture." Whether He will reveal the location of the Ark before the Rapture, only God knows. There is little question in our minds that it will be exposed at least during the tribulation, if not before. The author's book, *Revelation Illustrated and Made Plain*,[3] describes in detail the conditions of intense heat that will exist during the "trumpet judgments" when the sun scorches the earth with such an intensity men want to die. Such an event would obviously melt the glacier on Mt. Ararat sufficiently to leave the entire remains of the Ark "high and dry" for all the world to see. Certainly, if parts of the Ark are exposed now when the climate is just right (several years of low precipitation and hot winds from the desert floor below), it seems reasonable that the heat of the tribulation period will be sufficient to remove the ice protection from the old craft's surface, making it visible to even the most skeptical. One cannot help wondering what they will say in that day. If man's reactions to other divine revelations during the tribulation period, as foretold in the Book of Revelation, are any indication, we can expect man to turn defiantly against God and blaspheme His name, again illustrating that most atheists and agnostics are not unbelievers because of lack of proof but because of willful rejection of Christ and the ample evidence He has provided of His supernaturalness.

The Significance of the Ark

The real significance of the Ark in the days of Noah should be analyzed, since world conditions indicate we are living in the last days. The Ark reveals the attitude of God, not only for Noah's day, but our own. Consider the following:

1) God keeps His promises! Everyone has seen a rainbow and most folks, even though they know it isn't true, think of "the pot of gold" that some say is at the rainbow's end. Instead they should consider God's promise to mankind never again to destroy the earth by water and that He used the rainbow as His "token" or sign (Gen. 9:12-17). For well over four millenia of history God has kept that promise, and, characteristically, His future destruction of the earth will be by fire

not water. The thoughtful person should remember the principle that the Ark, the rainbow, and the Flood are all evidence that God keeps His word. That is why all men should remember that the God who kept His word to sinners who rejected His warning that He would send the rain is the same One who warns man to "repent, for the kingdom of Heaven is at hand." Even though in patience He waited 120 years, the vast majority refused to be ready, so, they perished. Men today need to see that God keeps His promises. Someday—it may be soon—He will surely destroy this world and judge all men who have rejected His Son.

2) God is merciful! The Ark of Noah is often called "the Ark of safety" because Noah and his family were safe in that Ark. There is a similar Ark of safety in these last days. It is a personal trust in God's Son, the Lord Jesus Christ. As Noah's family believed in the Ark to the point they climbed aboard before it started raining, so men today must believe on the Lord Jesus Christ as their personal Lord and Savior to the point of receiving Him (John 1:12) and invite Him into their lives. He has promised to be merciful to all such souls and save to the uttermost all who come to God by faith in Christ (Heb. 7:25).

3) You must make a decision. You don't have to make a decision about Noah's Ark—whether it will be found or even if it ever existed. But you do have to make a decision concerning the present-day Ark of Salvation, Jesus Christ. Jesus said, "I am the way, the truth and the life, no man cometh to the father but by me." In Noah's day those who delayed their decision until the flood came found it was too late to climb aboard. Remember, we have shown that we are already in the last days. Once the door to eternal life has been closed, it will be too late. That is why the Bible states "Now is the appointed time, now is the day of salvation."

Of course salvation through Jesus Christ cannot be exactly compared with climbing on board Noah's Ark. Eternal life is a gift of God in response to an inner heart cry from an individual. There are no magic words that can be repeated, for God looks on the heart. The heart cry that He hears comes from one who recognizes that he is a sinner and needs God's forgiveness and love, realizing that Jesus Christ by his sacrificial death on the cross paid the penalty for our sins. Receiving eternal life consists then of personally asking God to apply Jesus' death to your own particular situation and asking Jesus to come into your life, to take control, and turn you into the individual that God wants you to be.

Climb on board the Ark then. Receive Jesus Christ as your personal Savior and the Lord of your life. The authors know and love Him and heartily recommend Him to you. Only then will you know the peace and safety of His watchcare and be assured of an eternal home in heaven.

A Reasonable Conclusion

Logicians wisely tell us "the accuracy of a conclusion is dependent on the accuracy of the major premise and each additional premise." We believe Noah's Ark exists today encased in snow and ice somewhere up in the mountains of Ararat. We invite you to examine each of our premises and reach your own conclusion.

MAJOR PREMISE: The Ark of Noah is a fact of history! This fact is supported by the Bible, Jesus Christ, the apostles, universal flood stories, ancient flood inscriptions, and geological evidence that throughout the earth there was indeed a worldwide Flood.

PREMISE: Preservation of the Ark by freezing is possible. The ice region on upper Ararat could easily have set in within a few years after the Flood. The unique "gopher wood" from which Noah made the Ark, and which seems to have no known counterpart in post-flood days, carefully covered with "pitch" (probably as a preservative against water and deterioration) may have provided a protective coating, increasing this potentiality. To our knowledge, no scientific arguments have been proposed showing that preservation of the Ark by freezing is impossible.

PREMISE: Several honorable men in relatively modern times claim to have seen the Ark. Since the giant explosion of 1840 and the avalanche of 1883, there have been increasing reports by individuals, from Haji the Armenian, Nouri the Nestorian from Malabar, India, Resit the Turk, Greene the American, Navarra the Frenchman, and almost 200 other individuals—all of whose stories have many common details in spite of the glacial changes that understandably alter the body of ice that usually hides the Ark from view. Such similarity, without the possibility of collusion, seems most unlikely unless the Ark is really there.

PREMISE: Three men have found hand-hewn timbers in that area—150 miles from the nearest tree. Sir James Bryce (1876), Hardwicke Knight (1936), and Fernand Navarra (1955). The latter two reported vast amounts of timbers in the area, and Navarra's wood tested out to be of ancient vintage.

CONCLUSION: That Noah's Ark has been preserved; on certain occasions it has been sighted and is still up there covered with an icy mantle.

PREDICTION: That someday, when climatic conditions are just right, a significantly long dry, hot spell will melt that icy mantle back, at a time when the political conditions below are stable enough to allow a research team to methodically investigate the area—the Ark of Noah will be found.

We hope—and we believe—it will be soon!

[1]See Henry Morris, *Many Infallible Proofs* (San Diego: Creation Life Publishers, 1974), pp. 54-97.
[2]Tim F. LaHaye, *The Beginning of the End* (Wheaton, Ill.: Tyndale House Publishers, 1972).
[3]Tim F. LaHaye, *Revelation Illustrated and Made Plain* (Grand Rapids: Zondervan Publishing House, 1974).

What Can You Do to Help?

It's quite easy to see that much more work needs to be done before the Ark is located. Unfortunately, in the present political climate, exploration of the mountain itself will be kept to a minimum. And, even if a group of explorers is granted access to Mt. Ararat, there is no guarantee that the Ark will be spotted.

If, however, they knew precisely where to look, the search would stand a much better chance of success. Due to the difficulties involved there can be no promises, but exploration of only one particular area might just reveal the Ark even in the presence of heavy snow cover.

And so, we need to pinpoint the location of the Ark. Researchers have been able to narrow the possibilities down to a handful of sites, but none of these may be correct. Each new piece of information that comes in is analyzed and added to the puzzle and treated as though it might solve it. Needless to say, the research continues.

The reader might at this point ask the question, "How can I help? Is there anything I can do that might hasten the relocation of Noah's Ark?" The authors would answer without hesitation, "Yes, there is much you can do, and we welcome your participation!"

Fill in the Blanks

Didn't it strike you odd that there were so many ancient and medieval reports of Ark sightings, and yet none of them gave specifics of the Ark's location? Only meager amounts of time have been spent in this area of research compared to the numerous volumes of travel and study that could house references to the Ark. Both Turkish and Armenian archives are likely to be fertile hunting grounds, but have been barely touched by Ark enthusiasts. Many pertinent books and articles have appeared in English, German, and French and have been studied, but the supply of the potential sources has hardly been tapped. The interested reader would find this area of study fascinating under any circumstances, but with the incentives of possible new Ark information . . . Give it a try, check your local library for new material. Look under subject headings of the various names of the Ararat region and under travel headings as well as archaeological studies, religion, mythology, deluge, etc. Libraries are organized in different ways, but this will get you started. Also, check periodical listings and rare book collections. Who knows, maybe you will uncover an account that will give precise details of the location of Noah's Ark.

Chapter 5 tells the story of Haji Yearam, the old Armenian who visited the Ark as a boy in the company of three unbelieving atheists. His detailed account is lost forever, but undoubtedly information on the three English scientists is still around. If the deathbed confession of one of them made the papers in this country, just think of the stories carried in London papers. If he could be identified, his memoirs of his family's account could be traced. Since today articles on the Ark are clipped out and treasured by many, it follows that the article must still exist, as well as British articles on the find.

Viscount James Bryce supplied us with detailed accounts of his research and exploration but not of the events that triggered his interest in the subject. Perhaps, in his travels among the Armenians, he encountered eyewitnesses. Perhaps he was acquainted with the British scientists who viewed the Ark about a decade before. Again, published articles or unpublished memoirs would come in handy. Several excerpts from the Proceedings of the Royal Geographic Society have been of help, but there must be more.

Chapter 7 recounted the find by Turkish avalanche investigators. The Turkish official report has never been seen and is presumed to be gathering dust in Turkish archives. It would be difficult but not impossible to find. Easier to find would be the original news release from Constantinople in 1883 from which the other accounts were taken.

John Joseph, Prince of Nouri, addressed the World Parliament of Religions at the World's Fair in Chicago in 1893, but his talks, remembered by many, were completely deleted from the official transcript. They must still exist. See if you can find them. Rumors have it that he had pictures of the Ark, but again they are missing. Several descriptive quotes have been ascribed to him, but the authors have not been able to trace their origin, and they have not been used in this book. But, they may represent a personal written account.

George Hagopian (Chapter 9) saw the Ark as a boy before the mass Armenian persecution in and exodus from the Ararat area. He migrated to this country and many years later told his story. Without question there are others with similar backgrounds in this and other countries.

The Russians thoroughly documented Noah's Ark in 1917, the documents being lost or destroyed as the Communists gained power. More than twenty years later, the bogus Roskovitsky account was written from the bare facts. Since then several participants have been researched, but this part of the puzzle does not yet completely fit. Perhaps the account circulated in San Bernardino would help. Remaining members of the Czarist household could provide information, as well as other Russian participants. A few members of that expedition might still be alive, as well as friends and families. At any rate, see if you can come up with anything.

During World War I, American Armed Forces were treated to the fledging newspaper *Stars and Stripes*. One of these issues carried pictures of Noah's Ark. The file banks of the newspaper are incomplete and have not revealed the article, but so many people saw it and clipped it out only to destroy it later there must be many remaining copies. A photo of Noah's Ark taken from the air in the hands of an experienced Ararat explorer would immediately pinpoint the location. The mountain is immense, but a few major landmarks are well known to Ararat veterans. Who knows how many such pictures are stuffed in scrapbooks in boxes in attics across the country? Check yours. Further checking might just turn up the "March of Times" newsreel, seen by thousands in the forties but not since.

Chapter 15 describes Russian involvement once again in World War II. Pictures have been seen recently, taken by Russian pilots on several occasions. Wouldn't it be helpful if detente opened the door to this Russian information? With even less firm documentation, there exists evidence that Russia has sponsored numerous trips to the Ark. In this same chapter were listed numerous sets of photos seen in recent years in the hands of soldiers, evangelists, missionaries, students, and others but never in the hands of Ark researchers. See if you can remedy that situation.

The present-day Kurds and Turks no doubt are a potential source of a wealth of information untapped by researchers. American service personnel and tourists should never miss an opportunity to ask for information from a Turk and should also approach friendly officials on the subject. A word stimulating their interest in the search might just play an important part in the sanctioning of foreign exploration or a Turkish launched investigation.

George Greene, who spotted the Ark in 1953, died suspiciously several years later. His pictures have not been seen since that time. Approximately thirty people alive today have been interviewed who remember the photos. Perhaps there are others who have more detailed information. Researchers are known for their willing ears.

Chapter 27 discusses the possibility of high resolution photographs taken from satellite or spy planes. How frustrating it is to know there may be pictures of Noah's Ark in government files that are as yet inaccessible to civilians. But public domain photographs are getting better all the time and may soon be sufficient to locate the Ark. The recent trend toward de-classifying nonessential material may also spring the evidence we are looking for. Those in positions with access to such material are asked to keep their eyes open and let us know if such information is available.

There May Be More

This book has detailed most of the research that has come to light. There is more, for one reason or another not yet ready for publication. If the Ark is not found soon, a sequel will be published. But no one thinks that researchers have uncovered all the sightings and are now just trying to fill in the details. In other words, as more people become informed and interested, we expect much more new and important information to mani-fest itself. Perhaps you, the reader, have firsthand knowledge that will solve this exciting but frustrating puzzle. Don't hesitate to share it. Perhaps you, the reader, just by keeping your eyes and ears open will run into some such person. At any rate let us hear from you.

One other task. At the risk of sounding too political, a necessary step for further exploration of Mt. Ararat is renewing American friendship with Turkey. It seems ridiculous for American politicians to purposely make an enemy out of our longtime NATO ally, especially since Turkey possesses the largest standing army in all of Europe. It would not hurt for you to remind your legislators of this fact.

But the most important thing that most of you can do is to pray. God has providentially preserved the Ark for these thousands of years. He must have a purpose for His actions. Seemingly, the most likely purpose would be to reveal it in the last days as a faith strengthener for Christians and a reminder to non-Christians that there is a coming judgment and a present day Ark of Salvation, Jesus Christ.

An event of such magnitude as the relocation of Noah's Ark must have a particular slot selected in God's eternal timetable. Most biblical scholars feel that the end of the world as we know it is just around the corner. If the Ark is to be relocated at all, it must be found soon. Pray with us, please, to that end.

Index